D1581510

advancing learning, changing lives

ART AND DESIGN LEVEL 3

BTEC National

Rachel Dormor | Sarah Holmes | Tony Mott | Jan Schofield
Llewellyn Thomas | Sara Wicks | Gill Wilson | Jan Wise

Published by Pearson Education Limited, a company incorporated in England and Wales, having its registered office at Edinburgh Gate, Harlow, Essex, CM20 2JE. Registered company number: 872828

www.pearsonschoolsandfecolleges.co.uk

Edexcel is a registered trademark of Edexcel Limited

Text © Pearson Education Limited 2010

First published 2010

13 12 11 10

10 9 8 7 6 5 4 3 2 1

British Library Cataloguing in Publication Data
A catalogue record for this book is available from the British Library.

ISBN 978 1 846906 37 4

Edited by Davina Thackara
Designed by Wooden Ark
Typeset by Brian Melville
Original illustrations © Pearson Education Limited 2010
Illustrated by Brian Melville
Cover design by Visual Philosophy, created by eMC Design
Picture research by Zooid and Elena Wright
Cover photo/illustration © Alamy Images / Asia Images Group Pte Ltd
Back Cover photos © iStockphoto/Joe_Potato, Ирина Татарникова; Shutterstock/Jason Stitt
Printed in Spain by Grafos

Websites

The websites used in this book were correct and up to date at the time of publication. It is essential for tutors to preview each website before using it in class so as to ensure that the URL is still accurate, relevant and appropriate. We suggest that tutors bookmark useful websites and consider enabling students to access them through the school/college intranet.

Disclaimer

This material has been published on behalf of Edexcel and offers high-quality support for the delivery of Edexcel qualifications. This does not mean that the material is essential to achieve any Edexcel qualification, nor does it mean that it is the only suitable material available to support any Edexcel qualification. Edexcel material will not be used verbatim in setting any Edexcel examination or assessment. Any resource lists produced by Edexcel shall include this and other appropriate resources.

Copies of official specifications for all Edexcel qualifications may be found on the Edexcel website: www.edexcel.com

Contents

Credits

The authors and publisher would like to thank the following individuals and organisations for permission to reproduce photographs:

(Key: b=bottom; c=centre; l=left; r=right; t=top)

p. **1** iStockphoto/Kristian Septimius Krogh; p. **3** Emily Gardner (tr, bl, bc, br), Gill Wilson (tl); p. **5** iStockphoto/ Catherine dée Auvil; p. **6** David Hockney Studio (t, b); p. **8** Emma Jacobs (l, r); p. **9** Emma Jacobs; p. **11** Shutterstock/Doug Stacey; p. **13** Alamy Images/The Art Gallery Collection; p. **14** Jack Pittard (tl, tc, tr, b); p. **19** Lynsey Harrison (1/tl, 2/tl, 1/tr, 2/tr, 1/bl, 2/bl, 1/br, 2/cr); p. **21** iStockphoto/Joe_Potato; p. **23** Bridgeman Art Library Ltd/© DACS/© Connaught Brown, London (b); Pearson Education Ltd/Jules Selmes (t); p. **25** Getty Images/Jim Dyson (l); Sara Wicks (r); p. **26** Shutterstock/AdrianCheah; p. **27** Kobal Collection Ltd/Heart of Europe/Lumen/Athenor; p. **30** Sara Wicks; p. **31** Shutterstock/Alberto Pérez Veiga; p. **33** Corbis/Burstein Collection; p. **34** Corbis/Richard Glover; p. **35** Rex Features/Tony Kyriacou; p. **38** Tanya Bonakdar Gallery NY; p. **39** Sara Wicks; p. **41** iStockphoto/Aleksandra Smirnova; p. **43** Shutterstock/Jason Stitt (t), Pres Panayotov (b); p. **46** Courtesy White Cube, London/Stephen White; p. **48** Corbis/Luke Macgregor/Reuters (bl), Gagosian Gallery (tl), Sara Fanelli/Walker Books (tr); p. **51** Shutterstock/catman (t), Sofia (b); p. **53** Shutterstock/Krylova Ksenia (t), Johan Swanepoel (c), Ewa Walicka (b); p. **56** Shutterstock/Daniela Illing; p. **57** Sara Wicks; p. **58** Sara Wicks (tl, tr, b); p. **61** Tina Roskruge (t, b); p. **63** Shutterstock/Tupungato; p. **65** Gill Wilson (tl), Lorna Doyle (tr, cr, br, bl); p. **67** Getty Images/Catwalking; p. **68** Alamy Images/Paul Melling; p. **69** akg-images Ltd/Erich Lessing (tl, tr), Corbis/ Francis G. Mayer (b); p. **70** Kobal Collection Ltd/BOLAND, JASIN/DAVIS FILMS; p. **73** Getty Images/Shaun Curry/Stringer; p. **74** Sam Lambeth; p. **75** Alamy Images/Photos 12; p. **76** Mary Evans Picture Library/ONSLO; p. **81** Katie Welsford; p. **83** iStockphoto/ Kris Black; p. **85** Christian Venkatasamy (br); Tony Mott (bl); p. **87** Shutterstock/Zheltikov Dmitriy; p. **88** Amanda Hayes (br), Shutterstock/Regien Paassen (bl); p. **90** Bridgeman Art Library Ltd/DACS (b), Getty Images/Michael Ochs Archives (t); p. **94** Bridgeman Art Library Ltd/Wolverhampton Art Gallery, West Midlands, UK/© DACS (b), David Hockney Studio (t); p. **95** Alamy Images/Directphoto.org; p. **97** Alamy Images/Sandra Baker (l), Tony Mott (r); p. **98** Daniel Ambrose; p. **99** Corbis/Humphrey Evans; Cordaiy Photo Library Ltd; p. **101** Alamy Images/Blaine Harrington III; p. **103** Shutterstock/Andrea Haase; p. **105** Alamy Images/DWD-Drawing (tr), iStockphoto (cr, b), Pearson Education Ltd/Studio 8/Clark Wiseman (tl); p. **106** Shutterstock/Brian Chase; p. **107** Shutterstock/KUCO; p. **108** Shutterstock/Suzan Oschmann; p. **111** Alamy Images/David Hancock (b), Rhys Stacker (t); p. **113** Getty Images/Jon Feingersh; p. **115** Gill Wilson (t), Max Beardon (b); p. **118** Gill Wilson; p. **119** Gill Wilson; p. **121** iStockphoto/Chris Schmidt; p. **122** Alamy Images/ Hugh Threlfall; p. **123** Gill Wilson (t), Rob McDonald (b); p. **125** iStockphoto/Dean Mitchell; p. **127** iStockphoto/ Michael Griffin (r), Shutterstock/hfng (l); p. **128** Zooid Pictures; p. **129** Shutterstock/Yuri Arcurs; p. **130** The Maureen Paley Gallery; p. **131** Ashley Eagle; p. **132** Gill Wilson; **p. 133** Neil Bottle; p.**135** Getty Images/Hiroyuki Yamaguchi; p. **136** Shutterstock/Stepanov (r), Rui Vale de Sousa (bl), Tom Etherington (tl); p. **137** Gus Russell; p. **138** Alamy Images/Steve Photo; p. **139** Grant Waters (l, r); p. **140** Gill Wilson (tl, tc, tr, br, bl); p. **141** Photo12/ Archives du 7eme Art; p. **143** Brett Breckon (t, b); p. **145** Shutterstock/Jorge Cubells Biela; p. **146** Kirsty Doyle (t, b); p. **147** iStockphoto/Ирина Татарникова; p. **148** Alamy Images/Image Source (t), Getty Images/ Jupiterimages (b); p. **149** Press Association Images; p. **150** Getty Images/Jon Feingersh; p. **154** Jacob Donnelly (r), **155** Paul Robinson (t, b); p. **157** Shutterstock/Leegudim; p. **158** Lesley Davies-Evans; p. **159** Alamy Images/ Tetra Images; p. **160** Getty Images/Robert Nickelsberg; p. **161** Chris Lee; p. **162** George Wilson (tl, bl, bc, br, tr); p. **163** Getty Images; p. **164** Getty Images/Dominique Charriau (r), Shutterstock/Coka (l); p.**165** Science Photo Library Ltd/TED KINSMAN; p. **166** Aaron Dixon; p. **167** George Wilson; p. **169** iStockphoto/sabrina dei nobili; p. **170** Rutter and Bennett (t), Cass Sculpture Foundation (b); p. **171** iStockphoto (t), Joe_Potato (b); p. **172** Bridgeman Art Library Ltd/Musee d'Art Moderne de la Ville de Paris, Paris, France/© DACS/Roger-Viollet, Paris; p. **173** Shutterstock/Graça Victoria; p. **174** Kevin Jones; p. **175** Shutterstock/Lakatos Sandor (l), bioraven (r); p. **176** Sara Wicks (b), Shutterstock/Leo (t); p. **177** Alamy Images/Stan Pritchard; p. **178** Andy Malone; p. **179** Ian Bottle; p. **181** Alamy Images/ArcadeImages; p. **182** Anthony Bliss (t), Kobal Collection Ltd/Touchstone (b);

p. **183** Jannuzzi Smith Ltd/Richard Smith; p. **184** Shutterstock/c. ; p. **185** akg-images Ltd; p. **187** Ben Price; p. **189** Studio Tonne (t, b); p. **191** Alamy Images/Dennis Hallinan; p. **192** Alamy Images/LHB Photo (b), Shutterstock/Yuri Arcurs (t); p. **193** Alamy Images/Justin Leighton (tr), Corbis/Louie Psihoyos (br), Rex Features/ Sipa Press (l); p. **194** Alamy Images/moodboard (r), Rex Features/Solent News & Photo Agency (l); p. **195** Anglepoise Ltd (l), Zooid Pictures (r); p. **198** Corbis/Adam Woolfitt; p. **199** Alamy Images/Libby Welch (b), Shutterstock/Andresr (t); p. **201** Shutterstock/InavanHateren; p. **202** iStockphoto/Catharina van den Dikkenberg (bl), Shutterstock/ Yuri Arcurs (t), Richard Ortolano (br); p. **206** iStockphoto (t), ciseren korkut (b); p. **207** Nina Fraser; p. **208** iStockphoto/Silke Dietze; p. **210** Cressida Bell (l), Rex Features (r); p. **211** Caroline McNamara (t, b); p. **212** Getty Images/AFP; p. **213** David Guthrie (t, b); p. **215** iStockphoto/Alex Potemkin; p. **216** Tanvi Kant (t, b); p. **217** Getty Images/Colin Hawkins (t), Rachel Galley Jewellery Design LTD (b); p. **218** Alamy Images/BUILT Images; p. **219** Rachel Galley Jewellery Design LTD; p. **220** Alamy Images/MARKA; p. **221** Dan Logan (t), Rachel Dormor (b); p. **222** Rachel Dormor; p. **224** Dan Logan (t, b); p. **225** Hannah Lobley Paperwork.

All other images © Pearson Education

Pearson Education and the authors would like to acknowledge the contribution made by the staff and students of the University for the Creative Arts (UCA) to this resource. Many of the images and examples of work have been included with their kind permission.

The authors and publisher would like to thank the following individuals and organisations for permission to reproduce their materials:

p. **99** Quote from Eduardo Paolozzi first published in *Paolozzi Portraits*, 1988, National Portrait Gallery Publications © National Portrait Gallery, London.

Case studies (Professionals)
p. **139** Grant Waters; p. **150** James Nolan; p. **153** Michelle; p. **154** Jacob Donnelly; p. **166** Aaron Dixon; p. **183** Richard Smith; p. **185** Andy Edwards; p. **187** Ben Price; p. **206** Dr Paul Holdstock; p. **207** Nina Fraser; p. **219** Rachel Galley.

WorkSpace case studies
p. **19** Lynsey Harrison; p. **61** Tina Roskruge; p. **81** Katie Welsford; p. **101** Paul Greenhalgh; p. **123** Rob McDonald; p. **133** Neil Bottle; p. **143** Brett Breckon; p. **155** Paul Robinson; p. **161** Chris Lee; p. **167** George Wilson; p. **174** Kevin Jones; p. **178** Andy Malone; p. **179** Ian Bottle; p. **189** Paul Farrington; p. **211** Caroline McNamara; p. **213** Sara Impey; p. **224** Rachel Dormor; p. **225** Hannah Lobley.

Professional voices
p. **136** David Carroll; p. **136** Tom Etherington; p. **146** Kirsty Doyle; p. **158** Lesley Davies-Evans; p. **170** Chris Rutter and Evelyn Bennett; p. **182** Antony Bliss; p. **216** Tanvi Kant.

Every effort has been made to trace the copyright holders and we apologise in advance for any unintentional omissions. We would be pleased to insert the appropriate acknowledgement in any subsequent edition of this publication.

About the authors

Rachel Dormor

Rachel completed a potter's apprenticeship after art college and has successfully combined teaching BTEC courses with a career as a ceramic designer-maker. She currently works freelance for several awarding organisations (as a writer and moderator) and creates functional porcelain tableware which is exported around the world.

Sarah Holmes

Sarah is a lecturer in Art, Design and Media at a northern college, where she teaches Art and Design Contextual Studies as well as leading the BTEC Creative Media Production (video production) course. She is also an experienced author and trainer, working with leading publishing houses and awarding organisations.

Tony Mott

Tony studied fine art and sculpture at Goldsmiths and The Slade School of Fine Art and continues to work in mixed media. His current imagery is concerned with the identity and recognition of facial characteristics. He has extensive experience of teaching in further and higher education and is a Senior Lecturer at the University for the Creative Arts (UCA). For many years, he has been interested in landscape design.

Jan Schofield

Jan is currently working as Head of Section for Fashion Innovation at Liverpool Community College and as an Associate Inspector for Ofsted, as well as working closely with awarding organizations. She has previously taught on a range of fashion-based courses from Level 1 to Foundation Degree, and also manages a number of employer-related courses.

Llewellyn Thomas MA(RCA) MA LCC MILT FHEA AWG

Llewellyn is a wood-engraver by trade but has worked in many fields including theatre design and illustration. He has taught at the Maidstone College of the University for the Creative Arts (UCA) for over 20 years. During this time he has led the BA course in Illustration and the HND in Multimedia. He is currently a Senior Lecturer in Further Education. He is a brother of the Art Workers Guild.

Sara Wicks BA (Hons)

Sara is a practising artist who has exhibited widely in the UK and abroad, and whose work is in many private and public collections. She has worked as an artist -educator for the past 18 years, undertaking residencies in schools, museums and galleries in conjunction with exhibitions of her work. She has been teaching the Level 3 BTEC National Diploma for the past seven years and is currently a Senior Lecturer at the University for the Creative Arts (UCA).

Gill Wilson BA (Hons), MA (Ed), FHEA

Gill is a practising graphic designer and has been teaching on Level 3 BTEC National Diploma courses for the past 12 years. She is currently a Senior Lecturer at the University for the Creative Arts (UCA), a National Teaching Fellow of the Art, Design and Media Centre of the Higher Education Academy and is also studying for a Doctorate in Education.

Jan Wise

Jan taught textiles and fashion on BTEC courses for many years as a Course Leader and Head of Faculty. Jan is currently a writer, researcher and textiles and art history teacher and works as an examiner for textiles and fashion. In her spare time she designs stained glass panels for gardens.

University for the Creative Arts (UCA)

Pearson Education and the authors would like to acknowledge the contribution made by the staff and students of the University for the Creative Arts (UCA) to this resource. Many of the images and examples of work have been included with their kind permission.

About your BTEC Level 3 National Art and Design course

Choosing to study for a BTEC Level 3 National Art and Design qualification is a great decision to make for lots of reasons. Art and Design can lead you into a whole range of professions and sectors and allows you to explore your creativity in many different ways.

Your BTEC Level 3 National in Art and Design is a **vocational** or **work-related** qualification. This doesn't mean that it will give you all the skills you need to do a job, but it does mean that you'll have the opportunity to gain specific knowledge, understanding and skills that are relevant to your chosen subject or area of work.

What will you be doing?

The qualification is structured into **mandatory units** (ones that you must do) and **optional units** (ones that you can choose to do). How many units you do and which ones you cover depend on the type of qualification you are working towards.

Qualifications	Credits from mandatory units	Credits from optional units	Total credits
Edexcel BTEC Level 3 Certificate	10	20	30
Edexcel BTEC Level 3 Subsidiary Diploma	40	20	60
Edexcel BTEC Level 3 Diploma	50	70	120
Edexcel BTEC Level 3 Extended Diploma	50	130	180

You may have chosen a general art and design pathway or you may be following an endorsed route, and the units you study will reflect this. Whatever your choice, you will need to complete a mix of mandatory units, optional professional specialist units and optional endorsed route units.

General art and design pathway, *or*		
Endorsed routes:	Fine art	Graphic design
	3D design	Interactive media
	Design crafts	Photography
	Fashion and clothing	Textiles

How to use this book

This book is designed to help you through your BTEC Level 3 National Art and Design course.

- All of the Art and Design **mandatory units** are covered in this book. Your programme of study may cover these in different ways, and the projects that you work on may cover learning outcomes and content from a range of units. However, this book will help you to develop the knowledge, skills and understanding that you need.

- A selection of the optional **professional specialist units** are also included. The focus of these is to help you to realise your art and design projects, whatever they are, in an effective and work-ready way.

- We have also included information on the sectors that underpin the **endorsed routes**. Here you'll find invaluable insights into the multitude of interesting careers and pathways that are open to you.

This book contains many features that will help you use your skills and knowledge in work-related situations and assist you in getting the most from your course.

Introduction

These introductions give you a snapshot of what to expect from each unit – and what you should be aiming for by the time you finish it!

Assessment and grading criteria

This table explains what you must do to achieve each of the assessment criteria for each unit. For each assessment criterion, shown by the grade button **P1**, there is an assessment activity.

Assessment

Your tutor will set **assignments** throughout your course for you to complete. These may take the form of projects where you research, plan, prepare, make and evaluate a piece of work, sketchbooks, case studies and presentations. The important thing is that you evidence your skills and knowledge to date.

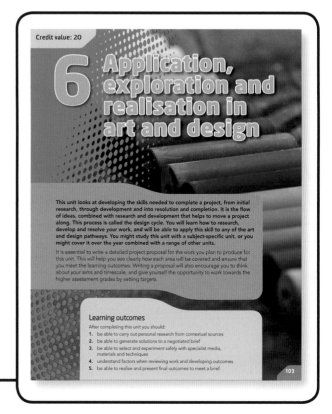

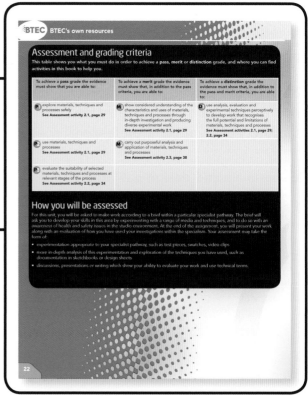

Stuck for ideas? Daunted by your first assignment? These learners have all been through it before…

Nemii

I came straight to the BTEC Level 3 National course from GCSE. Previously, we were told what to do and how to do it, but now, although the tutors teach us new ways of looking at things and new skills, we're expected to make decisions ourselves.

Our tutors say creativity does not come in a flash of inspiration, but develops from working, looking at the world more carefully and being open to new ideas.

When I first began to make visual recordings of the cathedral, I found it hard not to stick to pencil work and to come up with anything exciting, and blamed it on the subject matter. But we were encouraged to use lots of different materials and experiment, and I found everything I tried led on naturally to something else, like a kind of snowball – the more work you produce, the more ideas you seem to get. I was pleased with the composition I developed, because it looked contemporary and a bit wacky, even though it was based on a cathedral!

When we started using architectural influences to develop fashion ideas, I used some of the techniques and imagery I'd used in previous work, but adapted them to a different outcome.

Nemii's composition was developed from her visual recordings of the cathedral.

I no longer feel like I don't know what to do. If I start creating images from resources around me, ideas just follow.

Over to you!

- Are you confident in making your own design decisions?
- What helps you to generate visual work?
- Have you tried to work with unfamiliar media to extend your skills and try new techniques?

These sketchbook pages show how Nemii has drawn on her visual recording, and applied the same principles to experimental work for a project to develop a fashion piece from architectural influences.

3

Activities

There are different types of activities for you to do: **Assessment activities** are suggestions for tasks that you might do as part of your assignment and will help you develop your knowledge, skills and understanding. **Grading tips** clearly explain what you need to do in order to achieve a pass, merit or distinction grade.

Assessment activity 3.2: Knowing how to generate ideas P2 M2 BTEC

Research artists who use sequencing within their work such as film-makers and illustrators, and investigate the different approaches they use. Now select a short story or piece of text – for example, from a novel or well-known fairy story – and highlight eight sentences that intrigue you. Take a piece of A1 paper and, using ink, make some experimental marks on it – try blowing it through straws, and/or mixing it with washing-up liquid and blowing bubbles on the paper. Then take five minutes to respond to each of your sentences. Try to use a range of media, but stick to monochrome, using collaged pieces of paper, graphite or working into the surface with white paint.

You should now have a visually interesting sheet. Take another piece of A1 paper and divide it into 16 sections, making a sequence of images inspired by your first sheet. Do these drawings in ink so that you work fast and don't get over complicated – you have to think how to link the rectangles, whether through narrative or aesthetics.

Once you have completed your rectangles, look at your sheets and decide how you could develop these further.

1. Could you develop your work as the storyboard for an animation? If so, do you have the time and expertise to make a couple of seconds of film, i.e. 24 frames?
2. Would your work be more successful in book format? If so, will you incorporate text and how?
3. How else could you develop this piece?

Grading tips

- Be experimental in developing your storyboard and show that you have lots of ideas for generating techniques. Repeat your image-making using other media, such as collage and colour P2.
- You could then try to develop this piece further into one of the formats suggested above: if you do this successfully you could achieve M2.

There are also suggestions for **activities** that will give you a broader grasp of the industry, stretch your imagination and deepen your skills.

Activity: Exploring and extending

This activity will help you develop transferable skills and solve problems using different materials and techniques.

Task 1
Produce an A2 sheet of line drawings from observation of an organic structure, such as leaves, rocks or plants. Make sure you fill the sheet.

Task 2
Make a viewfinder, select an A5 area of your drawing and photocopy this section four times. Now recreate three 3D versions of your selected section using the following techniques and materials:
- copper wire and lead solder
- string, thread and sticks
- stitching, gluing, soldering found objects and mixed materials.

Task 3
Set up a plaster frame the same size as your photocopied section, mix some plaster and fill the frame to make a plaster slab. When this has set, carve the motif from your photocopy into the plaster and leave to dry.

Task 4
Roll pieces of soft clay over your plaster slab and manipulate them to make soft cylinders and forms. They will have a raised area to match the carving on your plaster slab, which can then be decorated with slips and scratched on to develop designs.

To make constructed clay pieces, roll slabs over your plaster work and leave them to dry until they are leather-hard. They can then be cut to size and joined with clay slip to form boxes and frames.

Task 5
In your sketchbook, take photocopies of your drawing and develop your ideas in two dimensions. Enlarge, reduce and repeat sections; add colour and mark- making; rip edges; add found materials; weave paper sections; and stitch, glue and fold, to make 20 alternative samples from the same starting-point.

Task 6
Identify which outcomes were the most successful and why. What health and safety issues did you encounter during this activity?

Personal, learning and thinking skills

Throughout your BTEC Level 3 National Art and Design course, there are lots of opportunities to develop your personal, learning and thinking skills. Look out for these as you progress.

PLTS

Independent enquirer

When working for a client, it is your responsibility to identify and research the information you need to fulfil the brief. This may involve consulting the client, industry experts, the public and end-users.

Functional skills

It's important that you have good English, mathematics and ICT skills – you never know when you'll need them, and employers will be looking for evidence that you've got these skills too.

Functional skills

English

Write a bullet list of the main points of your presentation. Put it into a logical sequence and include key words to act as a trigger when talking about your work in greater depth.

Key terms

Technical words and phrases are easy to spot. You can also use the glossary at the back of the book.

Key term

Visual language – how you communicate meaning in your work through mark-making and using the formal elements – line, tone, form and colour.

WorkSpace

Case studies provide snapshots of real workplace issues, and show how the skills and knowledge you develop during your course can help you in your career.

There are also mini-case studies throughout the book to help you focus on your own projects.

WorkSpace Ian Bottle
Fine artist

Ian Bottle works in a range of media and formats. Before taking a degree in Fine art at Newcastle Polytechnic his work revolved around ideas for environments for which he made maquettes, but at college his focus shifted to painting.

While still a student, he took part in the Northern Open and was subsequently awarded a student bursary and a solo exhibition at the Northern Centre for Contemporary Art in Sunderland. He was also selected for 'One Year On', a feature section at the International Contemporary Art Fair at Olympia in London.

One of Ian's paintings, which combines shapes and forms referred to in his sculptural pieces.

The experience of having a solo show and stand at a prestigious event led to other exhibitions and gallery contacts. Ian's work consisted of large-scale figurative imagery that served as allegories for wider personal and political concerns. Ian went on to do an MA at Chelsea School of Art where he was awarded a Boise travel scholarship to study Italian painting.

Since then, Ian has established his own studio in Kent and works fulltime as a lecturer. Although he still paints, digital media, particularly digital photography, is now an important component of his work, which he manipulates in Photoshop to create grounds for his paintings. He also projects photographs of fragmented shapes and forms in his studio, which become the basis for paintings as well as sculpture. Computer programs such as InDesign allow him to translate paintings into layouts for artist's books, which he sells as an affordable alternative to paintings and drawings.

Think about it!

- Can you think of any other formats for Ian's work that could combine his interest in sculpture, painting and digital media?
- How would you exhibit a diverse body of work like this in an empty gallery space?
- How would you price the different types of work that Ian makes?

179

Just checking

When you see this sort of activity, take stock! These quick activities and questions are there to check your knowledge. You can use them to see how much progress you've made or as a revision tool.

Edexcel's assignment tips

At the end of each unit, you'll find hints and tips to help you get the best mark you can, such as the best websites to go to, checklists to help you remember processes and really useful facts and figures.

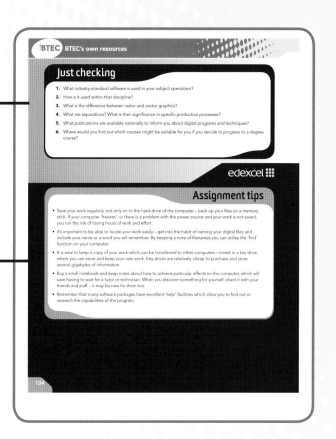

Have you read your **BTEC Level 3 National Art and Design Study Skills Guide**? It's full of advice on study skills, putting your assignments together and making the most of being a BTEC Art and Design student.

Ask your tutor about extra materials to help you through your course. You'll find interesting videos, activities, presentations and information about the Art and Design sector.

Your book is just part of the exciting resources from Edexcel to help you succeed in your BTEC course.

For more details visit:

- www.edexcel.com/BTEC
- www.pearsonfe.co.uk/BTEC 2010

1 Visual recording in art and design

You have probably had the experience of seeing something extraordinary and wanting to make a visual response to it. Most of us will have been disappointed by our lack of ability to do so, but the luckiest of us will occasionally have been reasonably pleased with the results.

This unit will encourage you to see as an artist/designer. Throughout the BTEC Level 3 National course you will research other artists, have opportunities to work with unfamiliar materials and learn new processes and techniques. This will help you to recognise the creative potential of less obvious primary sources. It is up to you, the artist, to make the things that surround you exciting, re-interpreting them in different media and juxtaposing them with other items to open up new meanings.

The acquired ability to draw, record and visually communicate what you see remains a fundamental skill in art and design. Your developmental studies and experiments are an integral part of the design cycle and will inform your final outcomes.

All your research and developmental work should become a valuable and growing resource for you, stimulating ideas for assignments and aiding your development as an artist.

Learning outcomes

After completing this unit you should:

1. know how to identify sources for visual recording
2. be able to record visually
3. understand visual recording in others' work
4. understand own visual recording
5. be able to develop visual recording to produce outcomes.

Assessment and grading criteria

This table shows you what you must do in order to achieve a **pass**, **merit** or **distinction** grade, and where you can find activities in this book to help you.

To achieve a **pass** grade the evidence must show that you are able to:	To achieve a **merit** grade the evidence must show that, in addition to the pass criteria, you are able to:	To achieve a **distinction** grade the evidence must show that, in addition to the pass and merit criteria, you are able to:
P1 identify primary and secondary sources for recording **See Assessment activities 1.1, page 7; 1.2, page 10**	**M1** research and respond to independently selected sources, consistently showing effective visual recording skills **See Assessment activities 1.1, page 7; 1.2, page 10; 1.4, page 15; 1.6, page 17**	**D1** demonstrate independence, innovation and individuality in evaluating and using sources, integrating visual recording skills and in-depth understanding in communicating information **See Assessment activities 1.1, page 7; 1.6, page 17**
P2 record visually **See Assessment activities 1.1, page 7; 1.2, page 10**	**M2** show an individual approach to communicating, comparing, illustrating and expanding information and presenting work in a coherent and appropriate creative format **See Assessment activities 1.2, page 10; 1.4, page 15; 1.5, page 16; 1.6. page 17**	
P3 discuss visual recording in others' work **See Assessment activities 1.3, page 13; 1.5, page 16**		
P4 review own visual recording **See Assessment activities 1.4, page 15; 1.5, page 16**		
P5 develop visual recording to produce effective outcomes **See Assessment activity 1.6, page 17**		

How you will be assessed

Your understanding of visual recording will be evidenced from work set specifically to meet the learning outcomes of the unit, but will also be drawn from project work. There should be evidence that you have met the criteria for all or some of the learning outcomes in all the core units in your creative work.

Your evidence for assessment will be in the form of different types of visual recording, and should demonstrate exploration and understanding of:

• creative ways of presenting images and ideas drawn from the natural or constructed environment

• analysis of the properties of different media

• scale

• two- and three-dimensional formats

• lens-based visual recording methods

• composition and development of outcomes.

Nemii

I came straight to the BTEC Level 3 National course from GCSE. Previously, we were told what to do and how to do it, but now, although the tutors teach us new ways of looking at things and new skills, we're expected to make decisions ourselves.

Our tutors say creativity does not come in a flash of inspiration, but develops from working, looking at the world more carefully and being open to new ideas.

When I first began to make visual recordings of the cathedral, I found it hard not to stick to pencil work and to come up with anything exciting, and blamed it on the subject matter. But we were encouraged to use lots of different materials and experiment, and I found everything I tried led on naturally to something else, like a kind of snowball – the more work you produce, the more ideas you seem to get. I was pleased with the composition I developed, because it looked contemporary and a bit wacky, even though it was based on a cathedral!

When we started using architectural influences to develop fashion ideas, I used some of the techniques and imagery I'd used in previous work, but adapted them to a different outcome.

Nemii's composition was developed from her visual recordings of the cathedral.

I no longer feel like I don't know what to do. If I start creating images from resources around me, ideas just follow.

Over to you!

- **Are you confident in making your own design decisions?**
- **What helps you to generate visual work?**
- **Have you tried to work with unfamiliar media to extend your skills and try new techniques?**

These sketchbook pages show how Nemii has drawn on her visual recording, and applied the same principles to experimental work for a project to develop a fashion piece from architectural influences.

1. Know how to identify sources for visual recording

Not always the obvious

Think about the unlikely subjects artists in the past have chosen which have challenged the way they are perceived by the viewer: René Magritte's painting of a pipe, *Ceci n'est pas une pipe* (This is not a pipe); Salvador Dalí's lobster telephone; Marcel Duchamp's urinal; Andy Warhol's prints of soup cans; Damien Hirst's creatures in formaldehyde and pharmaceutical installations. Research some of your own examples.

Look at your own environment and choose an everyday object. How many ways can you represent that object, or use it as a primary source to create exciting images? Make a list or draw a mind map of different materials, techniques and processes you could use. You may produce two- or three-dimensional pieces, animations or videos, digital images from scanning the object, or a combination of all methods. What could the object be used for other than its original function?

1.1 Identify primary and secondary sources

Visual recording from primary sources involves capturing an image of a person, landscape or building, or any other object in your immediate field of vision. This process requires you to take into consideration issues outside your control, such as movement or a change of light. This may make it a demanding process, but it could also offer opportunities to move around and capture different angles and background information and to focus on the whole object or just details. In this way, you have more scope for personal interpretation, and for building a range of resources from which to develop work later. For example, you might draw or photograph images of plant forms to help develop a painted composition; you might use studies of pattern or texture on a building to develop a design for a fabric; or you might use photos of an object to create a sculpture.

Secondary sources such as books, journals, film, video or the Internet are useful sources of reference material. Apart from fostering an important skill in research methods, often creative ideas involve a combination of primary and secondary inputs, and secondary sources can set off tangential lines of creative activity.

PLTS

Creative thinker

As a visual artist, you will make decisions about your choices of primary and secondary sources and the way you choose to represent them in your own work. As a creative thinker, you should develop the ability to view things from new and innovative perspectives.

Case study: **The most unlikely objects...**

Polly's self-study assignment required her to choose a household object as a primary source and use it to generate a diverse body of work. She struggled to find something with the right potential until she spotted an old-fashioned wooden 'dolly' clothes peg on a visit to her nan.

- She made a number of drawings of the dolly peg, using various media to see how she might exploit its various properties: soft tonal pencil to examine the surface and form; quick charcoal drawings to capture the quirkiness of the shape; multiple images using ink and wash.

- She then produced colour pencil sketches and watercolour studies by juxtaposing the pegs with floral fabrics to evoke an atmosphere of past times, inspired by the children's picture book *Peepo!* by Janet and Allan Ahlberg.

- This gave her the idea to create patterns from the pegs themselves, so she arranged the pegs into different shapes on a variety of backgrounds and photographed them.

- The three-dimensional qualities of the photographic images gave Polly the idea to scan the pegs directly into the computer, arranging them in different patterns and compositions.

- Looking at the structures gave her the idea to build with the pegs, linking them together to produce strange three-dimensional forms.

- She then photographed the objects on a white background, and used some of her landscape photographs to compose images exploring their potential as large-scale sculptures.

- Noticing the negative space, she focused on the basic shapes of the pegs and created a series of 'cut-out' compositions inspired by Henri Matisse.

1. Look through one of your completed sketchbooks. Take one example of a visual record of an object.

2. How many ways could you explore and develop work using this object?

3. How many ideas and experiments have you discarded, forgotten or not developed? Can you identify at least three or four examples of visual recording that could be developed to produce new and diverse outcomes?

Polly managed to produce a range of outcomes, recording her original object in different media and employing a number of techniques. In so doing, she reached greater understanding of the properties of her media, and developed ideas for how to take them further. As a result, she is increasing her level of skills and has produced a bank of experimental work to draw from for other projects. These studies also have the potential to stimulate solutions to design briefs within other disciplines, such as illustration, fabric design, public art or fine art.

You might also consider the effects of light, tonal qualities and time. Look at David Hockney's recent paintings of Woldgate Woods, which depict the same scene at different times.

When images of artwork are accessed through books or the Internet, the issue of scale can easily be overlooked. You are viewing Hockney's work here at 7.3 x 3.6in and 3.6 x 1.8in, whereas the true size is 72 x 144in (6 x 12ft). The impact of that kind of scale can only truly be appreciated at first hand, so you should try to visit exhibitions and view the work yourself, whenever possible.

PLTS

Independent enquirer

Get into the habit of visiting galleries and exhibitions and being aware of cultural activity in your area. By doing this, you will get invaluable stimulus for ideas and knowledge of creative practice. Read arts reviews in your library on a regular basis and keep yourself up to date with current trends and work.

Hockney's series of paintings of Woldgate Woods was produced at different times of the year from the same viewpoint. Each work is made up of six canvases.

Assessment activity 1.1: Identifying potential

Examine as many ways as you can of mark-making, using a wide range of traditional and non-traditional materials and methods. Select subject matter drawn from:

- the natural world – human form, animals, insects, plants, land, seas, skies, water, fire
- the constructed world – built environments, architecture and urban environments, machinery, industry, manufactured products

- cultural elements – decoration, clothing, textiles, artefacts, arts
- the reported or captured world – film, photography, documentary, virtual.

You may also want to consider how your work could be applied in your preferred discipline areas.

Capture this process in your sketchbook or design sheets. Evaluate and annotate where appropriate, documenting areas for potential development.

Grading tips

Remember to keep an open mind and be sensitive to the potential offered by the most unlikely primary sources. When making visual recordings, also consider your own physical relationship to them, and how this affects what you see.

It's often handy to have a viewfinder, particularly in an environment where there is a lot of visual information. This can help you isolate interesting areas and aid your composition skills (P1) (M1) (P2).

You can use this activity to fulfil the criteria for merit or distinction grades. At merit level (M1), you would be expected to produce skilful

visual records using a broad range of media and techniques, drawn from primary and secondary sources that you have selected yourself. Assessors would want to see that you had thought carefully about viewpoints, and thoroughly explored the ways a subject could be recorded with reference to similar or contrasting work by other artists and designers.

This investigation could contribute towards a distinction (D1), although you would need to produce work that was innovative and individual, and show how your recording method could be used to convey information.

Case study: Developing individuality

Ali has a passion for comic books and animated film, and has just joined the BTEC Level 3 National course in Art and Design. His first assignment is to produce images of the local cathedral. He visits the cathedral to draw and collect a range of visual references, but doesn't understand how this is relevant to what he hopes to do in the future.

Wandering around the building, he notices a strange gargoyle decorating part of the stonework, which he draws a number of times in different media and from different positions. Back at the studio, he uses the drawings to create three-dimensional models, and starts to think about how these could be displayed. He also remembers that the cathedral architecture could look quite sinister, and goes back to make

more drawings, take photographs and make small video clips on his mobile phone.

By the end of the assignment, he has a vast range of exciting visual work and has explored a range of materials, techniques and processes. He has also made connections between his work and contemporary practice, and discovered work by artists he did not know about, such as John Piper.

1. **Can you think of an assignment that you found uninspiring? How was this reflected in your outcome?**

2. **Think about Ali's experience – how could you have made it work for you?**

2. Be able to record visually

Once you have developed an open mind with regard to sources for visual recording, you need to be creative in your exploration of the options available. It's important that you are not constrained by convention, or intimidated by what might be expected of you.

This aspect of your practice is where you are expected to test the parameters of your media, and use opportunities to try out, and push the potential of, techniques and processes. Take creative risks and have fun.

2.1 Recording and mark-making

Emma is a BTEC Level 3 National student in her first year of study. The examples below show some of Emma's work – some was produced specially for this unit, while other pieces formed part of one of the professional units. These pages document a process of testing materials for a final composition.

PLTS

Self-manager

You will have read about Nemii's difficulties in adapting to an independent learning style on page 3. Some students love to have more creative freedom, but others are concerned about the lack of prescribed activities. As an arts practitioner, it's important to develop the ability to think and work independently, and to plan and manage your workload. These skills are highly valued in the workplace and will also give you the autonomy to pursue more creative options.

Emma has intuitively combined the mysterious visual qualities of traditional charcoal rubbing techniques with a ground created from coffee stains and layered with tissue paper.

Emma extends her studies using a wide range of materials, a stained ground and layered tissue, bringing in bold watered-down ink brushwork with a marker pen for emphasis. Subtle use of charcoal adds to the ghostly feeling.

Layered grey tissue creates a textured background surface as a focus of the composition, and Emma works into this to explore the depth of the architectural forms.

This experimental piece combines a collaged newsprint ground with a detail from a window.

This piece was produced as part of Unit 7, but you can see how Emma's experimental recording work has been drawn on and extended for this interim design sheet.

Case study: Jack, first year BTEC Level 3 National student

Jack has done extensive research on the artist Gustav Klimt for Unit 5, 'Contextual influences in art and design'. He is particularly drawn towards Klimt's *The Kiss*, and made a critical examination of the work.

Jack is passionate about fashion and textiles, and has focused on the patterns used in the painting, identifying what Klimt used as a basis for each pattern and reproducing a selection in different colours and media.

Throughout this process, Jack develops his visual recording skills to build an individual and versatile body of work to draw on for the fashion and textiles units. He annotates his work, capturing the process in words and images:

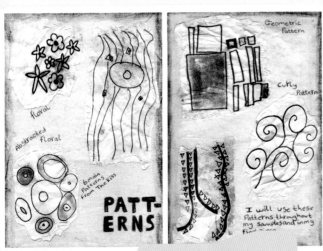

Jack identifies six main patterns from Klimt's *The Kiss*.

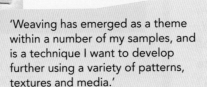

'A poly-block print on calico, using black printing ink. Newspaper is then collaged on to the pattern and gold fabric paint applied to the background.'

'A gold poly-block print on brown paper. The gold paint is quite subtle, so I outlined the design with black biro, and coloured some sections with pencil or watercolour paint.'

'Weaving has emerged as a theme within a number of my samples, and is a technique I want to develop further using a variety of patterns, textures and media.'

Jack's visual recording inspired by Klimt's artwork has generated work that he will be able to use in his specialist units.

1. How could you draw from the influence of artists in one discipline for work in a different field?

2. Can you think of any artists who are known for work in more than one discipline?

3. Can you find any of your own experimental work that could be developed to produce outcomes in more than one discipline?

4. Understand own visual recording

This section takes the same principles used in understanding the visual recording methods of other artists, and applies them in the examination and evaluation of your own work. In the previous case study you saw how Jack began to develop his practice through visual interpretations of Klimt's work, and to analyse how different materials subvert, extend and push visual ideas.

4.1 Examination and analysis of visual recording

This level of analysis will prepare you for generating ideas for final outcomes, ultimately in the context of professional work for clients. It will also help you to become self-reflective, and to evaluate the effectiveness of your visual recording, both from your own perspective and that of your target audience.

PLTS

Reflective learner

Reflection is an important aspect of the design development cycle, and should be part of each stage of the process. Reflective thinkers assess their own work and that of others in order to help inform future progress and identify opportunities for improvement and development.

Assessment activity 1.4: Drawing influence

Using Jack's case study as a model, deconstruct the work you selected for Assessment activity 1.3 and develop visual recordings in which you explore:

- visual elements of your chosen work or works, such as colour schemes, textures, forms, sequences, repetition

- structural elements, such as size, shape, materials

- emotive aspects, such as atmosphere, feeling

- practical elements or functionality

- context, intention and audience.

How much does your personal response affect your evaluation? How is your visual recording developing? How has it progressed from the original work? Make sure you document the process.

Now examine what you have done so far. How might it contribute towards the development of work within a discipline of your choice?

Grading tip

Reviewing your visual recording skills with reference to the factors identified throughout this section **P4** will help give your work direction. Jack's work illustrated the information he had selected from Klimt **M1**, through exploring the effects of materials, colour and texture. He also annotated and documented his process, incorporating an analysis of the techniques used and potential for further development **M2**.

4.2 Evaluation

In many respects, your increasing understanding of the role of visual recording in others' work will help you to understand and make sense of your own recording practices. Working in partnership with others will help develop this understanding, and your contributions to peer reviews, critiques, tutorials and seminars, whether in a formal or informal setting, is a highly valuable part of your practice.

PLTS

Team worker

As part of your practice as an artist or designer, you will often work with others, which will require you to make constructive judgements about their work. You will also need to respond to others' criticism of your own work. Working collaboratively is more about supporting than competing, in order to produce outcomes that contribute to the success of the group.

Functional skills

English

As part of the evaluation, you may find it helpful to discuss your work informally with your peers. Discussion can often generate responses that you might not have thought of, and will get you used to giving and receiving constructive criticism.

Assessment activity 1.5: Evaluating your work

 M2 P3 P4   **BTEC**

Based on your project work, review what you have achieved, taking into account the results of your visual recording.

Consider the following questions:

What are you conveying about the subject?

- What kind of information are you providing to the viewer?
- Are you exploring form, shape, surface, scale, spatial relationships…?

Are you taking a formal approach, such as:

- analysing, investigating, explaining, representing, documenting, illustrating, demonstrating…?
- using traditional materials, methods, techniques, processes…?

Are you taking an informal approach, such as:

- experimenting, evoking atmosphere, expressing a feeling, provoking responses, challenging stereotypes, creating an impression, subverting pre-conceptions…?
- utilising non-traditional materials, such as found objects, abstract concepts, light, sound, smell, touch…?

Grading tips

Reviewing your visual recording by examining what you are trying to convey and how you have set out to do it means you will be more likely to explore a wide range of possibilities, make well-considered decisions and produce effective outcomes M2. You will also be better equipped to discuss your work and that of others P3 P4.

5. Be able to develop visual recording to produce outcomes

As part of this unit, you will have produced a diverse body of work in which you have explored a broad range of primary sources and some secondary sources, and experimented with capturing images from those sources using a wide variety of media, techniques and processes, in different formats and scale. How are you going to utilise this work in the development of outcomes?

Assessment activity 1.6: Developing outcomes

Dungeness is a headland on the Kent coast, sheltering the low-lying Romney Marshes. Featured in numerous films and books, it is a rich and diverse environment that offers exciting opportunities for visual recording: vast shingle beaches littered with boats and fishing ephemera, a power station, lighthouse, light railway and small dwellings all scattered around a single main access road. The late artist and filmmaker Derek Jarman lived there, and his famous garden has been the focus of much attention.

After a series of field trips to Dungeness in which students recorded their visual responses to the environment, an interim studio critique was held of the work produced in order to develop final outcomes.

Reflecting on all the ideas presented in this section, imagine that you are one of those students.

- How would you start?

- What process would you go through in order to generate and develop ideas from your work?

Identify and document the stages that you would go through in the development of your ideas.

- Can you identify an environment in your area that would offer rich opportunities for visual recording?

- Spend time there making visual recordings to capture the sense of the place, using a wide range of media. Once you have done this, think about the visual outcomes you might develop.

Grading tips

The more work you produce, the more effective and diverse your outcomes will be. Always examine the potential of your experimental work for further development **P5**. Self-initiated work that demonstrates commitment to your practice will contribute towards gaining merit and distinction grades, and will help you develop an individual and innovative style of working and a sophisticated approach to presentation **M1 M2 D1**.

5.1 Develop

Think back to the first learning outcome, which looked at identifying sources for visual recording. Polly used a variety of means to make visual recordings from a primary source. Look back at this section (page 5) and consider the final outcomes she could produce from that body of work.

Analyse and explore your visual recording to identify the potential for creating outcomes. This may involve refining ideas and techniques, and modifying the work. You may be reviewing the work on your own or eliciting the opinions of peers or tutors. Look at the composition and consider:

- viewpoint
- cropping or selecting areas of an image for further development
- rearranging elements or re-sizing to adjust the balance or relationship of one element with another
- structure.

Your development of the work may involve editing, clarifying, refining, enhancing and re-interpreting, using other media or changing the emphasis or mood.

5.2 Produce outcomes

Working towards outcomes may involve developing your visual recording work for an art and design specialism. This could be part of a series, such as a fashion collection, advertising campaign, photo essay or elements of a website, and will need to be adapted and customised for its target market. As part of the design cycle, you will be developing plans, prototypes, test pieces, maquettes and models, and reviewing and refining these as you move towards your final outcome.

In considering final outcomes, it is essential to reference all the core units: Visual recording in art and design (Unit 1); Materials, techniques and processes in art and design (Unit 2); Ideas and concepts in art and design (Unit 3); Communication through art and design (Unit 4) and Contextual influences in art and design (Unit 5). Although there are separate sections covering these topics, they are inter-related and form the core of art and design practice.

Remember

When you are given project work there is sometimes a temptation to focus on just one idea to develop to a final outcome, whereas you should look for multiple opportunities through careful and critical examination of the potential of your visual recording. If you were presenting your ideas to a client, and they did not appreciate your interpretation of their brief, you would need to have alternative options for consideration.

Signpost

Look at the design development process as defined in Unit 7. This is not a definitive model, and elements such as reflection, evaluation and review are likely to occur at multiple points of development within the cycle.

Lynsey Harrison
Sculptor

Lynsey studied for a National Diploma in Art and Design before graduating with a BA (Hons) in Fine Art in 2008. In 2007 she worked as a technician for Antony Gormley, installing his first London solo show, Blind Light, at the Hayward Gallery. Like many young artists, she has a career profile of working in diverse creative and educational settings. She describes her visual recording and the importance of this process in the development of her work.

'Throughout my experiences and since completing the National Diploma, I have used visual recording to document my thought process, ideas, research and final outcomes, and have observed it used for major projects and exhibitions. Whilst working with Antony Gormley on *The Waste Man*, a 25m-high man constructed from the detritus of modern consumer society, made for the film *The Margate Exodus* (2006), visual recording was of utmost importance. Initial sketches of the man, small-scale photographed models and professionally drawn engineering plans of the skeletal structure were all used to communicate the process of development through to the final outcome.

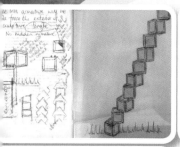 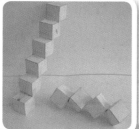  

My experience on *The Waste Man* helped me understand how important visual recording is to the development of a finished work, and for recording information that could be lost or forgotten. I used a similar process for my final degree show, and will continue to do this in the development of future pieces.'

The images above show the visual recordings for Lynsey's final degree show piece. They include drawn images, visuals and plans, maquettes constructed from different materials at each stage and photographs of prototypes and final pieces.

Think about it!

- Look at the documentation of Lynsey's work. Could you find similar examples in your own work?
- Can you map the design process to Lynsey's final work for her degree show?
- What do you know about Antony Gormley? What is the name of his famous sculpture in Gateshead? Research this artist.

Just checking

1. From the ideas outlined in this section, what do you feel is the purpose and pleasure of visual recording?

2. What do you understand by primary and secondary sources? Where might they be found?

3. How many different ways of making visual recordings can you think of?

4. What aspects would you look at to gain a greater understanding of an artist's visual recording practice?

5. How could you apply your own visual recording work to develop outcomes in response to a brief?

edexcel

Assignment tips

- Keep an open mind when you identify primary sources for visual recording – sometimes the most unlikely things can generate really exciting and innovative work.

- Remember that secondary sources are useful. The involvement of secondary source material varies enormously across the spectrum of art and design, some areas of design, such as furniture, are heavily reliant on established practice and data, while in fine art much greater emphasis is placed on personal creativity.

- Keep in mind all the ways you can adapt your visual recording – think back to Jack's case study and the way he created different effects from the same pattern by using a range of materials and colours.

- Remember to apply what you have learned about visual recording to all your project work.

2 Materials, techniques and processes in art and design

Artists can draw on an enormous range of traditional and contemporary materials and processes to develop their work. Indeed, some of the most exciting designers working today have built their practice on subverting established craft methods, by using unexpected and innovative media. However, behind these art works lie rigorous specialist training and carefully considered investigation of the possibilities inherent in materials.

To develop your own work in an exciting and creative way you will need to expand your range of materials, techniques and processes. As a practitioner it is vital to have a safe studio environment to work in, and you will need to consider carefully any health and safety issues before starting. As you increase your understanding and skill base you can be more ambitious in your investigation and experimentation. Documenting and evaluating your findings is also an important aspect of successful practice, and will enable you to apply your new skills and outcomes to future projects.

This unit underpins the other units you will be studying, and may be delivered in conjunction with others rather than as an independent assignment. You will soon realise how essential Unit 2 is in preparing you for your future career in art and design.

Learning outcomes

After completing this unit you should:

1. be able to explore materials, techniques and processes safely
2. be able to use materials, techniques and processes
3. understand the suitability of materials, techniques and processes.

Assessment and grading criteria

This table shows you what you must do in order to achieve a **pass**, **merit** or **distinction** grade, and where you can find activities in this book to help you.

To achieve a **pass** grade the evidence must show that you are able to:	To achieve a **merit** grade the evidence must show that, in addition to the pass criteria, you are able to:	To achieve a **distinction** grade the evidence must show that, in addition to the pass and merit criteria, you are able to:
P1 explore materials, techniques and processes safely **See Assessment activity 2.1, page 29**	**M1** show considered understanding of the characteristics and uses of materials, techniques and processes through in-depth investigation and producing diverse experimental work **See Assessment activity 2.1, page 29**	**D1** use analysis, evaluation and experimental techniques perceptively to develop work that recognises the full potential and limitations of materials, techniques and processes **See Assessment activities 2.1, page 29; 2.2, page 34**
P2 use materials, techniques and processes **See Assessment activity 2.1, page 29**	**M2** carry out purposeful analysis and application of materials, techniques and processes **See Assessment activity 2.3, page 38**	
P3 evaluate the suitability of selected materials, techniques and processes at relevant stages of the process **See Assessment activity 2.2, page 34**		

How you will be assessed

For this unit, you will be asked to make work according to a brief within a particular specialist pathway. The brief will ask you to develop your skills in this area by experimenting with a range of media and techniques, and to do so with an awareness of health and safety issues in the studio environment. At the end of the assignment, you will present your work along with an evaluation of how you have used your investigations within the specialism. Your assessment may take the form of:

- experimentation appropriate to your specialist pathway, such as test pieces, swatches, video clips
- more in-depth analysis of this experimentation and exploration of the techniques you have used, such as documentation in sketchbooks or design sheets
- discussions, presentations or writing which show your ability to evaluate your work and use technical terms.

James

Last term, we made a series of self portraits influenced by the work of other artists.

Exploring materials and techniques

We started by making quick drawings from looking at our faces at different angles. Pulling faces made me think of Francis Bacon's paintings. I found out that he did some of his early studies on pages from boxing magazines, so I made mono-prints of my face by drawing on to inked-up Perspex and using newspaper and magazine pages to print them on. These were messy, so I painted the ink directly on to the Perspex and printed this off – the results were much better. Some of the inky lines made me think of linocuts, so I copied one of the prints in lino. This was fiddly and I had to be careful not to cut myself, but I was pleased with the print and started experimenting by printing on different papers and on top of some of the mono-prints I'd already done.

Using suitable materials

Francis Bacon is particularly famous for his triptychs, so I tried to make a series of paintings on paper. We only had acrylic paint which didn't look good when it dried, so I went to the workshop to cut some wood panels. I had to have an induction to use the band saw. I primed the wood and painted on it, and was really pleased with the outcome, so I went back to the workshop to learn how to make a canvas stretcher.

Evaluation

Painting on canvas made me feel like I had moved from being a student to being a serious artist, and my tutors were pleased with how I kept on pushing my ideas. I'm now really excited by painting and want to experiment with different kinds of paint. I also plan to investigate different kinds of supports and primers to see how this affects my work.

Over to you!

- **What else do you think that James could do to explore materials and processes with the media available to him?**
- **Which artist would you research if you were doing this project, and what kind of experimentation would you do after looking at their work?**

A Francis Bacon triptych used by James for his research.

1. Be able to explore materials, techniques and processes safely

Exploring painting

You have probably seen sheets of paint colour samples in DIY shops. Try making your own sample sheets, but instead of different colours, select one colour only and try applying it to the paper in as many different ways as possible.

- Dilute the paint and instead of a brush, apply it by sponging, blotting, blowing or splattering, or with a feather.
- Try applying thick paint with a dry brush, palette knife, stick or piece of card – or straight from the tube!
- Try wetting the paper first and see how building up delicate layers changes the intensity of the colour.
- Try adding a different material to the paint, such as PVA glue or sand, or draw into the paint with the handle of the brush.
- See how many different kinds of mark you can make with your brush – long fluid strokes, short marks, scratchy marks, etc.

Experimenting with materials, techniques and processes safely is a key element of every assignment, as is carrying out research to help you develop exciting artwork. So this learning outcome will encourage you to investigate as many different media as possible, experiment widely and work safely whilst undertaking different techniques.

1.1 Variety of materials

When you make a new piece of work, you need to consider the range of materials available to you. You also need to think about the constraints of the brief – such as the requirement to work in two dimensions only – and how to use your materials creatively and imaginatively within these constraints. Looking at the work of other artists who have embraced a wide range of media will give you ideas and help you contextualise your work.

There will be lots of 2D materials which you are already comfortable with, such as paint, paper, charcoal, pencil, etc., but try to approach these

with fresh ideas. Use them in conjunction with new media, such as foils or plastics. You might want to explore everyday materials such as those encountered in the work of the Italian Arte Povera movement, which explored materials and effects inspired by the commonplace and banal, such as wood, rope and cloth; or, you could look at industrial materials such as concrete and steel. You could also explore the contrast between natural and synthetic fibres, or fragile materials such as glass and card in contrast to heavier media such as wood and clay. If you are following a photographic brief you might choose to explore time-based media – film, video and sound – or exploit still imagery through digital or wet photography, or a combination of the two. You could even use photographic emulsion to develop images on to three-dimensional materials such as Perspex and canvas. Use your computer to develop your imagery further and find out which software and hardware programs will increase your range of outcomes.

Try researching artists who use a wide range of media in their work to give you ideas, such as the American artist Robert Rauschenberg, who combined objects with painting and print, or the French artist Annette Messager, who makes installations combining text, photographs, textiles and machinery.

Detail of an installation by Annette Messager incorporating toys and taxidermy.

1.2 Mark-making

To explore materials successfully, you need to develop your own vocabulary of mark-making. Try experimenting with each medium in as many ways as possible, provided it is safe to do so. Whenever possible, contain your experiments in an appropriate format. This might consist of a:

Sketchbook – You might use your sketchbook for investigations in different media, such as those suggested in the starter stimulus and pursued in more depth. Your sketchbook should also contain drawings of your ideas, observations and others' work, as well as any additional visual information that interests you.

Box of 3D experiments – Keep a box or container of small samples of gluing, welding, riveting, tying, carving, casting, etc. You could look for small objects from around the studio, such as screws, pieces of card, wire, scrap plastic and metal, and find ways of transforming them by connecting them, or by making replicas through modelling or casting.

Range of fabric-based samples – Keep samples of experiments of dyeing, printing, warp, weft, etc. Try dyeing with natural materials alongside man-made chemical dyes; try printing on a wide range of surfaces, from silk to coarse sacking, to see how a design translates on different ground; try weaving with wire cable or plastic bags.

Folder of examples of different exposures – Keeping a record of different exposure times will be useful for photographic projects; try experimenting with different exposures to see how it affects your imagery.

3D experiments exploring structures of bird and wasp nests.

1.3 2D processes

If you are working in two dimensions, try to explore techniques outside your comfort zone. You could try some of the following:

- Instead of drawing in pencil, use mixed media and draw in a variety of scales, from large to thumbnail. Try drawing with your opposite hand, or attach your drawing material to a long stick so you have to draw at arm's length. Time your drawings – try making very fast drawings, allowing only ten seconds to begin with, then gradually increasing to longer times.

- Explore simple print processes such as mono and relief printing. If you enjoy lino-cutting try using other surfaces to cut prints from: try woodcuts or dry-point on Perspex. Then move on to more complex processes such as screen printing and etching on metal plates.

- Develop ideas in fabric by investigating tapestry, machine embroidery and weaving; contrast this with hand sewing and knitting. You can achieve an enormous array of stitched effects on a sewing machine – explore these by sewing on different kinds of materials.

- Experiment with lens-based processes, such as lighting, capture, exposure, manipulation, development, printing and different presentation possibilities. Alongside this, try working with less complex processes, such as light-sensitive paper to make cyanotypes, and juxtapose these with other photographic outcomes.

1.4 3D processes

If you are working in 3D you should start by making small samples and **maquettes** before producing a more considered piece of work. To make something that functions in three dimensions, consider the following:

- Will it be free-standing?

- Will it be wall-mounted, i.e. some sort of relief?

- Will it be suspended?

- Will it be a multiple or unique?

If you are using a CAD/CAM program, your design will be technically accurate, but you will still need to think about translating this into different 3D materials and which of these function best, both practically and **aesthetically**. Some 3D processes you may want to explore are:

- construction – you will need to consider the weight of the material, and whether your model requires **armatures**

- mould-making

- casting

- mixed-media work

- **toiles**

- paper engineering

- model-making.

A piece of fabric exploiting surface texture through embroidery, cutting and layering.

1.5 Time-based processes

Time-based media offer huge scope for exploring media and processes, because you can incorporate other work outcomes as the subject. For example, if you look at the work of the Czech animator Jan Svankmajer, you will see that many of the props and puppets he makes for his films are wonderful sculptures in their own right. If you decide to make an animation you will need to have a carefully thought-out storyboard; flipbooks are also a great way of sequencing ideas.

You could use video or film to generate a time-based outcome, or you may prefer a computer-generated outcome. You will also need to consider whether to have an audio component; your piece could even consist entirely of sound or music – investigate the work of the American artist John Cage, who explores sound and silence. You could use web design to make an interactive site where an audience responds to your work.

You will need to consider the format for presenting your outcomes, and here you could also be innovative. Instead of using a screen, try projecting your outcome onto the side of a building or a 2D artwork you have made your 'screen'. You could even create a specific environment, which might constitute a giant *camera obscura* – check out the chambers made by land artist Chris Drury.

1.6 Exploration

Although exploration is a key component of this learning outcome, it should be central to your practice as an artist. Whenever you make work, in whatever medium, you need to constantly experiment with, investigate and combine materials.

Experimentation

You need to make lots of experiments with materials to see all the possibilities within them. Test their parameters – how malleable is your medium, and how far can you work it? Do you encounter resistance between materials – and if so, can you exploit this? If you are using water-based materials, what are the extremes of wet and dry you can explore? Try to use as many traditional methods as possible – and then subvert them. Work with as many different surfaces as you find. Analyse your experiments to generate further ideas.

An animated still showing the use of traditional puppetry and painted cut-out forms to provide a striking set.

Key terms

Maquette – a smaller, preliminary model made by an artist, before embarking on a full-scale, final piece of work.

Aesthetics – when we talk about how aesthetically pleasing an artwork is, we mean that we find an enjoyment or appreciation in its formation.

Armature – a metal framework onto which a material such as clay or plaster is moulded to form a sculpture.

Toiles – the different cloth surfaces, such as canvas and linen, used to paint on.

Investigation

This is where you will need to think carefully about equipment, technologies and processes. You may have limited facilities and may be looking to investigate straightforward, 2D processes, such as painting and drawing. If you have access to mechanical processes, you will be able to achieve a more complex range of outcomes – using electronic and digital processes in combination with hand-made pieces can generate extraordinary outcomes. For example, the British artist Paul Morrison uses digital programs to transform photographs of landscapes, which he then magnifies and hand-paints onto gallery walls as an installation. This is an exciting way of using digital and hand-based processes together.

Combination

A lot of exciting exploration comes from putting unexpected materials together. Some combinations you could try are:

- drawing on unexpected surfaces, such as film
- stitching unconventional materials together
- collaging different materials together
- making an installation with a range of materials
- responding to a particular place, which could suggest materials to use, as in a site-specific work.

1.7 Health and safety

All work environments contain potential hazards, and in the studio you will often be using equipment and materials that could be harmful if used incorrectly. At college, tutors are required to make a risk assessment before undertaking workshop sessions, and in the workplace employers should have a health and safety policy in place. It is vital that you follow any guidance on using materials and equipment safely and sensibly, and that you make your working area as safe as possible.

Can you make a risk assessment?

1. Make a list of all the hazardous materials and equipment you will be using.

2. Itemise any potential risks from these.

3. List what you can do to minimise this risk.

An example might be:

- using a Stanley knife or scalpel for cutting paper
- danger of cutting oneself if the blade slips
- place a cutting mat beneath the paper, use strokes cutting away from the other hand resting on the paper and from the body.

Activity: Hazardous artworks?

Try looking at the Tate Modern website and scrolling through the A–Z of artists in their collection. Find three pieces of work, each by a different artist, and imagine that you are the curator responsible for hanging these in the gallery.

What are the risks connected to these works:

- from members of the public? For example, if accidentally touched, how would the artwork be affected? Or could it be inadvertently unplugged?

- to members of the public? For example, could someone bang their head on a low level artwork, or trip on a cable protruding from it?

Assessment activity 2.1: Exploration and use of materials, techniques and processes

P1 P2 M1 D1

BTEC

Think about the enormous range of shapes, colours and textures that surround you in your home environment as the starting point for a set of drawings. To prevent yourself being overwhelmed, make a viewfinder by cutting a small rectangle in the middle of a piece of paper and use this to focus on different viewpoints in your house. Divide an A1 piece of paper into 16 sections and use each of these to make a drawing inspired by one of the views. Try and make each drawing in a different medium.

You could use:

- biro, pencil, felt tip, marker pen
- charcoal, chalk, pastel
- ink, paint
- collage, cut-outs, rubbings
- random finds from around the home – shoe polish, make-up, tea, coffee, etc.

You could also take photographs and use one as the basis for a section. Also think about collaging and cutting into the image, or drawing over it rather than just sticking it down.

Now select five of these outcomes to translate into a range of panels approximately 30 x 30cm to mount within an exhibition context. Be inventive in the way you use materials and draw up a health and safety checklist, outlining any potential hazards with the media you will be using.

1. You could make a relief for one of your panels – explore available 3D materials.
2. You could make a fabric-based panel, using different sewing machine techniques and a range of threads and wires.
3. Try projecting a photographic image, film or video clip on to either a white 30 x 30cm panel or on to a wall space.

Grading tips

To achieve **M1** try to present a sketchbook full of ideas and experiments: if you have worked in 3D include samples and maquettes too. Try and show that you really understand the materials you are using. If you push each media to the limit – and you should try using your materials in unexpected ways – and support this with a review and analysis of your work, you will achieve **D1**.

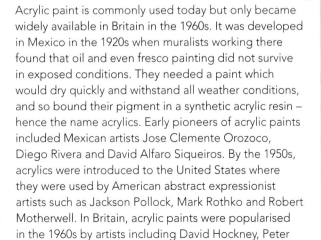

Did you know?

Acrylic paint is commonly used today but only became widely available in Britain in the 1960s. It was developed in Mexico in the 1920s when muralists working there found that oil and even fresco painting did not survive in exposed conditions. They needed a paint which would dry quickly and withstand all weather conditions, and so bound their pigment in a synthetic acrylic resin – hence the name acrylics. Early pioneers of acrylic paints included Mexican artists Jose Clemente Orozoco, Diego Rivera and David Alfaro Siqueiros. By the 1950s, acrylics were introduced to the United States where they were used by American abstract expressionist artists such as Jackson Pollock, Mark Rothko and Robert Motherwell. In Britain, acrylic paints were popularised in the 1960s by artists including David Hockney, Peter Blake and Bridget Riley.

Case study: Preparing a studio for a printmaking session

Christian and Jo are students who will be working with 15 Year 8 schoolchildren on a project their college is organising for local secondary schools. They will be assisting their tutor in running a print workshop in one of the college studios. The morning will start with a **monoprinting** session, which will then lead on to a simple screen-print workshop.

Both Christian and Jo have done a lot of printmaking but haven't had to assist in setting up a space for working in before, and neither has worked with this group of children. They will have to prepare the studio and lay out materials, and will need to work out a list of materials and equipment required in advance with their tutor.

1. What would you include on this materials list to give pupils the widest possible opportunities for experimenting with specific processes?

2. What are the risks attached to the materials and processes that they will be using, and what can Christian and Jo do to ensure that the studio environment is as safe as possible?

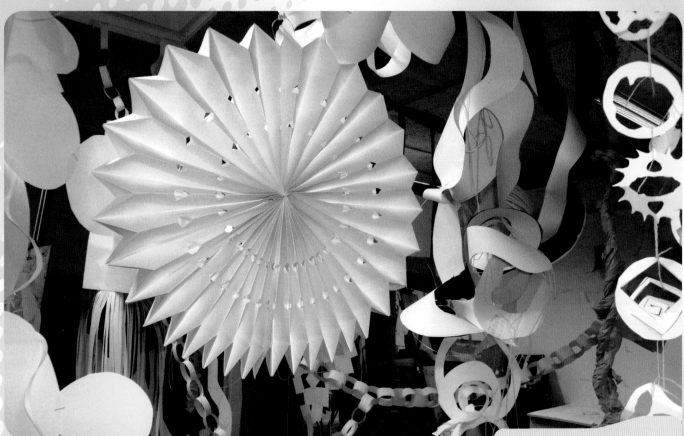

Paper structures made and installed by students as a stimulus for a printmaking workshop.

Key term

Monoprint – a straightforward means of making a simple print by rollering printing ink onto a flat, wipeable surface, such as glass or Perspex, and laying a piece of paper on top. By drawing on the back of the paper a mirror image of the original drawing is achieved on the reverse side. Although the name suggests that only one print can be achieved, it's usually possible to get at least one additional print – the 'ghost' print – from the residual ink remaining on the wipeable surface.

2. Be able to use materials, techniques and processes

For Learning Outcome 1 you will have explored a wide range of media and experimented with different techniques and processes. You will now be developing work towards a specific outcome and building upon the knowledge you've already gained. You will have learnt the possibilities and limitations of your materials and will be applying this knowledge to ensure a dynamic outcome.

This learning outcome asks you to demonstrate the knowledge you've gained from your experimentation. The key areas are limitations, potential and investigation.

2.1 Apply knowledge

Limitations

All professional artists have limitations imposed upon their work, usually either by venue, budget, materials, or time; and they will strive to deliver an exciting piece of work within these constraints. You are going to have limitations imposed on you by the following.

1. Selection – you will need to make a selection from your initial experimentation and ideas, and pursue these more thoroughly. You will have to be ruthless in discarding ideas that are at a tangent to your main thought process.

2. Intentions – your own ideas for an outcome will set some of your limits – for example, if you are working towards producing a wearable garment or structure, you will need to temper innovative materials with wearability.

3. Context – again, there will be constraints here. For example, if you are making a piece of work for exhibition the gallery space will impose parameters: likewise, an illustration project is likely to be in response to a specific text or idea.

4. The brief – this may limit you in terms of media – for example, you may be required to make a lens-based outcome – and you will certainly have a limited amount of time in which to produce your piece of work. You will need to plan your studio time carefully to achieve the most you can within the work schedule that you have.

How would you present your work within this space?

Potential

Recognising the strengths and possibilities within materials is vital to making a successful art work. Some of the greatest artists have been those who know how to exploit the potential of their materials and processes – think of the impact of the designer Issey Miyake's experimentation with pleating on the fashion industry. In exploring the potential of the materials that you are using, you should think about the following.

1. Experiments – manipulate media and apply your knowledge in as many ways as possible. Look at the particular properties and characteristics of the materials you are working with and think how to investigate these – you might want to challenge preconceived ideas of what is possible. Even if an experiment doesn't achieve what you originally hoped for it could still provide new ideas. Remember to make a risk assessment and maintain safe studio practice at all times.

2. Testing – what can you actually do with the medium? Make samples to see how to be adventurous and take risks!

3. Surfaces – whatever the media, you will be able to experiment with a range of surfaces. Think about opposites – smooth/rough, natural/man-made, hard/soft and how you can exploit these. Conversely, you may wish to work with as many types of similar surface as possible – for example, find different types of filament, such as thread/wool/rope/wire/string/cord.

4. Supports – again, be experimental, but make sure your support will hold the medium you are applying to it. For a sculptural piece it is essential that you take advice from a tutor or technician about armatures and/or underpinning: and if you decide to work on an ambitious scale make sure that you will be able to move your work easily and safely at the end of the project.

5. Wetness – investigate how far you can saturate the materials you are working with in order to effect interesting results.

- Paper is amazingly resilient even when wet – you could load watercolour paper with paint and achieve intense outcomes. Or you could pulp newsprint and add other materials, such as leaves or feathers, to create your own paper if you have a screen to mould it on.

- Try experimenting with clay at different levels of wetness – you could contrast organic manipulated forms using very wet clay with more controlled pieces.

6. Dryness – see how you can manipulate dryness. Look at the experiments with wetness and work in reverse. For example, use paint without the addition of water so you have dry, scratchy brushstrokes, or very thick paint that is like toothpaste in texture; make very delicate and brittle clay experiments that exploit their fragility.

7. Malleability – the word 'malleable' means flexible or pliable – you might explore how malleable you can make the materials you're working with.

- Try beating or hammering lightweight metals such as aluminium or copper to see how you can transform their shape and texture.

- Stretch and contort fabrics – see how this affects any sewing or printing you work into them.

8. Workability – for some materials to be workable, you will have to treat or prepare them first. Some examples might include:

- Canvas – this needs to be primed before you paint on it.

- Etching plates – unless you are making a dry-point etching, you will need to lay a waxy ground on your plate to draw into before immersing it in acid.

- If you are making a cyanotype you will need to coat the surface of your paper or fabric in the appropriate chemicals in a darkened space, and allow these to dry before you can make your images.

- You will need to heat wax safely before it is workable, and you will almost certainly be required to have a fire blanket in your studio if you are using a wax pot.

9. Resistance – exploring the resistance of materials can lead to dynamic results. However, you must ensure that all your experimentation is conducted safely, especially if outcomes are unpredictable – such as when using contrasting three-dimensional materials.

You could do some very straightforward experiments using wax crayons or candles to generate wax resist. Look at the three-dimensional drawings that the British sculptor Henry Moore made for his sculptures using wax resist and ink, or his powerful studies of the underground made during the Blitz.

Investigation

Learning Outcome 2 requires you to demonstrate how you use materials, techniques and processes, so you will need to show how you have undertaken your investigation. Your final outcome will almost certainly begin as an idea in your sketchbook,

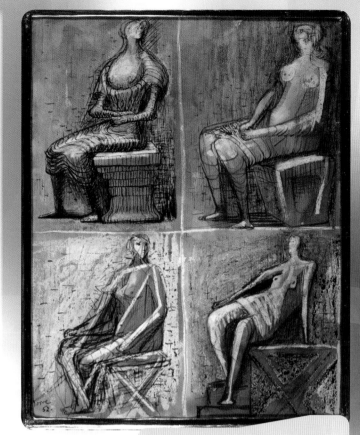

Henry Moore's use of wax resist in these drawings has enhanced the three-dimensional qualities of the figures.

which you will then develop through drawing into a sequence of sketches or designs. Depending on your brief and the equipment and technologies available, you will start making samples, models, maquettes or visual imagery to show the development of your ideas. Recording the progression of your work will not only be beneficial to your assessment, but will act as a useful document for developing future ideas that explore similar materials. Keep test pieces and other examples of your experimentation, as these will help link the investigation, from initial stimulus to finished pieces.

Did you know?

Rachel Whiteread's 1993 work *House* – a life-size cast of an empty East London house which had been demolished – was one of the most controversial pieces of art of recent years. Although she used a relatively modern material – concrete – and a monumental scale, the basic principles of the casting process have remained unchanged since the Bronze Age.

Assessment activity 2.2: Apply your knowledge to explore potential

For this activity you will be exploring painting supports, applying the paint handling you developed in the Exploring painting activity to a range of surfaces. Start by cutting several pieces of wood, Perspex and metal to a similar size – you could also look for more readily available materials such as different thicknesses of card and paper, fabric and plastic lids from packaging. You might even try making a small canvas stretcher or casting a block of plaster.

Try priming some of these supports – certain surfaces may be resistant but this will help you understand the limitations of the materials. You could also try soaking fabric or paper supports, or adding wax resist to your surfaces. You are now ready to paint on these surfaces and exploit the paint effects you explored before – don't forget your experiments with mark-making. Once you have obtained some results, try combining them, such as by stretching fabric over part of a wooden block, or joining different supports together to make a more interesting structure. Record your findings in your sketchbook – it's a good idea to take photographs so you have a visual record, and to compare your results with those of fellow students. By evaluating these you will have a thorough record to help generate a dynamic final piece.

Grading tips

Look at other artists' work to give you ideas, so that your outcomes are really adventurous. Document your workings thoroughly – you could almost treat your records of your experiments like recipe cards, so that you will know how to create similar effects in the future. Analyse these in depth to show that you have pushed your work as far as you can.

3. Understand the suitability of materials, techniques and processes

By now, your wide-ranging experimental work will have led to some exciting final pieces, and you will have demonstrated the skills and knowledge gained from your initial exploration of materials, techniques and processes. Learning Outcome 3 requires you to show that you have understood the possibilities of the media by evaluating the development of your work, and the decisions taken to progress your ideas. Try to be self-critical in your evaluation and use new terminology to show the development of your vocabulary.

3.1 Evaluate suitability

Being able to evaluate work successfully is essential to progressing your ideas and outcomes. Today's most innovative artists and designers constantly provide statements about their practice and, in doing so, analyse past outcomes in order to move forward with new concepts. When reviewing your work, you will need to assess whether you have fulfilled your intentions. Be honest and realistic about this – learn to be self-critical.

Try this

You might try evaluating someone else's work to help you consider your own. For example, the Design Museum holds examples of iconic 20th- and 21st-century design work, revered for its aesthetic quality, innovation and construction. Using either the library or websites (such as that of the Design Museum – www.designmuseum.org), research a piece of modern furniture design that inspires you, such as Arne Jacobsen's 'Egg' chair, or Tord Boontje's lighting pieces; then contrast this with an everyday example of the same type of furniture, such as a park bench or bedside lamp. Make drawings of each and

Tord Boontje's lighting forms are inspired by simple cut-out shapes but rely on high-precision cutting techniques for manufacture.

consider the following questions.

- What are the qualities of each piece? Are they fit for purpose?

- What do you think inspired the designer, and how do you feel the design works aesthetically?

- How would these pieces of furniture translate into different materials, such as metal to fabric, or glass to waxed paper?

- How would you develop these designs further with unlimited time and resources?

Now consider your own outcome for this unit, and try to answer similar questions. If you find this difficult consult your peer group – you need them to be truthful and constructive in their criticism. You could even present them – or yourself – with a checklist or questionnaire, to include the following questions.

Qualities

- Does your piece work aesthetically, and what are its characteristics?

- Does it have uses or effects?

- Is it fit for purpose?

- What are the limitations of your piece of work?

- What is its creative potential?

Alternative options

Look at your work and consider other options for its manufacture. Review this in conjunction with your earlier experimentation and the ideas you chose to pursue. Think about James in the case study at the beginning of this section and imagine him questioning his outcomes. For example, he could consider the scale of his canvas paintings, and whether a different size might have been better. Would his painting have been more successful in oils? Could he use different combinations of materials, such as a support made of collaged canvas and wood?

Working methods

Analyse your working methods – what do you think was successful, and what could you have done differently? You should look at other artists' work and make comparisons between their working methods and yours, and acknowledge their influence – as a professional artist you will need to see your work in the context of others and be aware of new ideas within your field.

Correct terminology

You will probably have learned new technical terms for this assignment. Make sure you always use the correct terminology – check with your tutors if you are unsure. Your critical vocabulary will expand, too, as you become more confident and practised at evaluating.

Decisions

Throughout the making of your work you will have made many decisions. Make clear in your evaluation why you opted for particular choices. Your evaluation should include your decisions concerning:

1. use of materials

2. techniques used in conjunction with these

3. equipment needed to make your work

4. crafts and technologies used

5. other processes you have incorporated

6. judgements made about suitability.

Activity: Developing ideas

Can you find an artwork and a supporting sketch or maquette by a famous artist? For example, see if you can find a drawing by Matisse and a painting which he then developed from this or a sculpture by Giacometti and the preliminary ideas for this. What kind of decisions did the artist have to make between having the idea and the final outcome?

3.2 Stages of the process

Your evaluation of your work will usually be in a written format, although there may be occasions when you make a presentation, an audio-visual taped discussion, or complete a questionnaire or evidence sheets. Whatever form it takes, you should keep a visual record of your assignment. An annotated sketchbook is vital to all assignments, but you could also have worksheets and examples of experiments, such as samples, test pieces and video clips. This visual record should include the following:

Initial experiments – the starting point for your exploration of media.

Ideas – the stimuli for your work.

Raw state – photographs or examples of media in its raw state before your intervention, for example, the type of clay you used to create a ceramic piece.

Setting and drying time – keep a visual record of work in its unfinished state, such as a plaster cast being taken, and document the result as it sets.

Preparation and planning – show any preparation or planning you undertook in producing your work.

Storage – you will have to consider storage carefully, especially as most studios have limited space – this is one reason why good documentation is vital. If you are storing computer files, back up work regularly and put all supporting work on to one disk.

Problem solving – you are likely to encounter problems while developing a piece of work – show what these problems involved, and how you attempted to resolve them.

Development – show any changes to your work outcome; a piece of work doesn't always develop in the way you hope, and having a record of an earlier stage is useful for comparison.

Finishing – show the various ways that you have approached finishing your work.

Presentation – make sure that you present your work as professionally as possible – this will be an important part of your future practice. Poor presentation will undermine your assessment, however good the content of a work.

Case study: Emma, second year BTEC student

Emma has made a series of stoneware vessels that have been shortlisted for a student competition run by the local museum. The competition winner will be asked to make a piece of work in response to the museum's ceramics collection, which ranges from medieval pottery to Wedgwood to a vase by Grayson Perry. Emma will have to present her ideas to a selection committee comprising four established ceramicists. Emma is worried about how to prepare for this, as there is little time available to make new work, although she has good documentation of previous work and always keeps test pieces from kiln firings.

1. **What could Emma show the panel to give them an idea of how her work could develop?**
2. **How should she present this?**
3. **What kind of language should she use in her presentation?**
4. **What should she consider when looking at the museum collection as a source of ideas?**

Assessment activity 2.3: Stages of the process

Think about the 'Try this' activity at the beginning of this learning outcome, in which you were asked to select an innovative piece of furniture design and contrast it with an everyday version of a similar object. Using the evaluation you have already undertaken, try to design your own piece of furniture. Your choice of material should be inspired by recycling and incorporate salvaged substances. Once you have made some drawings, make some small maquettes and samples to give an idea of your design in 3D. You could start by manipulating paper in different ways to trigger ideas, and then translate these into other materials. Try to evaluate your work as critically as you have the designer and everyday pieces, and imagine the potential and limitations of your media were your models to be translated to full size.

1. Try different combinations of recycled materials available, and consider carefully how you can transform these within a safe studio environment.

2. Take some photographs of these models. This could give you some ambiguous images, where the scale of your maquettes will be unclear – your work could even appear monumental.

3. Present one outcome as a final idea, and describe the process of making it either visually or through a written evaluation.

Grading tips

To achieve a merit for this unit, try to consider really carefully the different types of furniture that exist. By researching a wide range of possibilities, from historical to contemporary, and then trying to link these together through drawing, you will achieve some really dynamic designs which will inspire a more experimental approach to the media you use. If you make a really ambitious series of designs and maquettes, and review your work thoroughly, you could achieve a distinction.

Did you know?

Tate Thames Dig by the American artist Mark Dion was the first work to be commissioned by Tate Modern, in 1999. Objects, fragments and shards were recovered from the Millbank and Bankside areas of the river Thames, and the finds then presented in a 'cabinet of curiosities' at the museum. The work looks at the relationship between art and archaeology, and at forms of collecting and display, and is an innovative approach to creating a portrait of London.

Why do you think Mark Dion's *Tate Thames Dig* is an interactive artwork? How would you present archaeological fragments in a gallery context?

Sara Trillo
Fine artist

Sara Trillo's *Swan Maiden Dress*.

Sara trained as a painter at Norwich School of Art in the mid-1980s.

Her early work consisted of colourful semi-figurative paintings on paper, but since having twins in 2000, she has made mainly site-specific work or worked to commission. Her work is still paper based but now takes the form of fragile constructions and drawings, usually in delicate or muted colours. Her interest in paper has given her an understanding of different paper weights, and how these are affected by materials.

'I often use handmade papers and sometimes very ordinary paper, such as sheets from exercise books or brown parcel paper, but always experiment rigorously with the paints, inks and glues. One commission was for a group show in Belgium when I was heavily pregnant and using a lot of bird symbolism, so I decided to make a life-size work in the shape of a maternity dress. In folklore, swan maidens were women who changed their shape; as my shape had changed during pregnancy, I decided to incorporate swan feathers. I first made small paper maquettes of the dress and attached feathers to it, either gluing or pushing the feather quills into the surface. These looked too tribal, so I experimented with trapping the feathers between layers of tissue paper. I liked the result but felt that it might tear easily. I then experimented with gluing layers of tissue paper together to strengthen the paper while maintaining the delicate appearance. I also investigated different kinds of glues to see which would be most robust, and explored different makes of tissue paper, as some were flimsier than others; I wanted to use acid-free paper so the work would be easier to conserve. I then made a pattern of the dress and collaged pieces together to form the dress.

'The dress was surprisingly strong, but when suspended from the gallery ceiling had the delicate fairytale quality I'd hoped to achieve.'

Think about it!

- Could you rework this idea, using the same materials, to make something less labour intensive?
- Could you present a fragile work in a gallery that would work equally well in the home of a potential purchaser?

Just checking

1. Make sure you have thoroughly reviewed all your materials, techniques and processes. Ask yourself how you could rework your outcome with:

   - more time

   - more materials

   - different scales

   - different contexts, such as presenting your work in a gallery or museum space.

2. Have you made an in-depth investigation of your materials and processes?

3. Have you used materials, techniques and processes safely? If you dislike writing, make diagrams or drawings showing potential hazards, and how these can be managed safely.

4. Show a well-considered approach to materials, techniques and processes. Ask peers and tutors for suggestions of what else you could do with your work – they may suggest possibilities you haven't considered.

5. Make sure you manage your studio time effectively so you don't miss out on workshops and facilities with limited availability.

edexcel

Assignment tips

- Keep all your preparation material, even if you are unhappy with it. It will show your ideas and thinking, and demonstrate how hard you have worked.

- Present all your work neatly and professionally. If you have swatches or small studies on loose paper, mount them on large sheets of paper or thin card. Don't overload this sheet, and use a non-permanent glue such as Pritstick, as you may want to re-use examples of your work later. Label everything clearly.

- To achieve **M1**, **M2** and **D1** you will need to show in-depth investigation of materials and techniques and understanding of how to exploit their characteristics. A photographic record of the project is especially useful if your work is impermanent or to be reworked. You could ask someone to film or video you at different stages.

- Review your work at each stage and make sure you present a thorough evaluation at the end. A good analysis of how you could have improved your final outcome will help achieve a merit and distinction grade **M1**, **D1**. Contextualise your work with that of other artists and designers and be ambitious in your thinking. If you find writing difficult, record yourself talking through your outcomes, such as on a mobile phone downloaded to a CD-ROM.

3 Ideas and concepts in art and design

For all artists and designers the essential starting point in creating successful work is generating and developing ideas. We often see art works or design products in galleries and museums that impress us by their innovation, originality and imaginative qualities, but we are rarely aware of the ideas and experiments that have been refined or discarded in the process of creation.

To be successful in your work you need to understand how central creative thinking is to all artists and designers. You also need to contextualise your work by comparison with that of others: by researching and analysing the ideas and concepts behind contemporary and historical art and design you will discover the skills practitioners have used to develop their ideas; you should use this research to influence your own outcomes. As a practitioner, it is essential not only to generate ideas but to be able to refine your ideas to suit a given brief, and to present your ideas and outcomes coherently to an audience or client.

Learning outcomes

After completing this unit you should:

1. understand how ideas and concepts inform art and design work
2. know how to generate ideas
3. be able to generate and refine ideas in response to given briefs
4. be able to communicate and present ideas and outcomes to different audiences.

Assessment and grading criteria

This table shows you what you must do in order to achieve a **pass**, **merit** or **distinction** grade, and where you can find activities in this book to help you.

To achieve a **pass** grade the evidence must show that you are able to:	To achieve a **merit** grade the evidence must show that, in addition to the pass criteria, you are able to:	To achieve a **distinction** grade the evidence must show that, in addition to the pass and merit criteria, you are able to:
P1 compare ideas and concepts in art and design work **See Assessment activities 3.1, page 49; 3.3 page 60**	**M1** use the results of purposeful research and investigation to inform own ideas and concepts, demonstrating coherent direction in originating and developing ideas **See Assessment activities 3.1, page 49; 3.3, page 60**	**D1** independently analyse and interpret research to generate personal ideas and concepts, applying sophisticated thinking in generating, modifying and synthesising original ideas **See Assessment activities 3.1, page 49; 3.3, page 60**
P2 investigate ideas generating techniques **See Assessment activities 3.1 page 49; 3.2, page 54; 3.3, page 60**	**M2** demonstrate a considered approach to producing purposeful ideas and solutions in response to briefs, presenting work coherently and effectively **See Assessment activities 3.2, page 54; 3.3, page 60**	**D2** demonstrate an individual and perceptive approach to producing and communicating innovative and engaging work using sophisticated presentation methods **See Assessment activity 3.3, page 60**
P3 generate and refine ideas in response to given briefs **See Assessment activity 3.3, page 60**		
P4 communicate and present ideas and outcomes to different audiences **See Assessment activity 3.3, page 60**		

How you will be assessed

You will be asked to make work in response to a brief which may have an actual or fictional client. You will need to generate lots of ideas and use research to enrich, refine and contextualise the development of these workings. By the end of the project you will need to present your outcome to an audience which might include your tutors, peers and client, so you will have to adopt a professional approach in communicating your ideas effectively, and in choosing a relevant presentation method.

Tamsin

For this project I had to make a piece of headwear inspired by contemporary architecture. My tutor suggested I look at the work of Frank Gehry, as his initial ideas are often made with simple pen or pencil marks, and his maquettes use everyday materials such as tape and corrugated card. This gave me confidence to make 3D samples myself, so I started to explore stitching papers and card together.

I also looked at fashion designers to explore headwear, using the library and Internet to research individuals and museums with fashion and design collections. I researched the artist Lucy Orta, who uses protective clothes to initiate her ideas, which led me to look at protective headwear, particularly bee-keeping wear and veils, and encouraged me to experiment with unusual materials in the workshop, such as beaten metal.

At first my pieces looked clumsy, but the technician showed me different ways of working the metal, until I decided to combine metal with fabric. I began attaching pieces of calico to squares of aluminium, and ended up with a final piece that looked amazing but was uncomfortable to wear!

I then had to present my ideas, experiments and final piece to my tutors – one of whom was acting as a gallery client – using notes and PowerPoint®. They were pleased that I had produced an outcome which was really different from my previous work.

Over to you!

- How would you begin your research if you were doing this project?
- Can you think of other artists and architects that Tamsin could have looked at?
- What would you do to prepare for a presentation in a project like this?

Researching innovative artists, such as Frank Gehry, will give you lots of ideas for working with more ambitious materials.

1. Understand how ideas and concepts inform art and design work

How can concepts inform your art work?

This short activity will help you to think about how a different reference can influence your ideas.

In the studio, play a short piece of classical music (about five minutes long). Play it again and, using brush and ink, try to make marks in response to the music. If there seems to be a narrative to the music, you could add figurative forms or shapes – whatever seems relevant.

Now put your sheet aside and, using coloured pastels and paints, listen to the music again and try and interpret it in terms of colour. Try to incorporate shapes or imagery conjured up by the music, such as sweeping marks or layers of colour.

Now return to your assignment brief and listen to the music while working on it.

1. Has the music affected your previous approach to this project? Will you reconsider some of your previous ideas?

2. Can you use the mark-making and colour you developed while listening to the music?

3. How might different kinds of music, such as jazz or world music affect your idea?

A rich and diverse range of ideas is the starting point for any piece of work, but ideas do not stand alone – they refer to other **concepts** and need to be put into context. In addition to thoroughly researching and refining your ideas, for this learning outcome you will need to show references to other artists, movements, art forms and cultures, and understand how they are communicated. While this is a key component of Unit 3, it is also fundamental to all your other work.

1.1 References

It is impossible to set out here all the potential reference points that surround you. We live in a society constantly bombarded by visual imagery, much of it referencing other art works, historical events or topical issues and iconic cultural moments. Some of the references you could explore within your work are set out on the following pages.

Key term

Concept – the notion or idea that underpins and is communicated by an art work.

Visual

You may be given a brief that asks you to respond to your immediate environment. It is also likely that you will be asked to make work from first-hand observation, in order to develop your ability to look at and communicate visual information. Alongside observational work, you will also be making abstract or imaginative imagery. Rather than providing subject matter, these references may be an excuse for drawing, by triggering memories, associations and ideas for mark-making, or suggest a particular concept or investigation.

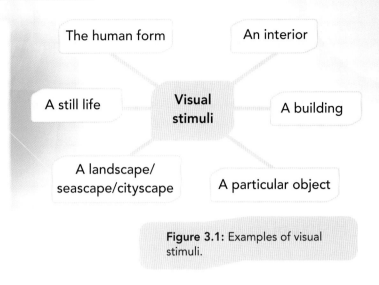

Figure 3.1: Examples of visual stimuli.

Non-visual

It is often useful to respond to non-visual material as a means of freeing yourself from convention and developing your visual language. The table below lists some of this potential material.

Table 3.1: Types and examples of non-visual material.

Types of non-visual material	Examples
Text and the spoken word	A piece of writing, fragment of text or speech, such as a paragraph from a newspaper or magazine, or an overheard conversation.
Emotions	You could make a series of drawings in response to the same subject matter while imagining yourself in a different emotional state – angry, subdued, excited, sad, etc. You can use different media and will need to think carefully about the kind of marks you are making and how they reinforce the emotion you are trying to convey.
Music	Experiment with seeing how different music affects your outcomes by contrasting listening to rock and pop with listening to jazz and classical music.
Touch	Try using your media in as many ways as possible without worrying about a particular result. The Catalan artist Antoni Tapies makes paintings using abstract motifs inspired by his surroundings and memories of the Spanish Civil War. His work is extremely physical and develops in accordance with the way materials interact. When making a large-scale work, he might lay the canvas on his studio floor and use a broom to sweep pigment over it, before sprinkling other matter onto the surface, and then making large gestural marks suggested by the wet paint.

Contemporary

When developing ideas, it is important to look at contemporary art and culture. You need to make connections between your work and that of other artists, and examine how they relate to modern life and society. Whatever your specialism, try to be as wide-ranging in your reference points as possible – linking apparently diverse references will help make your work more innovative.

Historical

When looking at contemporary art works, you will frequently see that the artist may have made references to historical events, trends or artists. For example, Jake and Dinos Chapman collaborated and came to prominence as part of the Young British Artists movement supported by Charles Saatchi. Their work explores disfigured human forms, torture and grotesques, some of which were inspired by Goya's 18th-century etchings depicting scenes of terror, called 'The Disasters of War'.

Signpost

Looking at different art movements from the past will provide you with a huge range of stimuli. The 20th century witnessed extraordinary technological advances, and these were mirrored by art movements such as Dada and Constructivism, which challenged the conventions of the time. See Unit 5.

Sustainability

If you are making a design outcome you will need to think about wider global concerns, such as whether your product can be manufactured from **sustainable** resources. Consider how your ideas impact upon the environment, and whether you have made a piece of work that is environmentally friendly. Can you incorporate recycled materials into your product, or make it recyclable? Does it use sustainable materials and does it require a large amount of energy to manufacture? If you are making a work to site outdoors, is it sensitive to the location?

Did you know?

The collections of the acclaimed British fashion designer Vivienne Westwood, who became famous for her punk clothing, have frequently been inspired by 17th- and 18th-century costume.

Use local museums and national collections, such as the British Museum and the V&A, to explore historical ideas and artefacts – you will be amazed at how 'modern' many of them seem – and gain lots of ideas and information to support your project brief.

See if you can find references to Goya in this artwork, *Sex*, by Jake and Dinos Chapman.

Art and society

How does art impact on society? Are you making something which will be elitist, accessible to only a tiny proportion of the population (such as an artwork exhibited only in a private gallery), or are you hoping to reach a wide audience (such as an advertising campaign screened on prime-time television or printed in the daily newspapers)? How do you want your work to be perceived by this audience?

You may want to make a piece of work that exploits the media in some way, in order to target a particular audience. A younger audience will be highly tuned to contemporary technologies and can be easily accessed via blogs and websites. It may be easier to target an older audience through radio, television or newspapers. You could also consider a project that uses:

• billboards

• empty shop windows/spaces

• leaflets.

Performing arts

You could also explore references from the performing arts for your work outcome. Since the Renaissance, many artists have tried to create the illusion of a stage set within their paintings. The 16th-century Spanish artist Juan Sánchez Cotán positioned fruit and vegetables in a highly theatrical manner. Others, such as Edgar Degas and Henri Matisse, have tried to express the movement of dancers in their paintings. Film has allowed artists to document movement, and many animations refer to theatre and dance, or use music as an integral part of their construction. You could even consider designing your work as a performance and investigate artists who make this the focus of their practice.

Philosophy and religion

Use the research you undertook earlier into art movements to generate ideas about how philosophical and religious beliefs can influence visual imagery. Whether or not you share the thinking of the artists behind these artefacts and paintings, you might find a rich source of narrative to stimulate your ideas, and an insight into different thought processes.

Activity: Create a storyboard

Look at a figurative painting that intrigues you. Create a storyboard based on the narrative you think could be unfolding in the painting, and use this as the basis for a performance.

Key term

Sustainable – the word sustainable is applied to materials and manufacturing processes that can be easily obtained and replaced and therefore have a less harmful effect on the environment. If you are using timber, for example, look for wood that comes from a sustainable source.

Activity: Other artists

You will need to contextualise your work constantly against that of other designers. See if you can research someone who is known across several areas. For example, William Blake was a famous artist and poet known as a visionary – why? What is a visionary? Can you give examples of any of the mythologies he referred to in his work? Which artists, designers, musicians and writers have subsequently been influenced by his work?

Oral and written sources

Oral and written influences could also inform your art and design work. While some artists, such as illustrators, are required to respond to specific texts, others also make text central to their practice, or use writing as a stimulus for ideas.

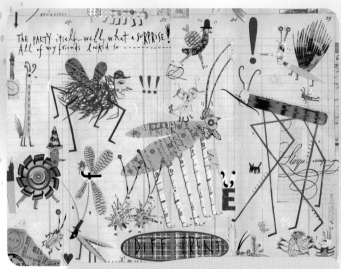

The Italian-born illustrator Sara Fanelli often uses text from old diaries, shopping lists and school exercise books as a surface to draw on, or uses lines of text to reinforce the power of her illustrations.

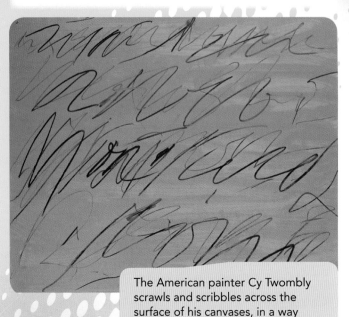

The American painter Cy Twombly scrawls and scribbles across the surface of his canvases, in a way that often seems unintelligible to the audience.

Jenny Holzer is an American conceptual artist, who since the late 1970s has installed texts in public spaces on plaques, billboards, projections and LED signs.

Activity: Communication and language

Catalogues, books, television and film often use sophisticated language to describe and discuss works of art. Make sure you understand all the following terms, and try to apply them to examples of artists' works:

- meaning
- **metaphor**
- ambiguity
- concept
- **icon**
- vision
- **semantics**
- **myth**.

Key terms

Semantics – relating to meaning.

Metaphor – describing something in a way that does not have literal meaning, for example, 'raining cats and dogs'.

Icons – traditionally images of religious figures used for worship, but can mean anyone who is widely admired and looked up to. The term is also used to describe symbols or graphic representations, such as icons on a computer screen.

Myth – a traditional narrative involving supernatural or imaginary characters. It can also mean a widely held but false idea.

Assessment activity 3.1: Understanding how others' ideas can inform your artwork

Make a quick drawing in any media of a view from a window, such as from your college studio, a room at home, a car/bus/train journey, etc.

Find four very different artists or art movements from the 20th century. You need to focus on visual information rather than writing, so just keep a record of the title, date and media of the work. Although the Internet is great for accessing information quickly, you will find better reproductions in books. Look carefully at the concept behind each movement and try to make another drawing of your view using this idea as a starting point. For example, if you have drawn a street scene and have chosen to research Futurism, try to add a sense of movement to your next drawing. Use colour if appropriate – in the case of Fauvism this would be essential.

1. You should end up with five very different versions of the same view. Without referring to them, draw your view again.

2. Has looking at others' work changed your way of seeing?

3. Have you approached your choice of media differently?

4. Has your research given you ideas about how to develop this further?

Grading tips

If your initial research is more thorough you could achieve a merit **M** or even a distinction **D** for the first part of this activity.

- When undertaking research you could make some drawings of the work of artists or movements that interest you; annotate these and think about why you have chosen particular images. Then consider carefully the connections between these and your own work through sketches and diagrams: how are you incorporating the ideas and thinking of others into your own outcomes? **M**

- Evaluate your research as it develops and show that you are developing your ideas in ways that successfully exploit your research. **D**

2. Know how to generate ideas

Ideas are at the heart of all creative thinking. Many different strategies are used by professional practitioners to trigger and develop starting points for work outcomes, ranging from imaginative and intellectual responses to making first-hand observational work from different sources.

others. Keep a record of all your initial thinking – even if you don't go on to develop all your ideas at this stage you will be able to refer to them in future projects, and having a record will enable you to see connections between different aspects of your practice.

2.1 Investigating techniques

There are numerous ways of generating ideas, some of which will work more successfully than

First-hand observation

For many artists and designers, looking at the world around them and responding to this through drawing from observation is the most useful way of starting an art work. We call this first-hand observation, because you are witnessing something directly. It is always a good idea to make drawings in this way, as it forces you to look hard at the subject in front of you and make decisions about the kind of information you wish to select. You will also be refining and improving your drawing skills and developing your way of looking at the world.

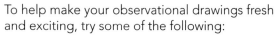

Activity: Create observational drawings

To help make your observational drawings fresh and exciting, try some of the following:

1. Make a series of grounds to work on – apply different media, such as collage, paint or ink, to a range of different types and sizes of paper, from cartridge to newsprint and tissue. You will have to think carefully about how you apply the information to the surface you are working on, which will force you to create more thoughtful drawings.

2. Time yourself – make drawings at different paces to bring spontaneity to your work. A quick drawing of three minutes will have more liveliness and capture the essence of your subject matter, but convey less information; a drawing of the same subject made over 30 minutes will have more information but could be laboured.

Key term

Ground – the surface that artists work on, usually applied to painting and thus referring to paper, canvas, wood or walls. Preparing grounds means making the surface suitable for painting on, such as by priming canvas for oils/acrylics or applying gesso for tempera painting.

Practical exploration

Use as many different media as possible to explore your starting point. For example, try looking at part of your college building. You could make a series of drawings on **grounds**, as already suggested, or use other media:

- Make rubbings of different surfaces on paper, then press clay against the surface and make a plaster relief from your impression. Think about the contrast between these outcomes.

- Use a camera to record the building at different times of the day, or to deliberately manipulate lighting.

- If you have permission, make quick paper and wire forms to install within a particular location – how does this transform the space? Or use the space as a setting to document another piece of work – how does this make you reconsider the environment?

- Think about scale – a drawing that you make on a piece of paper the size of a bus ticket will look completely different translated to A1 size.

Testing

Sometimes you can get exciting ideas just by exploring the medium you are working with, without trying to achieve a specific outcome. Being experimental and pushing parameters is vital – think back to the paint experimentation task (Exploring painting) in Unit 2. Even if you think your idea is impossible to achieve, try it – it may not work but you are likely to get another idea from the outcome.

It is also important to overcome preconceptions and develop the process you have undertaken. For example, if you are mono-printing, try using this process on other papers, such as found paper bags, text, etc., or on different surfaces such as fabrics. You could work outside and use mud as your ink; you could develop a range of stencils, from found organic matter to intricately cut paper stencils, or try working on a huge scale. Be inventive – and be ambitious!

Serial thinking

Another way of approaching ideas is through serial thinking, where one idea leads logically to another, producing a sequence. You could link your ideas through:

- a written list of ideas

- a visual list – use small thumbnail sketches or symbols

- a diagram with arrows leading to the next idea

- a storyboard format – progress your ideas within boxes as in a comic strip.

Free association

Free association is a great way of liberating ideas. You could think about doing this individually, but it also works well in a small group. One of you says a word that connects to your project, such as 'surface', and the next person says the first thing he/she thinks of, such as 'cleaning product'. Record all the words or phrases that you come up with and then try to describe them visually. Keep your drawings fast-paced – these are quick ideas – and vary media and scale. You should end up with an amazing sheet that will lead to further ideas.

Another way of producing unexpected outcomes is to think of bizarre combinations. For example, draw yourself as a piece of furniture – what would you be? As before, you need to make fast responses, which will help create spontaneous, lively work. This is a great way of freeing yourself from more cautious and over-worked ideas, and can produce some very exciting imagery.

Try drawing a parrot picnic – how would you describe this quickly in visual terms?

Activity: Lateral thinking

You have probably been told at some point to 'think outside the box' – this means making connections which do not form part of a logical progression and looking at ideas sideways; it is also known as lateral thinking.

Try researching the ideas of Edward de Bono, the key exponent of lateral thinking. He also introduced the term 'parallel thinking', which means trying to see both outcomes of a problem and use the differences constructively, rather than working towards a single 'correct' resolution. If you can make unusual and original connections between ideas, your art and design outcomes will be more exciting.

Instinct and intuition

Instinct is defined as an innate, usually fixed pattern of behaviour in response to certain stimuli. This means that you will have initial responses to a project that come spontaneously and naturally. You should document these instinctive responses, which could provide a vital starting point for subsequent work, but be aware that they will need to be supported by research and further ideas. Other ideas may arise intuitively or from your subconscious, rather than being derived from reason or logic. Think about the musical starter

stimulus (page 44) and your responses to this. There are numerous other experiences affected by emotions, such as joy or sadness, or by states such as beauty or horror. These intuitive responses may be very emotive and deeply personal.

Discussion

Often in the middle of a discussion with someone an apparently insignificant remark can lead to a good idea. Talking to your peers and tutors is a great way of examining ideas quickly, although you will usually need to find additional material to support them. It is vital that you keep a written record of your tutorials/seminars/studio crits – and even, as above, random chats which lead to ideas.

2.2 Focus

There may be a particular focus required for your ideas. You may want to convey a certain feeling in your work – inspired by something that has moved or excited you (see above and Figure 3.2 below) – or you may wish to convey a particular meaning or issue. To do this successfully you might find it useful to gather a small group of friends and give them a questionnaire to find out their response to your work. You will need to consider the questions very carefully, but remember that audiences interpret art in highly subjective ways – everyone will have a slightly different view or interpretation of a particular piece.

Mark-making – what kind of vocabulary of marks can you use to reinforce your ideas?

Colour – the choice of colour will affect the feeling you wish to communicate.

Think about…

Scale – do you want to make something small and intimate or large and powerful? How will the size of the work reinforce the feeling behind it?

Texture – what kind of surfaces would be most successful for your idea?

Shape – if your piece is three dimensional or irregularly shaped, this will require careful consideration.

Figure 3.2: Important points you need to consider to reinforce the feeling or meaning you wish to convey.

Signpost

You will find it helpful to refer to Unit 4 to think further about how your ideas can be communicated successfully.

Aesthetics

When we talk about aesthetics, we are referring to the visual appeal of something. You may want to give your work a strong aesthetic sense. You could do this by:

• limiting yourself to a particular palette of colours, or just monochrome

• using a carefully judged range of materials – perhaps by linking them in some way, such as natural or man-made

• imposing a specific constraint on your manufacture, such as making work that is deliberately fragile or heavy.

Resources

The materials available to you will inevitably influence your outcomes, but you can still be inventive even with limited resources. Look at recycling and all the possibilities this has given artists and designers over the past decade. Set yourself a project where you only use materials from your kitchen.

Use tea, coffee, etc., as ink or paint or use baking paper, packets, tin foil, etc., as papers or surfaces.

Use objects such as potatoes or fruit to print from, pour plaster into the hollow cavities of peppers or press other kitchen foodstuffs and equipment into clay to make reliefs.

Compile kitchen utensils to make constructions from and draw these, or use recycled packaging, corks, etc., as a starting point for constructions.

Assessment activity 3.2: Knowing how to generate ideas

Research artists who use sequencing within their work such as film-makers and illustrators, and investigate the different approaches they use. Now select a short story or piece of text – for example, from a novel or well-known fairy story – and highlight eight sentences that intrigue you. Take a piece of A1 paper and, using ink, make some experimental marks on it – try blowing it through straws, and/or mixing it with washing-up liquid and blowing bubbles on the paper. Then take five minutes to respond to each of your sentences. Try to use a range of media, but stick to monochrome, using collaged pieces of paper, graphite or working into the surface with white paint.

You should now have a visually interesting sheet. Take another piece of A1 paper and divide it into 16 sections, making a sequence of images inspired by your first sheet. Do these drawings in ink so that you work fast and don't get over complicated – you have to think how to link the rectangles, whether through narrative or aesthetics.

Once you have completed your rectangles, look at your sheets and decide how you could develop these further.

1. Could you develop your work as the storyboard for an animation? If so, do you have the time and expertise to make a couple of seconds of film, i.e. 24 frames?

2. Would your work be more successful in book format? If so, will you incorporate text and how?

3. How else could you develop this piece?

Grading tips

- Be experimental in developing your storyboard and show that you have lots of ideas for generating techniques. Repeat your image-making using other media, such as collage and colour **P2**.

- You could then try to develop this piece further into one of the formats suggested above: if you do this successfully you could achieve **M2**.

3. Be able to generate and refine ideas in response to given briefs

Just as important as having ideas is the ability to refine these to suit your given brief – you will need to constantly review your ideas and select those which seem most appropriate to develop further. You will also need to ensure that they conform to the criteria for the project and meet your personal objectives. Refining ideas will probably mean adapting your initial workings, which is a vital part of the creative process: as a project develops, you will see the need to modify unsuccessful elements, by making adjustments to form, scale or materials. If you have a client, their input could also lead to changes in your ideas, and you will need to allow sufficient time in your plan to complete the brief to as high a standard as possible.

3.1 Analysis of brief

To refine your ideas successfully, you will need to thoroughly analyse the brief. If you are working for a client it is important that everything is clearly understood by both parties from the outset. The client will have a set of requirements and, crucially, a timescale. Ideally, you will show your client work in progress as you proceed, to ensure your ideas are compatible with their concept. Some clients are very demanding and liable to change their thinking, so you may need to develop strategies for dealing with this. Equally, others will give you plenty of freedom, so you will need to keep checking you have not wandered too far from the original brief.

Make sure that you understand the objectives of the brief, so that a) there is no confusion in the later stages of the project, and b) you have a clear idea of the criteria by which you select and develop your ideas. For example, if you are asked to design a chair from recycled materials, your ideas should suit the form of seating required and the scale.

You may have a particularly challenging brief which requires you to think creatively. Alternatively, you may need to work with unfamiliar materials or a demanding scale, or there may be other difficult constraints imposed.

The following suggestions will help you:

• Keep notes of meetings and send a record of these to clients so that everyone is clear about the creative process.

• Make a timetable for the development of the work and stick to it rigorously.

• Ensure that you are clear about the payment structure for your work – portrait painters, for example, would require a partial payment before starting work; most designers invoice on completion of a job, but may require a portion of this beforehand if they need to buy expensive materials.

Action planning

Once you have had met the client, or established some initial ideas, you will need to make an action plan to pursue these further and review your ideas.

Which ideas do you want to progress forward?

What is the timescale available to you?

Possible questions

Have you allowed contingency time for unexpected outcomes?

What materials will you need?

How and when will you liaise with the client?

Figure 3.3: Examples of useful questions to help you review your ideas.

55

Response to feedback

Responding to feedback constructively is an important aspect of your development as an artist. You will not always agree with the feedback and will sometimes be frustrated if your work hasn't been received as well as you hoped. There are several strategies for dealing with this:

1. Ask your peers and tutors for their views prior to presenting your work; keep a record of what they say and consider it carefully. Their ideas could be very useful.

2. If you feel feedback is unfair, write down why you feel your work has been misunderstood, but don't allow this become an angry rant – keep it to a simple list of bullet points outlining your view of the project.

3. If your client has reservations about your work, try to resolve these. You want to maintain a good relationship, and by demonstrating flexibility you are more likely to receive future commissions.

3.2 Generate and refine ideas

There are lots of ways you can refine ideas. Your first starting point might be to take notes; or, if you are uncomfortable with writing, keep an audio record of initial thoughts. Likewise, you might want to make video recordings of particular environments or situations that inspire you. Once you have some starting points, you can develop these further through:

- rough studies
- mock-ups
- lists
- flow charts
- mind maps
- thumbnail sketches.

Make quick sketches to record or make refinements to ideas.

3.3 Context

You will need to develop your ideas within a particular context. Before starting you should research your target market or audience. For example, you could compile a survey that includes the following:

1. If you are making a product to sell, is there a market for it? Or, in the case of fine art, will there be an audience for your work?

2. Who are your product's potential users or clients?

3. What are their likely preferences?

4. Are these preferences affected by **demographics**? For example, does the product have the same consumer appeal in both affluent and depressed areas?

5. You will then have to think about the particular needs of your product or outcome. Do you need particular environments for its realisation? Does it need to be located in a particular site? What will be the scale of your piece? This will have implications not only for production/construction, but also, if the work is designed for a particular setting, for **installation**. Finally, you will need to resolve a timescale for completion of the work and, if you are producing multiples, determine the exact quantities needed, and factor this into your deadline.

Key terms

Demographics – refers to a study of life in communities through looking at births/deaths/diseases/average income/average age, etc.

Installation – an artwork which is installed within a gallery or found space and as such relates to the entire specified exhibition area, as opposed to a single wall space or floor space.

4. Be able to communicate and present ideas and outcomes to different audiences

For Learning Outcomes 1, 2 and 3 you will have looked at how ideas and concepts inform art and design work and explored and compared a range of references. You will have used this research to develop your ideas in different ways, and refined them to meet the demands of the brief. Hopefully, you will have an exciting and innovative outcome, but you will only succeed if you can communicate your ideas and final product effectively, and can adapt your presentation skills to diverse audiences.

4.1 Visualising techniques

When explaining your ideas to a client or audience, you could use various means to illustrate your ideas visually. Your client/audience may not have a creative background, so your supporting material should communicate your ideas clearly and effectively. You will probably have a sketchbook or reflective learning journal, which will be vital for containing initial ideas and experiments. However, it may not be suitable to use in a presentation, so consider some of the following:

Ideas worksheets show the development of your ideas with annotated drawings. Include reference material which has inspired you and develop this into a mood board with samples of texture, colour palettes and found imagery.

Samples are great for showing constructed work before incurring costs, particularly if you use conventional materials or more standard materials in an innovative way.

Models give a clear idea of the intended structure of 3D work. Photographs of models can also be useful but may give an ambiguous sense of scale.

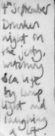

If your brief requires a narrative outcome, a storyboard is needed to communicate your piece succinctly, and could be supported by sample illustrations or video clips.

4.2 Communicate ideas

To communicate your ideas successfully you need to take an analytical approach to your work. Ongoing evaluation is always good practice, and for this unit is essential. When reviewing your work you might consider some of the following questions.

- Can you explain clearly how you arrived at your initial idea?

- Your audience will want an insight into your working practices – can you clarify the processes by which you developed your ideas into a final piece?

- What successes and failures did you encounter during the development cycle?

- What were the implications of your choice of materials and techniques?

- How do you feel about the quality of your outcome?

- Does it work aesthetically?

4.3 Presentation methods

A professional artist or designer will be required to present work regularly to galleries or clients, so try to get as much experience as you can at this stage to give you confidence. The key to a successful presentation is to be well prepared, with a presentation format that is relevant to the audience and venue. For example, if your brief requires an exhibition outcome you may need to mount and display your work. If you are required to talk to a client or audience, you will need to find out in advance if there are facilities for a computer slide show. You will also need to know how many people you are presenting to and how much time you will have; it may also be useful to make some notes to remind you of what to say. Keep your presentation as concise as possible and visually interesting so your audience remains engaged.

If appropriate, you could also consider other forms of presentation, such as a podcast, blog, performance or projection.

PLTS

Reflective learner, creative thinker, team worker, self-manager and effective participator

Present your ideas and outcomes to a group of fellow students and ask them to give you feedback. Then swap roles, so you give them feedback on their work. In your journal or sketchbook evaluate the connections and differences between your outcomes and approaches, and reflect on how you could modify or adapt your approach for a more formal presentation.

Functional skills

English

Write a bullet list of the main points of your presentation. Put it into a logical sequence and include key words to act as a trigger when talking about your work in greater depth.

4.4 Different audiences

Your assignment will clarify who your presentation audience will be and whether you need to modify your methods. Consider how you would present your ideas to:

• fellow art and design students or tutors

• very young or elderly people

• a prominent artist/designer/gallery curator, or successful company director or manager.

Did you know?

Picasso began his first sketchbook aged 13 in 1894, which he made himself by sewing bundles of paper together. By 1964, he had 175 sketchbooks documenting development drawings, experimentation and ideas of one of the greatest artists of the 20th century.

Assessment activity 3.3: Using your ideas to form an outcome

Create documentation in book form of all your ideas and workings for this unit. Record examples of other artists whose work has a connection to your own, and think about incorporating into the book any materials related to your outcome, such as for a cover. You should include photos of the development of your ideas and, in doing so, think about how to make the book visually stunning for both readers and possible gallery audiences. For example, you could print all your information on tracing or brown paper, or make pages that fold inwards or pop out, or even make a freestanding concertina. Although it contains ideas and information, this is not a sketchbook or a scrapbook – it should have more in common with an artist's book or even a sculpture. You should aim for an outcome that documents the project in an innovative way.

1. How can you link your material together in an aesthetically pleasing way?

2. What is the most suitable scale for your book – will it be hand size or more substantial in format?

3. Will you make multiple copies in order to reach a wider audience?

Grading tips

With this activity you could achieve **D1** and **D2** if you make a really well considered book. Do not allow it to become a scrapbook: make your sequence of ideas and documentation coherent and be imaginative with your placing of information on each page. If you can produce some original ideas, this will differentiate your work from that of others. Try to incorporate specific processes such as photocopy transfer/screenprint, etc. to make your book seem more professional and your presentation more sophisticated.

Tina Roskruge
Ceramic artist

Tina studied ceramics at Middlesex University in the late 1980s, then went on to make ceramic forms for exhibition and commission, while also working freelance for the Crafts Council.

Two years ago, Tina became involved in a collaborative project between an artists' group and a gallery, which has had a huge impact on her work. The artists are all parents of primary school-aged children, and have been examining the effect of their children's creativity on their own work. The gallery is hosting a series of exhibitions of work produced by the families with related public workshops. Tina and some of the artists are also writing a research paper about their outcomes.

Hearts (2009; pictured above) and *Guns* (2008; pictured below) by Tina Roskruge for *Generate*, a Turner Contemporary exhibition at Droit House, Margate.

Tina's practice now refers to the work of her three children, and she is also researching how other artists have worked in conjunction with their children.

She keeps a written and visual diary for research purposes, as well as films and recorded discussions of her children. As she has a kiln in her studio she also experiments with clay firing. The project has helped diversify her work: for the first exhibition she made constructed pieces alongside the children who were working to a similar format, as well as playful forms using ceramic and string inspired by her son's toy gun. This developed into an installation of 100 ceramic guns cast from toy guns. She has also documented her children's drawings digitally and incorporated text from her discussions with them to make artists' books.

Think about it!

- Can you think of any other references or ideas that Tina could explore in conjunction with this work?
- How would you generate ideas if you were collaborating with someone else on a project?
- Can you think of other ways Tina could develop and refine the different elements of her practice?
- How could Tina develop a different audience for her work beyond visitors to the gallery?

Just checking

1. Ensure that you carry out effective research at the start of your project. Look at other artists and designers to generate ideas, and find references to develop your thinking.

2. When you are ready to generate ideas, do this in ways that are most productive. While some people favour particular thinking exercises to stimulate creativity, others prefer to start with practical exploration to trigger ideas.

3. You will need to keep evolving and developing your ideas. Don't forget to check your ideas constantly against the brief and, if you are working for clients, liaise with them regularly. Be receptive to feedback from tutors and/or your client, and be prepared to make changes if necessary.

4. When presenting your final outcome, make sure that you do this in a professional way. Think carefully about your audience and choose the most appropriate method.

Assignment tips

- Record your ideas constantly – you should never be without your sketchbook; some artists and designers keep notebooks for writing in too.

- Try to document all your work outcomes through photography – you will have a great visual record of how a piece develops, even if it doesn't work out.

- Constantly evaluate your work. This will enable you to see if you are using references and research usefully, whether you are generating a sufficient number and range of ideas and whether you can refine them successfully to make an exciting outcome. Be completely honest, and never be complacent about your work.

4 Communication through art and design

Communication has never been more sophisticated, diverse and abundant. We are constantly exposed to a huge range of images which we process and interpret almost subconsciously. In order to do this we draw on our experience of the world, and the more we know and understand of the world, the richer our interpretations become.

In order to become effective communicators as artists and designers, you need to unpick the elements of visual communication, such as size, colour, shape, texture and structure, which cause us to respond in a particular way. This will help you to develop your own work in response to a brief and to be creative and innovative in your use of materials, techniques and processes. As well as thinking about how a piece of art makes you feel, you need to examine why you respond in that way.

Understanding how artists and designers use visual communication in their work will inform the development of your own work and help you to explain and justify your outcomes against the brief. As a practising artist, you need to be able to talk convincingly about your work to galleries or clients, and be able to persuade them that your work is of value.

Learning outcomes

After completing this unit you should:

1. understand how media, materials and processes are used in others' work to convey ideas and meaning
2. be able to develop visual language
3. know how art and design is used to communicate ideas and meaning
4. be able to communicate by using the language of art and design.

Assessment and grading criteria

This table shows you what you must do in order to achieve a **pass**, **merit** or **distinction** grade, and where you can find activities in this book to help you.

To achieve a pass grade the evidence must show that you are able to:	To achieve a **merit** grade the evidence must show that, in addition to the pass criteria, you are able to:	To achieve a **distinction** grade the evidence must show that, in addition to the pass and merit criteria, you are able to:
P1 explain how media and materials are used in the work of others to convey ideas and meaning **See Assessment activities 4.1, page 67; 4.2, page 71; 4.3, page 72; 4.6, page 76; 4.7, page 77; 4.8, page 80**	**M1** evaluate how media, materials and processes are used diversely to convey ideas and meaning, drawing on own experiments to make effective comparisons **See Assessment activities 4.1, page 67; 4.2, page 71; 4.3, page 72; 4.5, page 74; 4.6, page 76; 4.7, page 77; 4.8, page 80**	**D1** communicate an intended meaning cogently to a specified audience by imaginative use of the language of art and design **See Assessment activities 4.3, page 72; 4.4, page 73; 4.8, page 80**
P2 create own visual language by working with materials, media and processes **See Assessment activities 4.2, page 71; 4.3, page 72; 4.5, page 74**	**M2** communicate an intended meaning clearly to a specified audience by refined use of the language of art and design **See Assessment activities 4.3, page 72; 4.4, page 73; 4.8, page 80**	
P3 describe ways in which visual language is used to communicate ideas and meaning **See Assessment activities 4.3, page 72; 4.6, page 76; 4.7, page 77 ; 4.8, page 80**		
P4 communicate an intended meaning to a specified audience using the language of art and design **See Assessment activity 4.3, page 72**		

How you will be assessed

This unit will be assessed through internal assignments that will be designed and marked by the tutors at your centre. They are designed to allow you to show your understanding of the unit outcomes. The mandatory units form the basis of your practice, and the principles you learn in these should be applied to all your additional units and inform your future work as an artist or designer. In this unit your focus is to demonstrate your understanding of communication through visual communication in various forms.

Your assessment could be in the form of:

- evaluation and analyses of a range of others' visual work
- sketchbook work and developmental studies and experiments
- formal presentations or studio critiques
- final outcomes.

Lorna

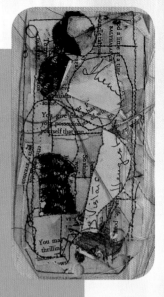

I began to understand how visual images communicate ideas when we had to produce work on the past, present and future of Margate. It was a 'live' project and our client was Turner Contemporary, an organisation overseeing the building of a new gallery there, which wanted work that presented a positive image of Margate.

We visited a warehouse full of second-hand goods – furniture, clothes and personal memorabilia. I noticed how particular features, colours and styles of lettering helped identify which decade the items belonged to. I was fascinated by postcards and photographs of people in Margate, and how they gave you a clue as to what sort of people they were. I made a collection of artefacts and started to construct a story about people in the photographs, using information from my research about life in Margate, and imagined their characters and lifestyle.

Visiting the Walpole Bay Hotel and looking through the signing-in book inspired me to research typography. I photographed various pages, generating many letterforms, signatures and messages, and embroidered over the photocopies of the signing-in book and photographs of Margate. Embroidering handwritten messages over the photographs added texture and a personal dimension. I also made luggage tags using different images and materials from Margate and dyed fabrics using tea and coffee to make them look old and worn.

My collection took the form of a box of items belonging to my imagined Margate family – some found items, but others constructed to look authentic. I presented the work in an old piano stool to make it look as if it had been found just as it was.

When I presented my ideas to the client, I already had a document of the research, development and design cycle, so I didn't struggle to explain my work. The amount of work I had produced surprised me, and I have a much better idea now about how to approach future projects.

Over to you!

- **Can you identify the era in which a piece of work was produced from the style?**
- **Can you think of events or visits which have triggered ideas for your work?**
- **If so, how can you replicate that in other work?**

Lorna's final piece is shown here with some samples of the individual components which show various elements that communicate ideas to the viewer. What is your response to the work?

1. Understand how media, materials and processes are used in others' work to convey ideas and meaning

Effective communication

Think about a piece of visual work that has made an impression on you and find a copy of it to refer to. It could be an advertisement, a piece of art or a scene from a film.

Make a document in which you:

• describe your response to the work and how it makes you feel

• identify the visual and verbal/written elements in the work that you think make it effective as a form of communication

• consider who you think is the intended audience

• try to find out other people's response and compare this to your own (this could be your peers, art critics or reviews)

• look at how it might be improved.

Lorna's experience demonstrates the excitement and stimulation of ideas that should come from looking at a broad range of visual work. We are influenced by everything that is around us, and extending your knowledge through research and enquiry will help you to develop as an arts practitioner. The memorabilia she found in the second-hand shop triggered further investigations and experiments that added new depths to her imagery, and developed new skills in a media which was previously unfamiliar to her.

1.1 Media, materials and techniques

If you are drawn to a particular design discipline, you might be tempted to ignore creative processes not traditionally associated with that discipline or those which fall outside your field of experience. This will limit the creative potential of your work and prevent you from developing additional skills. Boundaries are becoming increasingly blurred between arts disciplines; this unit encourages you to explore a wide variety of media, materials and techniques that artists and designers have used to communicate ideas, concepts and information.

PLTS

Independent enquirer

In order to take ownership of your work and develop an individual style, you need to develop a highly personal approach to your research, which means that you have to take the initiative when looking for sources of information. The ability to work independently is important in the working world.

The design for this garment draws from landscape and floral influences; the designer has exploited the properties of the fabric to create a three-dimensional texture, taking the concept of the floral dress to an extreme.

Key terms

The words below describe how to approach the work of other artists, and how to develop understanding of the visual elements of their work that communicate ideas and meaning.

Critique – a considered judgement of or discussion about the qualities of a creative work.

Research – a methodical investigation into a subject to discover facts, establish or revise a theory and develop a plan of action based on what is discovered.

Analysis – detailed and careful consideration of something in order to understand it better. This may be through examination of its individual parts, or study of the structure as a whole.

Reflection – careful thought, especially the process of reconsidering previous actions, events or decisions.

Did you know?

Artists sometimes focus on the sense of smell, too. Anya Gallacio produced a piece for the Turner Prize in 2003 composed of huge sheets of glass, in between which were dozens of gerbera (flowers). Over the three-month duration of the exhibition, the gerbera decayed. The smell became an important and integral part of the work. Can you think of any other examples of creative work where the sense of smell might be important?

Assessment activity 4.1: Innovation through subversion   BTEC

Within a chosen discipline, look for examples of art or design work that use media, materials or techniques which might not traditionally be associated with that discipline.

- Create some sketchbook pages or design sheets to explain, visually and through annotation how the subversive element of the work has contributed towards the construction of meaning.
- Try to find some **critiques** of the work from reviews, books, magazines, newspapers or the Internet. Do they all agree? How have different critics responded to the work?
- Record your own response to the work.

Grading tips

Always make sure you connect your research to your own work. Connections help you to understand clearly the context in which it is being produced. Connections help you to understand how your investigations can feed into the development and realisation of your work.

The subjective element of art and design should encourage you to share your opinions with others, read reviews and formulate convincing arguments to support your responses to works of art, as well as being open to different viewpoints **P1**. This will enable you to give good explanations as to how visual language works, to evaluate its effectiveness and apply these principles to your own visual work **M1**.

Case study: Touch

Touch is an important element of the language of art and design. As a fashion designer, you will consider the importance of the feel of a fabric as well as its other properties. Sculptural works such as Barbara Hepworth's are visually compelling and tactile.

In the 2003 Turner Prize exhibition, artists Jake and Dinos Chapman created a sculptural work entitled *Death*, which looked like two plastic blow-up dolls, but was in fact made of bronze, offering the sensation of touching something alien to expectation.

How your work feels, or looks as if it feels, is another dimension to the language of art and design.

Subversion through media, materials, techniques and ideas behind the work is a common feature of the work of the Chapman brothers.

1. Look at other examples of their work, and research the ideas behind them and the methods used. What is your response to their work?

2. Compare this with the work of other artists working with similar materials. How do the artworks exploit the properties of the media, materials and techniques to create meaning?

3. What kind of atmosphere is evoked by their work? How does it make you feel? What messages do you think they are trying to convey?

Two Forms (Divided Circle) by Barbara Hepworth. When viewing Hepworth's sculptures, it is almost irresistible to touch them, even if prohibited. Have you ever seen a sculptural piece and wanted to touch it?

1.2 How do artists and designers convey ideas and meaning?

In order to understand how meaning and ideas are conveyed visually, you need to examine works thoroughly and develop coherent arguments to support your views.

When you are examining the work of other artists, you should question, challenge and argue your responses to the work. **Research** and **analysis** will enhance your understanding and enable you to develop persuasive arguments, as well as feed into the development of your own work.

When looking at how artists communicate, consider the media used, including photography, painting, drawing, etching, graphics, interactive media, fashion, weaving, construction, casting and time-based media. How have the techniques affected the properties of the media?

How might materials, such as paint, plaster, graphite, paper, fabric, wood, stone, metal or digitally produced outcomes affect the mood and atmosphere of a work and the viewer's interpretation of its meaning? Examine the colour palette, texture, form, size, composition and construction and think about what impression this makes.

How do variations in technique affect mood? Look at the contrast between the three paintings on the next page. How does the use of light and colour create atmosphere? How do the different brushwork techniques contribute to the viewer's perception of the artist's intentions and feelings?

Comparing art works is a good way of identifying the visual elements that evoke responses or create meaning. You can apply the same principles in examining cinematographic techniques in film, fashion collections or any other visual discipline.

The Fighting Temeraire,
Turner (1839).

Coquelicots (Poppies),
Monet (1873).

Enclosed Field with Rising
Sun, Van Gogh (1889).

Case study: The importance of narrative

Throughout history, we have used stories to communicate with others. Stories have often been a vehicle for making a moral point, often using metaphor to illustrate connections to everyday living.

Celebrity culture and the rise in popularity of reality television shows and talent competitions have placed the personal stories of otherwise ordinary people in the public domain. Advertisements can be successful when they feature stories or ongoing serialisations, as in soap operas. Fine artists often use their own personal stories or those of others as a basis for a body of work.

News brought through video or photography can be edited to reflect either the artist's or commissioning agent's view of a reported situation.

Storyboards help an artist construct a visual narrative for television, video, animation or film. There is a high level of sophistication in the creation of comic books and graphic novels, such as in the use of lighting and extreme viewpoints.

Think of a story that you might like to tell.

1. **How could you tell the story visually?**
2. **What medium would you use?**
3. **How could you make sure that your storyline was clear to your audience?**

A storyboard is created to help the designer tell a story visually. Storyboards are used to set a visual style for a film and create atmosphere.

Evaluating the effectiveness of a visual work

Once you have identified the media, materials and techniques used in a piece of work, and considered what the intended message is, you should evaluate how well this has been communicated to the target audience. Critically analysing and evaluating other artists' work will help you to become self-critical and reflective in your own practice.

Functional skills

English

Interpreting images can be highly subjective. It is vital to try to find out what other people think about your own work and the work of others. Discussion helps you to clarify your own thoughts and discourages you from being narrow-minded.

Remember

Take every opportunity you can to visit art galleries and museums, go to plays and watch films. Read arts reviews in the media and record your own responses. Take a critical stance yourself, and think about how the artist, designer or filmmaker has used visual language to convey a message.

Assessment activity 4.2: Analysis into practice

Choose one piece of two-dimensional work, such as a painting, poster or fabric design, and one piece of three-dimensional work. This could be a sculptural work, a cutting-edge piece of design such as furniture, or a household object or theatre set design. Make an analysis of both, in the same way that you did with the Effective communication activity at the beginning of the section, explaining how the materials and features have been used to convey ideas and meaning effectively, and how you think this might have been improved.

Having done this, for the two-dimensional piece:

- Make some studies of your chosen piece in your sketchbook, using a completely different colour palette from the original.
- Re-create parts of your chosen work using a completely different medium and technique.

For the three-dimensional work:

- Make some drawings of the work, documenting how it might look if it were made in a completely different material, colour and texture.
- If possible, create a maquette with material available to you, and photograph it for your sketchbook.

- Evaluate the results, considering how the changes you have made affect the way the viewer would look at the work. Ask the opinion of your peers. Does it still communicate the same message? Does it still work as a piece of design? How does the way you have used visual language using different materials and techniques affect the work's mood or style?

Grading tips

This assessment activity requires you to focus on how you have perceived another artist's work and reinterpreted the meaning yourself through alternative visual means.

You have explained how the media, materials and techniques used in the selected pieces convey ideas and meaning **P1**, evaluated their effectiveness by drawing comparisons based on your own experiments **P2**, and broadened your own visual language by using a diverse range of techniques and evaluated these within the development of your work and through annotation and reflection **M1**.

2. Be able to develop visual language

Early art education is generally concerned with trying to represent or reproduce the visible world. However, younger children can be very experimental in their creative work, using colour, and sometimes the **physical** act of mark-making, to create meaning or feelings such as anger or enthusiasm.

It can sometimes be difficult to break habits and take creative risks with your work, but experimentation is a valuable part of your development as an artist. Exploit opportunities to be innovative – try out different materials and techniques, and try to work outside your comfort zone.

Key terms

Creativity – the ability to use the imagination, or to draw on your knowledge of a subject, to develop new and original ideas or outcomes.

Innovation – the act or process of inventing or introducing something new, or a new way of doing something.

2.1 Visual language

As an artist or designer, you will be developing methods and techniques to communicate your work visually, but when talking to clients you will also need to communicate verbally.

All professions have specialist words and phrases, and you will need to acquire a good knowledge of the **language** used in **art** and **design**. A useful way of building an art and design vocabulary is to read exhibition reviews in newspapers, or in publications such as *Visual Communication* (Sage Publications) or *Tate* etc.

Key terms

Language – a system of communication with its own set of conventions, encompassing spoken or written words, signs, gestures or sounds.

Art – works produced through creative human endeavour rather than nature, and which reflect the skill or ability to do something well.

Design – to create or plan a form or structure in a skilful or artistic way, usually for a particular purpose.

Remember

Keep a record of all your research, experimentation and evaluations. You can only be assessed on work that is seen by the assessor. Sometimes if you decide a piece of work you produce is not the right solution for the given brief, you may be tempted to discard it, but you should document your reasons for rejecting it and keep it for future reference.

Assessment activity 4.3: Define the language of art and design

BTEC

What is meant by 'the language of art and design'?

You might consider this by thinking about how to define 'art' and 'design'. Write down some thoughts in your sketchbook or journal, reflecting on the work you have done so far.

Working with a partner, select a piece of work each that you have produced. Reflect upon what you were hoping to communicate. How have you used the language of art and design, and how effective has this been as a means of communication? Do not share your thoughts with your partner at this stage.

Now look at your partner's piece of work and record your personal response – what does the work communicate to you? Compare the artist's intentions with your interpretation. Does it matter if a viewer perceives a different meaning, and, as the artist, does this add a new perspective for you? You could include contributions from more of your peers.

Grading tip

This activity requires you to think about definitions of art and design, and to examine how media, materials and processes contribute to meaning **P1** through visual experimentation **P2** and evaluation **P3**. By reflecting on these processes **M1** the ultimate aim is to harness this knowledge in the production of visual outcomes that communicate as they were intended **P4** with refinement and sophistication **M2**. Try to communicate with your target audience as imaginatively as possible **D1**.

Assessment activity 4.4: Learning the language

- Select and read an article from a specialist art publication, or a chapter from one of the books on your recommended reading list. Pick out words or phrases you don't understand and write them down. Find out what they mean and add the definition, so you can begin to build a glossary of terms in the back of your sketchbook or journal. Familiarise yourself with them and introduce this new vocabulary into your studio critiques, discussions, annotations, presentations and formal written work, where appropriate.

- Try to get into the habit of visiting the library and reading articles that interest you and continue to build your glossary of terms.

Grading tip

This activity offers practical ways to help you refine your communication skills, to explain and support your visual outcomes to an audience **M2** cogently **D1**. This includes developing an awareness of the vocabulary used in specific professional circles.

2.2 Methods, materials and media

This section should continue to help you to identify methods and materials to develop your own visual language. Try to avoid the obvious, perhaps by finding unusual drawing materials.

You could try drawing with natural or found materials in the landscape and photographing the results. Andy Goldsworthy and Richard Long both use landscape to make work and then record the outcome in photographs. How could you draw on their ideas?

This piece by Richard Long, constructed from slate, creates a sculptural path, juxtaposing the apparent randomness of the position of each piece of slate with the highly structured form of the piece itself. Much of Long's work is made from natural found materials and remains in the landscape, recorded through photography.

Reflecting on what you have looked at in the section covering LO1, think carefully about how materials, techniques and processes contribute to the construction of meaning in art and design, and build a wide body of work based on what you have learned. The illustrations should help you to consider how to combine traditional and non-traditional materials as means to communicate.

• Two-dimensional work: line, tone, texture, scale, colour, shape and form, using mark-making, drawing, painting, photography, collage, printmaking, digital media, type, illustration, composition, symbols and semiotics.

Sam made plastic moulds to form the word 'Ephemeral' (meaning 'lasting only a short time'). He filled them with water and froze them to create letters of ice, then photographed the word as it disappeared.

PLTS

Creative thinker

Creative thinkers will have the ability to innovate. How many times have you heard people say 'I could have done that' when discussing a piece of creative work that does not appear to have the requirement of an acquired specific technical or artistic skill. Perhaps they could – although the skills required are frequently underestimated – but they didn't. The concept came from a creative thinker.

Assessment activity 4.5: Exploring techniques

 BTEC

 P2 M1

Look at the list of techniques below:

• washes
• scumbling
• solarisation
• focusing
• composition
• layering
• cloning
• carving
• cross-hatching
• cutting
• juxtaposing
• contrasting.

Find and research at least one example of each of these in an artist or designer's work.

Now try out the techniques yourself, thinking how the properties of each could create meaning within your own work.

How might you apply this to specific design disciplines?

Grading tip

This task focuses on the development of your own visual language, informed by the work of other artists and designers. It should also encourage you to experiment with materials, media and processes not traditionally associated with your design discipline, and to 'think laterally' with a view to creating innovative outcomes P2. To extend this M1, you should evaluate how your work creates meaning, drawing on that of other artists.

- Three-dimensional work: maquettes, sculptural works, public art, models, film or theatrical sets, characters for animation through carving, modelling, casting, constructing, fabricating, cutting, juxtaposing and using effects of scale and space.

- Time-based media: film, video, multi-media, interactive media and games design, incorporating visual elements, sound, light, framing, timing, narrative.

- Fashion, clothing and textiles: paper, fabrics, dyeing, pattern, printing, decoration and garment construction to create a look, style, character or mood.

- Combined media: using any combination, including performance, to make connections between creative disciplines, such as fashion promotion, set-making and costumes, etc.

Analyse the design of this costume, in terms of materials used, style of construction and decorative touches. How do these elements work together to create a sense of character and mood?

Remember

If you want to use music that has been written/composed by someone else, you have to get permission from the publisher or record label that owns the copyright. If they are well known, this may be expensive. It is possible to obtain copyright-free music, or, better still, create your own using software such as Garage Band.

Case study: Sound

Bruce Nauman's installation in the Turbine Hall at Tate Modern (2004) was based on voices and required the visitor to move around the space to hear different spoken texts. This is an example of an art work based primarily on sound, combined with secondary elements such as text. Film is a more familiar medium where sound is used to evoke meaning, such as the famous shower scene in Hitchcock's film *Psycho*.

Whether you are working in film, animation or fine art, you may wish to incorporate sound into your own work. You will need to consider how the soundtrack works with visual images to create meaning, which could be either obvious or quite abstract.

1. **Think of some examples where sound plays a part in communicating meaning, other than through the spoken word.**
2. **How many examples can you identify from different disciplines?**

3. Know how art and design is used to communicate ideas and meaning

How many ways is art and design used to communicate and for what purpose? For example, in the Second World War a number of posters were produced to warn the public against talking too freely about the war in case an enemy agent overheard.

An example of one of the posters produced in the Second World War warning people to be discreet about the information they shared.

Assessment activity 4.6: How ideas and meaning are communicated

Make a list or a mind map to include as many ways as possible of how and why different forms of art and design communicate messages. Identify what the purpose of the work is and at whom it is aimed.

Cover the following specialisms and add your own:

- painting
- photography
- typography
- product design
- sculpture
- video
- animation
- pattern-making
- felt-making
- embroidering
- model-making
- printmaking
- dyeing
- illustration
- games design.

Select a number of reasons for communicating through art and design from your list or mind map, and find at least a dozen examples which illustrate your findings. Collate these in your sketchbook or journal, or produce design sheets incorporating your original mind map.

Annotate your work to include descriptions of the ways ideas and meanings have been communicated in the examples you have chosen.

Grading tip

As well as looking at how techniques can communicate messages **P1**, **P3**, this activity encourages you to reflect on techniques used in specific disciplines. It should open up possibilities for selecting techniques not traditionally used in the discipline and help you develop more innovative work **M1**.

What can you identify as contributing to the construction of meaning?

With reference to three aspects – appearance, context and form – think about how these contribute to sculptural pieces, for example.

Appearance – how have the visual elements contributed towards meaning? Consider the materials used to create the piece and how the look or feel of the fabric of the piece has made an impression on you. Why do you think the artist has chosen to use that material or materials to create the piece?

Context – how and where has the work been presented, and how has this affected the way it is viewed and interpreted? Some contemporary works can look almost incongruous when located in a prestigious gallery, so how does location affect the way you view the piece? Can you think of examples of work that would be viewed quite differently in different contexts?

Form – what significance does this have, and how does it affect the meaning? How much does scale affect the way a work is viewed? Do familiar forms in unfamiliar spaces take on a new significance? Think of some examples.

Assessment activity 4.7: Appearance, context and form

Select three examples of work from Assessment activity 4.6 and make a more detailed analysis, incorporating appearance, context and form into your observations. This could be in the form of an essay with illustrations and bibliography, a formal presentation with visual elements, or a video documentary with full commentary. Make sure you also take into account prior influences on the artist and related work.

- How have considerations of appearance, context and form enhanced your understanding of the art works?

- How will this affect your approach to creating work for a specific audience?

Grading tip

This activity is designed to help you understand the contextual as well as visual aspects of art and design **P1** and help you to examine how these elements shape an artist or designer's response to a brief **P3** applying this to your own work **M1**.

4. Be able to communicate by using the language of art and design

The learning outcomes for this unit encourage you to be experimental and innovative in your approach to communicating visually. The first three outcomes required you to:

- examine how others use media, materials and processes to convey ideas and meaning, drawing comparisons and taking account of the context of the work.

- experiment with a wide range of traditional and unconventional media and techniques.

- critically examine how different methods communicate meaning.

The final outcome requires you to consolidate this understanding. This will be evidenced in how you apply your knowledge of communication in art and design, and in your production of solutions that are effective in communicating with an intended audience.

4.1 Communicate an intended meaning

Analysing art works

You will have researched visual work produced by artists and designers in a wide variety of disciplines, employing a vast selection of materials, techniques and processes. You should also have experimented widely, reflecting upon how different methods contribute towards communicating ideas to an audience.

It is not enough simply to look at the work of other artists. Instead of a **tacit** response (a vague feeling of what a work is about), analysing how and why a work has been produced and evaluating its effectiveness in relation to purpose and audience will allow you to form an **explicit** response (as opposed to an **implicit** one). It will also enable you to support your response, and to use your knowledge about visual communication in your own work.

Your analysis of a piece of artwork, or reflection on your own practice, may provoke the following questions:

- What is the subject or theme of the work?

- Who is the artist?

- What ideas, concepts or messages is the artist trying to convey?

- What is the tone of the piece – is it angry, joyful, wistful?

- What is the atmosphere – peaceful, humorous, forbidding?

- How does the imagery contribute to the creation of meaning?

- What form does the piece take, and how has it been produced?

- What materials have been used?

- How have the techniques used contributed towards tone or atmosphere?

This is not a definitive list. Add your own questions as they arise and refer back to the work you produced for the Effective communication activity at the beginning of this section.

Key terms

Tacit – understood on an intuitive or subconscious level without being verbalised or consciously defined.

Explicit – clearly expressed, leaving no doubt as to the intended meaning.

Implicit, or implied – not obvious, but open to interpretation. (Meaning may be confined to a privileged or elite group of people with prior knowledge or experience, which gives them an advantage.)

The purpose

Now you need to think about the purpose of art and design. The following list gives you a number of possible options:

- to attract
- to inform
- to provoke or challenge
- to entertain
- to sell
- to be functional
- to be aesthetically pleasing (within an environment or independent of the setting)
- to decorate.

A work is quite likely to have multiple functions.

4.2 Specified audience

The work you are analysing may have been produced for a niche market such as haute couture, or be intended for wider consumption, as in a political campaign. In order to produce work for a specific audience, you need to know the characteristics and requirements of the market.

An advertising agency needs to able to forecast and evidence the expected financial return from an advertising campaign. Market research, perhaps commissioned as part of the campaign, provides that information, and the agency might also run a number of 'test' advertisements. Smaller agencies would be unlikely to have the budget to undertake intensive research, but would still need to gauge the financial viability of any work they produce.

Interpretation

The interpretation of an idea or meaning through reading visual images is dependent firstly on the person who creates the message, and secondly on the person who receives it. The person interpreting the message will be dependent on his or her prior knowledge, understanding and experience.

One example is the audience at a pantomime. Younger members of the audience might appreciate the jokes on an 'innocent' level of understanding, whereas adults might appreciate double entendre, which places a different meaning on the joke.

You can draw parallels with your own interpretation of visual communication. The greater your knowledge and understanding of the subject, the deeper and more complex your interpretation.

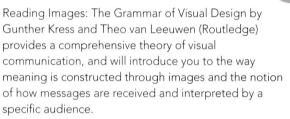

Did you know?

Reading Images: The Grammar of Visual Design by Gunther Kress and Theo van Leeuwen (Routledge) provides a comprehensive theory of visual communication, and will introduce you to the way meaning is constructed through images and the notion of how messages are received and interpreted by a specific audience.

Functional skills

Mathematics

Imagine you are asked to produce a small advertising campaign. As part of your research you access statistics of the population percentage that purchases a rival product to that of your client. The statistics are collated within particular age ranges. How are you going to organise the information into a format that will tell you about potential consumers of your client's product?

Collaboration

Collaboration gives you opportunities to work outside your own specialism, so you need to be aware of what is going on in the creative industries, as well as in science, technology and other disciplines that have a potential link with your own.

Writers often rely on visual artists to enhance their story-telling, and graphic novelists such as Neil Gaiman sometimes collaborate closely with artists. For this to be successful, both writer and artist need to have a good understanding of each other's craft.

Key terms

Cogent – forceful and convincing to the intellect and reason.

Imaginative – new and original, or not likely to have been easily thought up by somebody else.

4.3 Presenting your ideas

You will spend a lot of time talking about your work in discussions with peers, tutors and clients, and in studio critiques and presentations. The context and audience will determine the style and tone you adopt for this, and you will have to exercise judgment in terms of pitch and the degree of risk that is appropriate.

Functional skills

English

Adapting your style of presentation to suit a particular audience is a fundamental communication skill. Sometimes in a working situation, you cannot anticipate your audience and it is necessary to gauge their reaction to what you are saying and be prepared to adapt if you sense it is not being received well.

Assessment activity 4.8: Making meaning explicit BTEC

P1 P3 M1 M2 D1

Looking back over this section, reflect upon what you have learned in terms of how visual language can communicate ideas and meaning.

Go back to your initial research work in sketchbooks, journals or design sheets. Did you document your initial tacit response to the work you researched? How does that compare with your view of the work when analysed according to elements discussed in this section that contribute to the communication of meaning?

Be prepared to reflect on this and re-evaluate what may now be a more explicit response. By documenting your thoughts in the light of more information, you are providing evidence of your increasing understanding of visual communication.

Grading tip

This activity is designed to consolidate your learning on this unit and inform your future practice **P1 P3 M1 M2**. **D1** requires you to 'communicate an intended meaning cogently to a specified audience, by imaginative use of the language of art and design'. This requires you to be perceptive, analytical, informed, selective and visually sensitive and adept.

Katie Welsford
Artist

Katie Welsford's work is a combination of sculpture, fashion, jewellery and product design.

'The crossover of disciplines and blurring of conventional creative boundaries is something I find stimulating. I enjoy making work that is familiar but cannot be placed. In the studio or street I'm inspired by the internal/psychological and external/physical worlds in which we exist. I make work that questions our body's relationship with objects and space. The items I create are often part of a collection or series – sculptures that can be worn and that sit somewhere between jewellery and prosthetic limbs. My creations aid, assist, adorn and embellish the body.

Katie's work *Home Comfort.*

One such example is *Home Comfort – 2005*, which comprises a roll of wallpaper, padded and sealed with cotton, presented on the floor in a roll, or wrapped around the body, to provide domestic comfort.

Home Comfort is a response to the domestic environment and the way we subconsciously endeavour to recreate our initial home, the womb. Most of the spaces that we live in are created into environments filled with soft furnishings.

The work aimed to explore this theme and make real the idea of furnishings that create a homely, cosy environment and give us a sense of comfort and security. By getting inside the work and wrapping myself in it, I captured the feeling of being in a comfortable place, padded and protected by the wallpaper – a symbol of the home. The work was performed with and documented through photography, and is also a sculptural piece that can be displayed on its own. It was exhibited at the Bury Art Gallery near Manchester.

Think about it!

- **How much crossover of disciplines can you identify in your own work?**
- **Do you draw upon the way you view the world when making work?**
- **How much are you influenced by your physical environment?**

Just checking

1. Why is research so important?

2. What do you understand by the 'language of art and design'?

3. What is the difference between a tacit response and an explicit response?

4. Look back at this section again carefully. Can you construct a diagram that would help you plan your work for this unit?

5. Within the diagram you have created, can you identify the different stages you go through in your design development?

edexcel :::

Assignment tips

Examine the language used in the assessment criteria.

At pass level the key words are: explain (LO1); create (LO2); describe (LO3); and communicate (LO4). Make sure that there is plenty of evidence that you have done this in your work for assessment.

To achieve a merit or distinction the language is more complex.

- For **M1**, **evaluate** and **diverse** are key words as well as the need to **draw on your own experiments to make effective comparisons.**

- For **M2**, you need to show evidence that you have communicated an intended meaning clearly to a specified audience, by refined use of the language of art and design.

- For **D1**, you need to show evidence that you have communicated an intended meaning cogently to a specified audience, by imaginative use of visual language.

You can see from this exercise how important it is to understand the meaning of language. The definitions of words used in the assessment criteria are provided here, but you should adopt the practice of looking these up for yourself and including them in your glossary of terms.

5 Contextual influences in art and design

Art and design is a barometer of its time – the cultural dimension of a society that may be also experiencing technological and social changes. As you research developments in art and design you will be able to decide how important your subject has been in creating today's world. You will also discover the questions that are being asked and how artists and designers are helping to solve problems. For example, can an architect help improve society with well-designed buildings, or a product designer help solve the global-warming problem by designing more efficient machines?

You should be producing work for this unit throughout your course. Discovering the importance of contextual references in relation to your own work will give you a lifelong ability to enrich and stimulate your creative ideas as an artist or designer.

This unit covers just some of the key movements, artists and designers, and crafts people that may have an influence on your work. Hopefully, the information will provide inspiration for your research and the work that you create.

Learning outcomes

After completing this unit you should:

1. know about key developments in art, craft and design
2. be able to research and record historical, contemporary and contextual information
3. be able to review, produce and present outcomes from contextual sources.

Assessment and grading criteria

This table shows you what you must do in order to achieve a **pass**, **merit** or **distinction** grade, and where you can find activities in this book to help you.

To achieve a **pass** grade the evidence must show that you are able to:	To achieve a **merit** grade the evidence must show that, in addition to the pass criteria, you are able to:	To achieve a **distinction** grade the evidence must show that, in addition to the pass and merit criteria, you are able to:
P1 describe the characteristics and influences of key movements and the work of individuals **See Assessment activities 5.1, page 88; 5.2, page 92**	**M1** research and organise information about art, craft and design developments, effectively linking the contexts in which works were produced **See Assessment activities 5.1, page 88; 5.2, page 92; 5.4, page 100**	**D1** extract and analyse complex information independently, from comprehensive research **See Assessment activities 5.1, page 88; 5.2, page 92; 5.4, page 100**
P2 show how cultural contexts relate to historical and contemporary art, craft and design **See Assessment activities 5.1, page 88; 5.2, page 92; 5.3, page 94**	**M2** express coherent opinions, supported by examples drawn from established sources **See Assessment activities 5.2, page 92; 5.3, page 94; 5.4, page 100**	**D2** express informed judgements and argued conclusions, using specialist language fluently **See Assessment activities 5.2, page 92; 5.3, page 94; 5.4, page 100**
P3 produce primary and secondary research **See Assessment activities 5.1, page 88; 5.2, page 92; 5.4, page 100**		
P4 review information and produce outcomes **See Assessment activities 5.1, page 88; 5.2, page 92; 5.4, page 100**		
P5 present outcomes **See Assessment activities 5.1, page 88; 5.2, page 92; 5.4, page 100**		

How you will be assessed

Some of your Unit 5 assignments will be included in project briefs for other units. The research tasks will be carried out in conjunction with practical work, so it is important that you keep evidence of Unit 5 work in a journal or format that is identifiable. Evidence for assessment may take the form of:

* written assignments such as essays that may be illustrated

* presentations, by you or by a small group. You may include some computer-generated images or other visual material. These presentations will be assessed by tutors who will keep a written record

* research journals – these will probably be illustrated and can include a wide range of references. They may not be as cohesive as an essay or written assignment as you can use your research journal to gather all sorts of information that interests and inspires you.

Christian

In this project we had to work in a small group and make a one-minute-long animated film based on a visit to Dungeness. One of the themes we were given was 'What's in the box?', so we decided one of us would wear a box on our head with a question mark.

When we got to Dungeness we immediately got a sense of the place. There was a vast amount of open land and I personally felt loneliness, because there was very little civilisation there; it was like walking into what was once a restricted zone, where nuclear bombs were tested.

Before visiting the location, we researched the animator Jan Svankmejer and felt very inspired by his work. He used lots of found objects to make his films, which he moved about to make them look alive. We were also shown a film by Derek Jarman, who lived in Dungeness – we could see how he had used the beach as a background for scenes in the film. We improvised and tried to get as much footage as possible.

Over to you!

- What preparations would you make if you were going to visit a place being used for a project theme?
- How would you find information about the location?
- Would you prepare some pages in your sketchbook with 'grounds' so that you had colours and textures to respond to rather than blank sheets?

This abandoned tank at Dungeness no longer has a function but do you think it has a surreal quality in this context?

An animation still from student work relating to the Dungeness visit.

1. Know about key developments in art, craft and design

Working with the outdoors

Can an outdoor environment help you conceive an idea or narrative, and how can you begin to research this environment?

If a location is used to supply themes and ideas for a project, make sure that you do some research in advance – good preparation will give you insight. Your project brief will provide some references.

Make notes while you are in the location, where your responses will be fresh and not reliant on memory. You may need to write down information about photographs as you take them.

Look back at Christian's work on page 85. It demonstrates how the creative process can take place, but it also gives you an idea of how practical work can be mixed with personal experience and contextual research. Today, you are likely to start a research topic by sitting at a computer and searching on Google. However, armchair research is only one way to find out about something. In this case, research was about looking at real things and was a form of primary research. You should also judge physical qualities, based on things that relate to your senses, such as touch or smell, but also more general qualities such as atmosphere and sense of space, which can never be conveyed accurately by photography or film.

Unit 5 focuses on the late 19th century until the present day. The industrial revolution, which started in the late 18th century, led to a huge expansion of cities over the next 100 years. The British Empire generated the wealth to enable scientific advances and the development of manufacturing processes that supplied a growing consumer market. One example of technology's effect on the role of the artist was the invention of photography. By the second half of the19th century this new medium of recording was challenging the role of the artist, which helped spur the development of new painting movements such as Impressionism.

The following section covers some of the key movements of the 20th century, linked to their themes and influences:

- Art Nouveau
- Dada and Surrealism
- The Bauhaus
- Abstract Expressionism, Minimalism and Pop Art.

Consider the last 100 years and write down anything you know about the art, design and historical context of the period. You could write your ideas as a 'spider' diagram.

This would be good activity to do with a small group – you will be able to find out what others know and pool your knowledge.

When you have put down all the information you can remember, use research sources to make a timeline diagram that links major developments in art and design during the last 100 years to other significant events.

There are a number of good surveys of art and design history, but the viewpoint will reflect the period in which it is written – what is contemporary now will look very different in 20 years' time. Television documentaries seem to date even faster than books, with changing fashions and styles of programme.

1.1 Art, craft and design movements

Historical art and design is often divided into movements. These divisions help you to understand the chronological development of art and design, but they also need to be set in a broader context. Certain movements such as Pop Art never seem to have disappeared, so you need to consider the peak time of any key movement, the factors surrounding it and what contributed to its decline in importance. The Bauhaus school of art and design, for example, which flourished in Germany in the 1920s and 1930s, is a good example of a design ideal that peaked and then suffered a downfall for political reasons. It was thought subversive by the Nazi regime and was dissolved in 1933 before the Second World War.

We associate the birth of the modern movement with the early 20th century. A new millennium had never triggered a major cultural change before, but the fact that a fresh term – Art Nouveau (New Art) – was used shows that there was a desire to break with the past. Historical and classical styles were rejected and many new ones created. There was also greater use of materials such as steel and glass, and mechanisation increased the market for consumer goods and reduced the power of the state, the church and the aristocracy as patrons.

Pont Alexandre III (constructed 1896–1900) displays opulent Art Nouveau decoration including lamps, cherubs, nymphs and winged horses.

Art Nouveau

Art Nouveau was one of the first movements in art and design that can be described as 'modernist' – a term used to define the new art forms that developed in the first half of the 20th century.

Remember

Art Nouveau fact file

Key dates: 1880–1914

Key figures: Charles Rennie Mackintosh, Joseph Hoffmann, Antonio Gaudí, Victor Horta, William De Morgan, Aubrey Beardsley

Key concept: the rejection of historical styles and a desire to unify all aspects of design using shapes and structures inspired by natural forms.

Assessment activity 5.1: Key movements – Art Nouveau in Europe

:BTEC

Create a pictorial presentation with text.

Describe the characteristics and influences of Art Nouveau in Britain, France, Germany, Austria and Spain, and highlight the work of one artist or designer from each of these countries. Work on a separate A3 sheet for each country and collage together your notes, drawings, photographs and photocopies so the different styles can be seen. You might compare the austere, monochromatic work of Charles Rennie Mackintosh with the colourful, flamboyant designs of Antonio Gaudí, and compare the British and Spanish contexts.

For **P1** you need to give a visual overview for each country and highlight individual artists and designers.

For **P2** include a summary of about 500 words.

These pieces of work will fulfil the requirements for **P5** and your research journal will fulfil criteria for **P3** and **P4**.

Grading tips

To achieve a pass, you will need to describe the characteristics and influences of key movements and the work of individuals. Your work should include well-organised information and clearly listed references – be sure to look at more sources than Wikipedia! **P1**

To achieve a merit, you will need to link your research and information to the context in which works were produced and to the broader culture of early 20th-century Europe. You should consult a wider number of sources than for a pass and include your own judgements and analysis. You could also look at aspects of technology, politics or technology and comment on the importance of cities such as Paris, Vienna and Barcelona. **M1**

To achieve a distinction, you will need to evidence independent analysis of complex information derived from a wide field of research. You might also include some observations of primary sources, such as works in galleries and museums. **D1**

A view of the roof of Gaudí's Casa Mila apartment block in Barcelona.

The doorway of 29 Avenue Rapp, Paris (designed by Jules Lavirotte in 1901). The ceramics and brickwork are decorated with animal and flower motifs intermingled with female figures.

Dada and Surrealism

These two movements relied on the roles of accident and chance as part of the creative process and, in the case of Dada, rejected vigorously the cultural and political values that contributed to the outbreak of the First World War (1914–18). Dada released creative and inventive forces that had a lasting effect on 20th-century art, and led directly to the literary and artistic movement known as Surrealism.

Surrealism's reputation for creating strange images was based on its poetic invention and reliance on unconscious experience, partly influenced by the psychoanalytical theories of Sigmund Freud. The movement emerged in the1920s and peaked in the 1930s; some of its leading figures, such as Salvador Dalí, are among the best-known artists of any period.

Remember

Dada fact file

Key dates: 1916–1923

Key figures: Marcel Duchamp, Tristan Tzara, Man Ray, George Grosz, John Heartfield, Francis Picabia

Key concepts: anarchic, subversive anti-art that also involved poetry and political action.

The influence of Surrealism

Many artists such as Pablo Picasso and Alberto Giacometti, who did not belong formally to the movement, produced Surrealist works, while Max Ernst, Joan Miró and René Magritte continued to produce Surrealist imagery throughout their lives. Surrealist art relies on several visual devices, including the shock tactic of making the bizarre seem normal and mixing disconnected subject matter. Max Ernst, for example, created nightmarish scenes by using the collage process. Illustrations from a number of books were joined together to create an element of surprise and unrest. Surrealism has also been incorporated into graphic design and advertising. We continue to be shocked and disturbed by Surrealist images today, while the word 'surreal' has become attached to a wide range of unusual phenomena or images.

The impact of Surrealism on art and design has been enormous and continues more than 50 years after the movement ceased to have avant-garde status. Its imagery seems to reveal inner thoughts in which self-control and reason have been abandoned.

Remember

Surrealism fact file

Key dates: 1920s–1940s

Key figures: André Breton, Salvador Dalí, Max Ernst, René Magritte, Joan Miró, Giorgio de Chirico

Key concepts: dream images and expression, bringing the world of unconscious experience into art; incongruous juxtapositions of ready-made or found objects.

Activity: Dada, Surrealism and the found object

One of the most important legacies of Dada and Surrealism is the idea that the creative act on its own has as much value as a finished work, and that a found object can replace a work of art. Combining materials and objects that have no association with traditional art media revolutionised the way artists could work.

This mixing of materials and imagery, often referred to as **collage**, has been one of the most significant artistic developments of the 20th century. Collage has influenced a large body of art over the last 100 years, and has even given rise to computer-generated imagery using programs such as Photoshop.

1. Can you find and collect evidence of the influence of collage and the found object on practices in art and design? Start with obvious two-dimensional things such as advertisements, record covers and textile designs. Then extend your research to found objects and examples of 'new' things that have been made from existing objects. Is 'retro' styling a form of design by collage, where one design ideal is mixed with another?

2. Make sure that you record the names of the key protagonists of this way of working, such as Max Ernst (Surrealist collages) and, more recently, Robert Rauschenberg, who used collage in the second half of the 20th-century to create silkscreen prints.

Key term

Collage – the process of using fragments of sometimes unrelated printed matter and photographs to make compositions.

The photocollage or photomontage process used in this design by Peter Blake (for a Beatles album cover) began with the work of the Berlin Dadaists such as Raoul Hausmann and George Grosz in the 1930s.

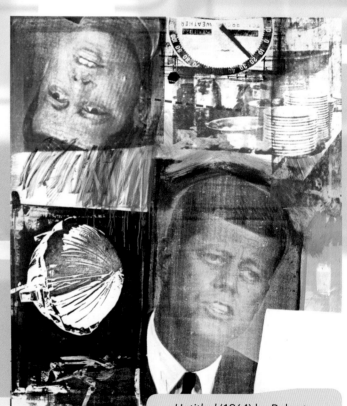

Untitled (1964) by Robert Rauschenberg.

Activity: Art, dreams and psychoanalysis – can you make the sub-conscious visible?

The Interpretation of Dreams by Sigmund Freud was first published in 1899. Freud's psychoanalytical theories were based on his work as a doctor and opened the way to a greater understanding of why we behave as we do.

- Can you research some of the basic categories of dream subject matter that he described?
- By looking at imagery by artists such as Dalí and Ernst, can you explain the idea that Surrealism depicts the world of the subconscious?

The wider cultural context: the Bauhaus

The Bauhaus had a lasting influence on art and design education and pioneered the idea that art and design should be taught in an integrated way.

Before the Bauhaus, artists worked in specific disciplines and were schooled mainly in the methods of classical art. At the Bauhaus all students studied painting, design and architecture, and followed a basic colour course initially taught by Johannes Itten.

The Bauhaus had technical and aesthetic instructors known as Masters, who ran different workshops. László Moholy-Nagy, for example, led the photography and **typography** workshops; his interest in new technologies has a parallel with the way that computers have transformed the teaching of art and design in the early 21st century.

In 1926 the Bauhaus moved from its first location in Weimar to Dessau, to a building designed by the architect and school's director, Walter Gropius. Gropius was succeeded by Hannes Meyer in 1928, whose Marxist philosophy put greater emphasis on the practical and sociological aspects of the school.

The architect Mies van der Rohe replaced Meyer for the last brief phase of the school, when it was based in Berlin from 1932. In 1933 the Nazi regime closed the school because of its political leanings. Teachers such as Moholy-Nagy and Gropius moved to America where they helped introduce the philosophy of the Bauhaus to Black Mountain College in North Carolina, and to Chicago and Yale universities. The Bauhaus revolutionised art education and its impact is still evident today.

Key term

Typography – letterforms and their use within graphic design and layout were an important aspect of the Bauhaus School, with influential work designed by László Moholy-Nagy, Herbert Bayer and Joost Schmidt.

Remember

Bauhaus fact file

Key dates: 1920s–1930s

Key figures: Walter Gropius, Herbert Bayer, Josef Albers, László Moholy-Nagy

Key concept: art and design school motivated by technical and aesthetic principles linking all fields of art and design.

Assessment activity 5.2: The wider cultural context – art education

Using books and websites, etc., describe the formation and development of the Bauhaus and compare it to the art school education of today. Why did it close?

To find out about current art school education you will have to do some primary research by talking to your tutors and other students. Some of your tutors may have experienced a very different type of art school that was not part of a large institution or university.

1. Are subject areas mixed together much?

2. Do students have workshops in different processes?

3. Look back at the recent history of art schools and find out how courses and colleges have changed in the past 50 years.

Grading tips

To achieve a pass grade (**P1**, **P2**) you should describe the formation and structure of the Bauhaus and the work of key artists and designers who worked there. You should also discuss why it was so successful and how it has influenced British art schools during the last 60 years. Break your information into decades or use major historical events such as the Second World War to help organise your material **P3** **P4** **P5**.

For **M1** and **M2** you will need to look at the Bauhaus in a wider cultural context, examining the reasons for its success and closure. By analysing current art school prospectuses you can compare aspects of past and present art education.

For **D1** and **D2** you could include primary research by interviewing your college staff and tutors about their experiences at art school from the 1970s onwards.

Abstract Expressionism

After the Second World War (1939–45), American culture acquired a new importance in the world and the US overshadowed Europe as a leader of the avant-garde. Many European artists emigrated to the US to escape the war and Fascism, and the paths created by Surrealism and Expressionism led to an increased exploration of the inner self. American artists of the 1940s and 1950s, such as Jackson Pollock, Willem De Kooning and Mark Rothko, worked on large-size canvases, where the process of painting itself became as important as the creation of images. Lavish exhibitions of this new work, known as Abstract Expressionism or **Action Painting**, gave American painting a dominant place in Western art in the 1950s and 1960s.

Key term

Action Painting – Jackson Pollock's working process, known as Action Painting, was a radical demonstration of the concept that painting was a series of highly physical actions and was no longer dependent on the easel.

Remember

Abstract Expressionism fact file

Key dates: 1940s–1960s

Key figures: Willem de Kooning, Jackson Pollock, Mark Rothko

Key concept: a form of painting where feelings and actions are manifested through the image and process of painting.

Minimalism

Minimalism, which became an important movement in the 1960s, played down emotional and aesthetic values in art. Form and material were explored in the simplest and purest ways through mainly three-dimensional objects produced by industrial processes, without reference to the human figure or the visible world. Some of the most important artists associated with Minimalism are Robert Morris, Donald Judd and Carl Andre. Minimalist values have also become adopted as a design philosophy, with decoration and ornament regarded as unnecessary.

Remember

Minimalism fact file

Key dates: 1960s

Key figures: Robert Morris, Donald Judd, Carl Andre

Key concept: the rejection of aesthetic values and personal expression, and the celebration of simple and impersonal forms, often industrially produced.

Did you know?

In 1972 the Tate Gallery purchased a work by Carl Andre, *Equivalent VIII*, which consisted of 120 fire bricks. Initially, the purchase remained unnoticed, but in 1976 it became a press sensation, which made Andre's work one of the most famous in the world. The press could not accept that Andre's bricks were worth any more than ordinary bricks.

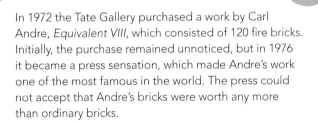

When visiting Tate Modern, look carefully at the way the architects Herzog and De Meuron have converted this huge building that was once a power station. They wanted a neutral space that allowed the art works to speak for themselves, and created a building with few architectural details (such as skirting boards) that might interfere with the works.

Pop Art

Pop Art emerged in the 1960s in Britain and the US and gave the everyday commercial object or image a new cultural importance. Imagery for Pop Art was drawn from popular and commercial art and the media, and was partly influenced by the success of pop music. Many critics of the time labelled Pop Art as vulgar and thought art was lowering its values.

British Pop Art tended to have a greater focus on painting than American and more narrative imagery. David Hockney, Peter Blake and Richard Hamilton are all well-known British Pop Artists. American Pop Artists, such as Andy Warhol, Roy Lichtenstein and Claus Oldenburg, transformed the objects of consumerism into symbols of glamour. Andy Warhol had been a graphic designer before turning to painting and printmaking, while the painter James Rosenquist had designed roadside advertisement hoardings. Claus Oldenburg had worked as a car designer, and his skills as a draughtsman can be seen in his proposals for monumental sculptures of everyday objects.

How many iconic everyday symbols can you think of (such as Mickey Mouse or the Coca Cola bottle)?

Andy Warhol celebrated fame and created iconic images of people such as Marilyn Monroe. Who would he choose from today's hall of fame, and what sort of image of them might he create?

Remember

Pop Art fact file

Key dates: 1960s

Key figures: Andy Warhol, Roy Lichtenstein, Claus Oldenburg, David Hockney, Peter Blake

Key concept: source material taken from mass culture, such as advertising and the media.

Assessment activity 5.3: World cultures

The Second World War (1939–45) left Britain in a poor economic state; it took more than a decade to regain industrial momentum and supply consumer demand. The United States had been less damaged, both financially and physically, and post-war consumer demand soon created a culture and environment very different from that in Britain.

Research the emergence of Pop Art in Britain and the US and explore the way cultural and environmental factors in each country produced different styles.

Grading tips

You should make reference to everyday things such as comics, cars, product designs and advertisements, to show the context artists were working in. **P2**

For **M2**, your research should include references to historical events, such as the development of space exploration, so that your opinions are not only defined by art works.

To achieve **D2**, look for primary sources in a museum or old magazines and examine the differences between post-war British and American cultures.

Your image research could be done on camera, using pairs of images to reinforce each point you are making. This could be a potential computer slide show presentation. Make sure that you take notes on your images.

David Hockney's subject matter led him to be classed as a Pop Artist. How does his work compare with that of contemporary Pop Artists?

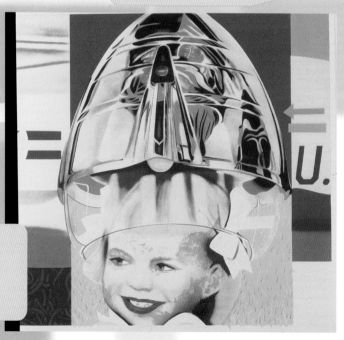

James Rosenquist's paintings have an obvious link with his previous employment as a billboard painter. He eliminates the idea of the artist's brush marks and gives the impression that the painting has been mechanically produced.

Postmodernism

This term is mainly relevant to developments in art and design from the 1980s. In architecture, the postmodern style applies to buildings where a modernist approach to form and function has been accompanied by other architectural styles, particularly classical. While the modernist architect Mies Van der Rohe said 'less is more', the American architect Robert Venturi, in his book *Complexity and Contradiction in Architecture* (1966), wrote 'less is a bore'. Venturi regarded decorative elements in architecture as adding vitality and richness.

In painting, postmodernism applies to work from the 1970s and 1980s, when the formalist and generally Minimalist values of modernism were substituted by a new style of Expressionist art. German artists such as Georg Baselitz, and the Italian Francesco Clemente, were making large paintings in a figurative style with highly visible brushstrokes. Gradually, a less Expressionist form of postmodernist art evolved, where the idea of 'meaning' was to become a central issue.

Remember

Postmodernism fact file

Key dates: 1970s–1980s

Key figures: Julian Schnabel, Georg Baselitz, Francesco Clemente, Robert Venturi

Key concept: a rejection of the formalist limitations of modernism which led to a new decorative freedom in architecture and figuration in art.

1.2 The impact of science and technology on art and design

Postmodernism developed in a world where the computer has had a major impact on art and design. Information is now easily accessible and anyone can put their work on a website. There is now a notion of reality termed 'virtual'.

Computers also enable complex design calculations to be made in fields such as architecture and car design. Two- and three-dimensional designs can now be sent electronically, and artists and designers can communicate from different parts of the world. Drawings no longer need to be made on paper, and in animation a new kind of pictorial depth and reality is now possible.

The exterior of the Centre Pompidou gallery is a focus of attention, as well as its contents. The concept of displaying the functional characteristics of a building on the outside established a new language of architecture. The architects were Richard Rogers, Renzo Piano and Gianfranco Franchini. Can you think of another building where the functional aspects are highly visible?

2. Be able to research and record historical, contemporary and contextual information

When researching your subject it is important that you find as many ways as possible to identify, select and record references that will be useful to your work and help you gain a broader understanding of your subject. This will help you develop your critical and analytical skills and add imagination and inspiration to your ideas. Presentations will help you learn about the main developments of 19th- and 20th-century art and design, and specialist unit assignments will help you discover the contextual aspects of your subject.

As well as referring to books and the Internet, you may find some useful DVD recordings in your college library. These may be specially made documentary films or recordings from television programmes. Contemporary writing and films are also useful, and for some subjects, such as fashion, magazines and even shops can be major research sources.

2.1 Research

Sources for research fit into two main categories – primary and secondary. Primary research is made from original sources such as art works, objects, original documents or interviews. With primary research you have to make sure that you record information carefully and in as much detail as possible – you may not get a second opportunity. Secondary research material includes books, the Internet, television programmes, etc., and provides information that has already been filtered and presented by another person.

The Internet is a very useful tool for preliminary research, but beware of its limitations and distractions. Your fellow students will be seeing the same information and it is now relatively easy to check whether information has been lifted from Internet sources. Your tutors and college librarians should be able to help you focus your research and direct you towards key sources. It is also important when researching a subject that you identify respected authors and eliminate irrelevant information.

Primary sources

- **Galleries and museums**

The most obvious source for your field of study is a gallery or museum. Apart from the works on display they also have reserve collections, study centres and libraries. Some of these facilities may need to be booked. Galleries and museums also have education departments which plan programmes for special exhibitions and are involved in the layout and presentation of work to make it more accessible.

- **Looking at primary sources**

You can find out more than you expect by looking carefully at something. You can see its size, colour, texture, finish and form much more clearly than in any photograph. An exhibition or collection may also provide a kind of visual continuity that cannot be appreciated any other way. Once you have seen the original work, a book or catalogue will probably make more sense to you.

- **Talking to artists and designers and visiting their studios**

Sometimes it is possible to talk to artists and designers directly about their work. Graduating design students exhibit at the New Designers exhibition in the Business Design Centre, London, every year in July.

'Open Studio' events allow you to visit communities of artists and designers who have studios in a large building. They are always willing to talk about their work and professional practice, and it may be possible to arrange a special interview with them for a research project.

Activity: How can you combine your primary research with secondary research?

As an example, see page 85, when Dungeness in Kent was used as an inspiration for a project, and look at ways you could apply similar research/context principles to another place. Many artists and designers have been inspired by a specific location – for a fine artist it may be a landscape such as St. Ives in Cornwall, where a colony of artists and craftspeople has been based in a small fishing village for nearly 100 years. Architects and designers have also been inspired by local materials and technical processes. This will have been evident if you carried out research on Art Nouveau illustrated at the beginning of this unit.

The work of the Art Nouveau architect Antonio Gaudí involved wrought iron and ceramics. Both materials are commonly used as decorative features in Catalonia.

In Derek Jarman's film *The Garden* (1990), you can see how he has used the environment as a backdrop, and created a kind of collage where crude special effects are used to give the natural landscape a sense of unreality. If you have visited a location used in a film, painting, design or novel, you realise how fact and fiction can be mixed for narrative effect and how the location inspires the creative process.

In his garden, Jarman created his own small paradise from driftwood and other objects collected from the beach. The plants he used are only those that will grow in this inhospitable environment but they evoke a fragile sense of optimism. With this example in mind, think about how the creative mind can be matched to reality as you walk around a landscape – your responses could be recorded photographically.

Have you ever been to a place and realised that the context makes something you already know more meaningful? It might be going to a country where a story or film is set or visiting a house where an author lived.

Pieces of driftwood and other found objects are used in Derek Jarman's garden at Dungeness. Can you think of other artists who have made 3D collages?

Gaudí's work is regarded as Art Nouveau but what style of architecture do these gates at Parc Guell remind you of?

2.2 Record

A research journal can be in written form, but you can also keep a photographic or digital record. Your journals will help you to record, generate and evaluate your ideas, and will provide evidence for your assessments and help you make links to other assignments. Some of your journal work will be first-hand responses, such as those made in a gallery. You could also make diagrams, add pictures, etc. The book does not need to look neat, it is more important that the information is meaningful to you and links to what happens next.

If you are recording information from a lecture you may have to use headings with short phrases to keep up with the flow of information. Make sure when you are recording information that you make a note of the source. A **bibliography** will list written and Internet sources. If you are referring to an object or a building, details of author and date are essential, but location and materials are also worth noting. Direct quotations from text should be identified by quotation marks.

Making a bibliography

The usual way to reference a book is:

Author (surname followed by initials), book title, place of publication (e.g. London), publisher, date of publication. This information is usually found at the beginning of a book, near the title or contents page.

Magazine sources should be referenced as:

Author, title of article, name of journal, date and page reference.

For a website reference:

Author, article/subject, website address, date of website access. Make sure that you record the URL (uniform research locator) information before changing sites.

Reference to DVD recordings should include the presenter, title, production company (this might be a TV channel) and year of production.

All of this detail makes your presentation look professional and thorough and shares your information sources with others.

2.3 Contextual information

Case study: Daniel

'In a project for a fine art unit we were asked to research how artists had used the self-portrait. We were shown a film about the artist Chuck Close and saw how he made his paintings from photographs by scaling up areas divided into a grid. I was amazed by the way the image turned into a photo as you moved away from it, yet up close looked like a painting. I also remembered how Chuck Close had said the shapes in each square were like hotdogs or donuts.'

1. **When was photography invented and what effect did it have on painting?**
2. **How many artists can you find that paint directly from photographs?**

Self-portrait based on Chuck Close's working method.

Case study: The Artist as Hephaestus, Eduardo Paolozzi

Paolozzi's sculpture alluding to the god of fire gives the artist an impression of mechanical power.

'What might describe the modern condition is that in creating a self-portrait today's artist (unlike Rembrandt or Van Gogh) will not stare at himself in a mirror but will try to capture his likeness by other means. The approach of a sculptor … either disguises the superficial facts of the self-portrait or, if the artist is lucky, reveals new personal insights. In my interpretation, the torso for example is an amalgam of shapes but the tension between the head and the limbs should guarantee that these inventions read either as an engine block or as flesh.'

Do you think this sculpture reflects early 20th century ideas such as cubism or collage?

1. **Can you think of any contemporary self-portraits that have not been made with the use of a mirror?**

2. **There are many bronze statues in towns and cities that were produced for very good reasons – can you find six examples in your own area and decide if they still have a context in the present day?**

Activity: Self-portraits

Choose 22 self-portraits from 1900 to the present day to research, using two examples per decade. A self-portrait could also include an image of the artist that has not been titled 'self-portrait'. Is it possible to define why the portrait seems to fit the period in which it was made? Is it in a particular style such as Cubist, or does the medium (such as frozen blood used in a cast of Mark Quinn's head) tell us something about the period? Can you select the most important self-portraits of each decade based on the significance of particular artists?

How many artists have made the self-portrait the main focus of their career, such as Antony Gormley?

You could also investigate the idea of design objects as a form of self-portrait. When choosing objects, how much are customers buying into a designer's personality (perhaps as outrageous or adventurous)?

Key term

Bibliography – a bibliography used to refer to the list of written sources used by an author but can now also include other sources such as the Internet and television broadcasts.

Your bibliography will demonstrate the breadth of your research and also point the reader towards sources for future study. It is important to try to identify the key works in any subject you are studying, including primary sources.

3. Be able to review, produce and present outcomes from contextual sources

Whatever form of presentation you are making, you will have to review and edit your collected information. This may mean reorganising the order or structure to improve the sense and flow of your work. Discuss your work with your tutors and fellow students and get their feedback.

Unless very short, most written forms of presentation will have an introduction and a conclusion. When considering these parts, ask yourself if you have kept your work focused on the main topic – for example, full biographical details

may not be necessary when you are looking at the ideas of a designer.

Presentations could be in the form of:

- written essays
- oral presentations using visual images (display boards or computer slide shows) supported by a written summary as additional evidence
- journals or sketchbooks with images and notes
- web pages
- pages for the course on-line learning facility.

Assessment activity 5.4: Art and design now

 **BTEC**

You are to make a visual presentation to a non-specialist audience about what is current and important in art and design and provide some contextual background. Your presentation will last about five minutes and show a selection of images accompanied by a commentary. The commentary should be in written form and have an introduction and conclusion.

You can choose any field of art and design – fine art, fashion, graphic design, photography, product design, car design, architecture, etc. For some of these subjects you could include your own photographs.

Primary sources

Visits to galleries, studios, shops, showrooms, locations, talking to artists and designers.

Secondary sources

Websites, magazines, newspapers, television programmes/reports, exhibition catalogues, brochures.

Grading tips

Because there is an emphasis on 'now' and information about your subject may not yet be fully documented, to achieve a pass you will need to research both primary and secondary sources.

To achieve **M1** and **M2** there should be greater analysis of the link between information and context.

For **D1** and **D2** this contextual analysis should include sociological comment and might cover more than one country.

Paul Greenhalgh
Director and president

Paul Greenhalgh studied fine art and art history at Reading University and took a postgraduate degree in history of art at the Courtauld Institute.

Paul has held a number of posts in both art education and museums – he was recently head of research at the Victoria and Albert Museum in London, and is now Director and President of the Corcoran Gallery of Art and College of Art + Design in Washington DC. His career path has been based on the view that research in art and design history is a creative field in itself.

'I trained initially as a painter, and alongside this began to study history of art.

I am convinced that the combination of academic work and studio activity gave me an extremely sound yet flexible grounding, which has allowed my career to develop in a fulfilling and productive way. My training has allowed me to work closely with artists and designers and with historic works of art of all types.

I have been employed in museums as a curator, researcher and exhibition designer, and taught art and design history in colleges of art. I have also worked as a commentator on the arts, and as an academic editor and author. I have no doubt that it was the combination of academic study with studio practice that facilitated my career.'

Paul has progressed from a degree in fine art and art history to his current role as Director and President of the Corcoran in Washington DC.

Think about it!

- Art galleries and museums are now a major part of our culture and tourist industry. Have you thought about job opportunities in this area?
- Research and writing can lead to new ways of looking at past and present cultures. Can you now see how these activities can also be creative?
- In London, the arts are one of the greatest generators of wealth and income. Did you realise they were so important?

Just checking

By the end of your course you will have gained a huge insight into the context of your chosen subject.

1. Why is it important to keep up with current developments in your subject?

2. When you visit a new place or country for the first time, do you now feel able to find ways of researching its culture?

3. Do you now realise how important galleries, museums and libraries are as places to find information?

4. Information and opinions are constantly changing, but you should now have greater confidence in your own opinions.

5. Do you have a general idea of how art and design developed during the last 150 years?

Assignment tips

- Understand the pass, merit and distinction criteria: pass level is achieved by assembling the evidence that a project brief has asked for. You can see how there are fewer criteria for distinction and that this level is achieved by personal analysis and a self-directed approach.

- Use a defined approach to your research: 'research, analyse, critique, reflect' (see Unit 4, page 67). It is important for you to list all of your research sources – remember that the most original outcomes come from your own ideas and conclusions, which are often derived from primary sources.

- Drawing conclusions: familiarise yourself with facts, but then draw your own conclusions after analysing your information. Your opinions and conclusions should be based on a number of sources to ensure a balanced viewpoint.

6 Application, exploration and realisation in art and design

This unit looks at developing the skills needed to complete a project, from initial research, through development and into resolution and completion. It is the flow of ideas, combined with research and development that helps to move a project along. This process is called the design cycle. You will learn how to research, develop and resolve your work, and will be able to apply this skill to any of the art and design pathways. You might study this unit with a subject-specific unit, or you might cover it over the year combined with a range of other units.

It is essential to write a detailed project proposal for the work you plan to produce for this unit. This will help you see clearly how each area will be covered and ensure that you meet the learning outcomes. Writing a proposal will also encourage you to think about your aims and timescale, and give yourself the opportunity to work towards the higher assessment grades by setting targets.

Learning outcomes

After completing this unit you should:

1. be able to carry out personal research from contextual sources
2. be able to generate solutions to a negotiated brief
3. be able to select and experiment safely with specialist media, materials and techniques
4. understand factors when reviewing work and developing outcomes
5. be able to realise and present final outcomes to meet a brief.

Assessment and grading criteria

This table shows you what you must do in order to achieve a **pass**, **merit** or **distinction** grade, and where you can find activities in this book to help you.

To achieve a **pass** grade the evidence must show that you are able to:	To achieve a **merit** grade the evidence must show that, in addition to the pass criteria, you are able to:	To achieve a **distinction** grade the evidence must show that, in addition to the pass and merit criteria, you are able to:
P1 carry out personal research from contextual sources **See Assessment activity 6.1, page 108**	**M1** research and respond to sources, showing clear, consistent direction and intention **See Assessment activity 6.1, page 108**	**D1** research informed, independently selected references, showing innovative personal thinking and creative direction **See Assessment activity 6.1, page 108**
P2 develop solutions for a negotiated brief, developing and extending visual language skills **See Assessment activity 6.1, page 108**	**M2** show initiative in selecting and using materials, equipment and techniques, applying understanding of the factors that influence the specialism in evaluating the work against the brief **See Assessment activity 6.1, page 108**	**D2** show perceptive critical appreciation, meeting the brief through applying an understanding of the factors that influence the specialism **See Assessment activites 6.1, page 108; 6.2, page 109; 6.3, page 110**
P3 select and experiment safely with specialist media, materials and techniques to develop visual communication skills **See Assessment activity 6.2, page 109**	**M3** show an individual approach to structuring, reviewing and presenting work in a coherent and considered format **See Assessment activity 6.2, page 109**	
P4 review work and develop outcomes **See Assessment activity 6.3, page 110**	**M4** produce effective and skilful outcomes that show a consistent level of knowledge, skill and understanding **See Assessment activity 6.3, page 110**	
P5 realise and present final outcomes to meet a brief **See Assessment activity 6.4, page 110**		

How you will be assessed

You have to write a proposal outlining where you will identify source material relevant to the theme or brief. It should also explain how you will approach each stage of the project to meet the learning outcomes and how research from contextual sources and media has helped refine your ideas. Work produced may include:

- initial research such as drawings, photos, information from a visit or talk, library, Internet, magazine research
- sketchbook work, design sheets, storyboards and plans showing development
- samples, models, tests, thumbnails, drafts
- evaluation, reviews, feedback, analysis
- final outcomes.

Gemma

I did this unit as my final major project at the end of the second year. My specialist pathway was textiles and the theme was 'Transport'.

For the research we visited a transport museum. I wanted to design a repeat fabric pattern for use in a children's room. After planning how much time to spend on research and developing ideas, and what materials to use, I took photos and drew some planes and trucks; I also used the Internet to research the museum and the work of artists with similar ideas, and looked at examples of children's fabric and wallpaper to see what was already available. Using different materials, I created some colourful designs, which I developed into ten sample ideas. I then surveyed my group to see which were the most popular. I chose the top three to develop further.

When my tutors reviewed the proposal, I wrote down what we talked about and any action plans made. I also used skills I had learnt in other areas, such as Photoshop, to scan my drawings and pattern repeats. I took pictures from magazines to create concept boards, but put my own print ideas on the wallpaper and curtains. At the end, I used both the mood and concept boards as part of my finished display, including the final pieces and all my sketchbook work.

Over to you!

- **What helped Gemma to get her project started?**
- **How did Gemma develop her ideas?**
- **What will you use as starting points?**

1. Be able to carry out personal research from contextual sources

Deciding what to produce

This unit is very open and you may choose what you produce. However, it is important that you show the stages that you go through on your creative journey.

Before you start, read through the learning outcomes. How do you think you can meet them? Make sure you understand the language used and that you know how to achieve them. Look at the Assessment and grading criteria and list what your project will need. Can you break your work into stages that relate to the learning outcomes and help you plan your time?

For this unit you will either be working to a set brief or to your own self-initiated brief. You will be working in a specialism and should show confidence with specialist materials and techniques. The first few weeks should be all about **personal research**.

There are four key stages to this unit: research, development, review and completion. You will follow the design cycle and keep going through the stages until the project is fully resolved. You might start with an idea, plan how to develop it, make some samples, get feedback on them and then decide you need to do some more research.

Gather as much information as possible related to your theme. Also use your visual recording skills to draw, take photographs, make rubbings, look for colour schemes, film recordings and match fabric swatches. Use different materials and alternative formats to gather visual information.

The next step is secondary research. Use the Internet to follow up ideas and look up artists and factual information. Use books and newspapers to find supporting information. Print off images and take photocopies. Remember to always credit where you found the information.

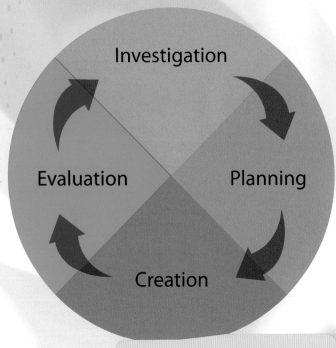

Figure 6.1: The design cycle.

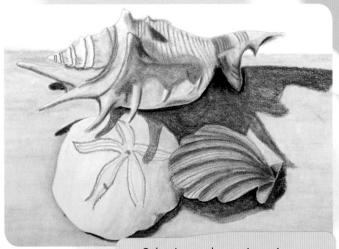

Selecting and experimenting with different specialist media.

Key term

Personal research – this is independent research supported by organised trips and visits to museums, galleries, etc.

Did you know?

Interviews and questionnaires are a great way to get a lot of specific information quickly.

Remember

The key theme of this unit, application, exploration and realisation, is the process of applying your knowledge, research and skills with specialist materials and techniques, exploring alternative ideas, and putting your ideas into a finished art and design outcome.

Case study: Alison Brown — freelance illustrator

I work from home as a freelance illustrator, often to very tight deadlines. I also work alone so it is important for me to be able to generate ideas quickly and research them effectively. Most of my commissions are from newspapers asking me to illustrate articles.

Where do you get your ideas from?

The illustrations have to reflect the article. I will choose a theme from the text and research it to find a strong visual that I can develop. I find out from the client what style of image they want and who it is aimed at. My work is very figurative, so if I am stuck for ideas, I will take my sketchbook to a busy place and sketch people.

Do you ever use secondary sources to get ideas?

Yes, I also collect images in a sourcebook from travel and interiors magazines. It helps me put the illustrations into context, and I read about other artists whose work I like.

1. Who are Alison's clients?
2. What does Alison do when she is stuck for inspiration?
3. How would you develop your ideas if you were a freelance illustrator?

Example of Alison's work – *figurative illustration*: loose sketches of people.

2. Be able to generate solutions to a negotiated brief

2.1 Negotiate and work to a brief

See your proposal as a flexible document that can evolve with the project and don't narrow down too quickly. Use the proposal as a guide to how you will manage your time and what resources you may need at each stage. Include information about how you will develop and experiment. What materials will you use? How will you maintain or improve the quality of your work? How will you make selections and refinements?

Show that you have considered your audience or have used methods such as interviewing and surveys to find out how they feel about the work.

Activity: Starting points

This is a great activity for the whole group so you can share ideas and starting points. Start your project by setting a theme or title. Creating a mind-map, try to think of at least 50 words related to the theme or stimulus word. Examples of starting points and stimulus words could be 'Containment', 'The Beach', 'Movement', 'Structure'.

Then work on your own or in pairs to stretch all your potential ideas. Think about how each one could be made, produced or designed. Write a list of all the materials and techniques available to you.

2.2 Generate ideas

Allow time in your proposal to develop your ideas and develop a focused approach. For example, you might be making a lamp base in clay but find that it shrinks or the light fittings don't fit properly. You may decide to research another material, as well as different types of clay to find out the shrink-rate percentage.

Personal style and approach will make your mark on the developmental work. Select materials and processes relevant to your specialist areas, and that will illustrate the skills you have developed. Keep experimenting. If things don't work out, you can still show that you have tried something and learnt from it. Use your **visual language** skills in your design and presentation work.

Key term

Visual language – how you communicate meaning in your work through mark-making and using the formal elements – line, tone, form and colour.

Example of visual language, using tone and mark-making to generate different moods.

Assessment activity 6.1: Possible outcomes

 **BTEC**

Look back at the work you did for the Starting points activity on the previous page. The next step is to come up with a range of different possible outcomes that you could produce – a lighting project, short film, media campaign or garment. Focus on projects that are realistic and achievable within your timescale and the resources available to you.

Once you have a range of possible ideas and outcomes, you will be able to narrow down areas on which to focus your research. Use the Learning Resource Centre and the Internet to look at other artists who work in similar ways. Also use primary sources to gather information. Include your thought processes in your sketchbook.

Grading tips

Your individual approach and personal style will be the element that helps to set your work apart from other people's. Look for creative and unusual starting points and generate at least ten workable ideas for further development. These will count towards Learning Outcome 2.

To reach the higher grades for this unit, you will need to look at ways of interlinking each stage of the project. Your research should be a thread that runs through the project, while developmental work should show the journey and the decisions you made. If something doesn't work or your ideas change, discuss how you overcame the problems or why things changed. Feedback and review are key factors too, so include evidence from discussions with your colleagues and tutors, and feedback from testing or surveys.

3. Be able to select and experiment safely with specialist media, materials and techniques

Your work should show that you are confident using different materials and that you are not afraid to experiment and find new ways of working. You should back up your experiments with notes or annotations about what you used and how it could be applied, such as smudging charcoal to look like shading.

3.1 Material, equipment and techniques

Specialist media and techniques also include all the 2D resources that you can use to develop the visual language element of your work. Your assessor will be looking for the way that you **visually communicate** ideas in your design work as well as the finished piece. This means how you choose colours and materials, being creative and experimental in generating ideas, and working to health and safety guidelines in studios and workshops.

3.2 Health and safety

Health and safety must be evident both in your proposal and in your developmental work. Include safety guidance relevant to the specialism you are working in, photographs of the tools and equipment you used, or images of you working safely.

Did you know?

You will be expected to work confidently and safely in the studios and you should be able to talk about the media and techniques you are using, with the correct technical terms.

Key term

Visual communication – how you communicate your ideas without words, such as by drawings, thumbnail sketches, working drawings, photos, photos of design development, design sheets, annotation.

Assessment activity 6.2: Scale up, scale down BTEC

It is easy to lose momentum a few weeks into a long project. This is the stage at which to go back into your research to come up with some fresh ideas.

Scale up/scale down: Take an element of your work and scale it up and then scale it down. This works well with pattern ideas, sculpture and drawings. When you scale up, think about new ways to use your idea. Could this be a form that works enlarged as a piece of public art or a building design? Scaled down, could it be a piece of jewellery or a logo?

50 from 5: Next, take five elements from your work to redevelop. This will vary depending on the type of work you are doing, but divide a design sheet into 5 columns, each with 11 rows. Place your chosen elements in the top rows and change each one 10 times. Simple changes can be colour, proportion and turning the image round. More detailed changes could be different materials, textures and techniques.

Grading tip

Make sure you explain why you chose to develop some ideas and why you rejected others. You could annotate photos along with your evaluations. Use the correct technical names for any materials and techniques you used so that you are working towards LO2. Don't forget to mention health and safety and refer to any relevant safety guidelines.

4. Understand factors when reviewing work and developing outcomes

4.1 Reviewing factors

How will you know if you are producing good-quality work? Here are some suggestions:

- **Comments** – include notes and feedback from tutor reviews.

- **Ask people** – ask them to vote for their favourite design or idea.

- **Add your own feedback** – this could be a page in your sketchbook every week where you review your progress.

- **Be creative** – if you hate writing, use stickers or parcel tags to put down a few key words to measure your progress; use 'traffic lights' to show where you need to develop.

- **Use a flow chart or a table** – if you have been problem-solving, use a flow chart to show where you changed your ideas.

5. Be able to realise and present final outcomes to meet a brief

5.1 Finishing and assessment

How will you know when you are finished? If you have followed all the stages carefully and regularly reviewed your work, you should be able to keep to the timescale. Leave yourself at least a week before the handing-in date to go through all your work and mount up final pieces, write evaluations, annotate your sketch book and tie up loose ends.

Reflect on your proposal. Did you meet your aims and objectives? If so, how, and if not, can you identify why not? Look again at the learning outcomes and the assessment and grading criteria – where would you place yourself?

Assessment activity 6.3: Review and feedback   BTEC

P4   M4   D2

In your sketch book or folder you should explain why things changed as the project went on. This might be a diary, a video diary, an image or a short evaluation at the end of every week. To push this further, choose a selection of ideas. Then ask ten different people which one they prefer and why.

Use the feedback to make changes and improvements and document all this in your sketchbook or work folder.

Grading tip

Each time you review your work or show that you have made a judgement you will be working towards P4 and M4.

Assessment activity 6.4: Resolve and finish pieces   BTEC

P5

This is the making and resolving of your project. You will present all the developmental and supporting work as well as the finished outcome.

Before you hand your work in for assessment, go through all of your research and developmental work and highlight key stages. Reviewing the content will help you to map your work against the learning outcomes and identify any areas to develop. Remember to label any sketches or photographs, and to include artwork and your sketchbook in your evaluation.

Grading tip

To gain a high grade there should be a clear link between originating, developing and finishing the project, with explanations of the journey you made, backed up by thorough contextual and specialist subject knowledge.

Lee McIntyre
Lighting designer

I work for a company that design and produce innovative lighting installations for public spaces.

Clients: Our clients have an idea of what they want and a planned budget. They are often local councils, schools or large businesses.

Design process: When we get the brief we first research the company or area, and its history and social context. We then develop a range of four or five ideas which can be presented to the client as a pitch. These include visuals with drawings, photographs and Photoshopped images.

Developing ideas: During the pitch, the clients will ask questions and give feedback about the ideas.

> What would you need to consider if you were going to create an artwork in a town centre?

We then research any points raised by the client (such as health and safety, materials, installation, etc.), develop the idea further and investigate construction methods, materials, costings and timescale. Once the idea has been approved, we start sampling and testing it out. We only start making the final pieces when all the testing and developmental work has been completed.

Success factors: Research, planning and development are the most important factors for a successful installation. Understanding what clients need and what their priorities are is key. Careful planning and research before projects start ensures that they run smoothly and stay on budget and within timescale.

> Using innovative technology and new materials to create exciting and engaging public art.

Think about it!

- Who sets the projects for Lee's company?
- How are ideas developed?
- What are the key things that make a successful project?

Just checking

1. What is the design cycle?

2. List four possible sources of inspiration for starting points.

3. Describe three ways that you can develop your ideas.

4. Write a project proposal and use the assessment and grading criteria to help you. If you are combining units, you must make sure your proposal covers all of the learning outcomes for each unit.

5. Include time to review your work every few weeks, ask for feedback, share ideas, talk about your work and include all the evidence of this in your sketchbook or folder.

edexcel ⠿

Assignment tips

Project proposal: Planning and preparation are crucial for this unit. When you write a project proposal make sure you look at the assessment and grading criteria to give yourself the best chance of getting a good grade. To get a distinction you need to show the way the elements fit together to produce creative, well-researched and well-presented work.

Research: Research doesn't just happen at the start of a project – make sure it goes all the way through. Show how your ideas have developed as the result of your research; talk about things that changed and factors that influenced you.

Development:

• Show how your ideas developed, make choices about materials and ideas and discuss in your work why you made those choices.

• Develop ideas through problem-solving, testing, making samples of models, asking for feedback, such as from a survey of the most popular idea, and include feedback from your tutor.

Presentation: Think about the best way to present your work: can the developmental work be presented in an innovative way? Will you give a presentation or display the work? Make sure design sheets and presentation sheets are appropriate and clearly labelled. Read through the assignment brief and the assessment and grading criteria before you hand your work in and see if you need to add anything or highlight key sections that could boost your grade.

7 Design methods in art and design

This unit provides opportunities to demonstrate your understanding of the design cycle: understanding and interpretation of the specifications of the brief; research methods; development of ideas and selection of those with potential for further development; production of visuals, maquettes and test pieces in order to test the suitability of materials, techniques and processes; presentation; reflection and evaluation in response to feedback; refinement and production of outcomes. As well as demonstrating your creative skills, there will be an emphasis on professional working practice, including time management and organisation, teamwork, interpersonal skills and the ability to work independently.

You will need to develop a wide vocabulary that reflects the conventions of your subject area, pay attention to the client's requirements and how these are met through your solution to the brief, be prepared to listen and respond appropriately to feedback, and review your work making any necessary adjustments.

You will also need to consider legal constraints such as copyright, building regulations, health and safety, and ethics, and how these affect your design solutions, planning and timeframe.

Learning outcomes

After completing this unit you should:

1. understand the design development process
2. be able to use the design development process in own work
3. be able to communicate ideas and intentions clearly
4. be able to work safely with others.

Assessment and grading criteria

This table shows you what you must do in order to achieve a **pass**, **merit** or **distinction** grade, and where you can find activities in this book to help you.

To achieve a pass grade the evidence must show that you are able to:	To achieve a **merit** grade the evidence must show that, in addition to the pass criteria, you are able to:	To achieve a **distinction** grade the evidence must show that, in addition to the pass and merit criteria, you are able to:
P1 describe the design development process **See Assessment activity 7.1, page 120 and project work**	**M1** consistently show a clear understanding and effective application of the design process **See Assessment activities 7.1, page 120; 7.2, page 121 and project work**	**D1** show independence and creativity in the safe application of the design process, producing professional outcomes based on highly-focused research and collaborative development of ideas **See Assessment activities 7.1, page 120; 7.2, page 121; 7.3, page 122 and project work**
P2 use the design development process in own work **See Assessment activity 7.1, page 120 and project work**	**M2** use both verbal and visual communication with others confidently and effectively **See Assessment activity 7.2, page 121 and project work**	
P3 communicate ideas and intentions clearly **See Assessment activity 7.2, page 121 and project work**		
P4 work safely with others **See Assessment activity 7.3, page 122 and project work**		

How you will be assessed

You will be assessed on the work you produce in response to a brief, which may be a live project, a client-led brief or a simulated professional brief.

As well as producing and presenting outcomes that answer the client brief, you need to demonstrate your understanding of the design cycle and the process through which ideas are generated and evaluated. You also need to consider the practical and financial constraints and any legal, ethical and environmental issues that affect your work. You will need to be a responsible and reliable practitioner, and to show a professional approach to working with others that takes account of their views.

Max

Our brief was to produce work for a client showing what it is to be a young artist living and working in Medway. The date of the private view was already set, and we were given a size and format to work to for display on the walls, so I felt pressure to generate ideas and produce something good enough to show. My family have lived in Medway forever, so I talked to my grandad about life in the dockyard, and how it has changed. Drawing ideas from history helped me connect family history to my art.

The dockyard influence and physicality of making in my design development resulted in a three-dimensional piece, which was outside the brief. My tutors suggested that I discuss my ideas with other students exhibiting, and make a convincing argument for deviating from the format. Two other students also had ideas that did not fit the brief, so we worked on our presentation together. The client was impressed that we had considered the aesthetics of the exhibition and the opinions of the other exhibitors, but they had also looked at wheelchair access and health and safety issues around the work and its interaction with the public. Exhibiting my work has given me confidence, but it has also made me realise how important it is to work responsibly with other people.

Over to you!

- **What do you think persuaded Max's client to move away from the original constraints of the brief?**

- **Max drew from his family history to develop his work. How much do you use your own cultural background and experience as a focus for creative work?**

Max's work had to be viewed from all sides and was suspended from ceiling to floor. This meant that he had to consider the space around the piece, any obstacles that might pose a danger to the public and whether there was sufficient wheelchair access.

1. and 2. Understand the design development process and be able to use it in own work

Planning your project

You are given a professional brief and expected to respond to this in a way that demonstrates your understanding of the design development cycle and how this would be applied in a real-life scenario.

You have received the following email:

Dear (designer),

I am planning to take a full-page four-colour advertisement in 'MacWorld' to promote a small range of computer accessories available through our outlets. The next deadline for artwork is three weeks tomorrow; as I have already booked the space there is no room for manoeuvre.

I have some shots of the products that must be included in the ad, which you should receive tomorrow. These are accompanied by a brief description and prices. Aside from these, I am pretty open to ideas regarding design and layout as we have not advertised before, so I would like to see some ideas before the ad goes to press.

You will need to contact the magazine about size and format in which the artwork should be supplied.

Please forward your schedule for production, as I need to plan meetings, and will be away on business the day after tomorrow for a week. I will need a price for the job before I leave.

Working in small groups, identify what is required and what you need to find out in order to structure a professional response to the email. Draft your reply to the client.

Interpreting the brief

Being absolutely clear about the specific requirements of the brief is critical, for both planning and production. You also need to be aware of the design and development cycle and allow enough time to meet the deadline. Figure 7.1 on the following page identifies each stage of the cycle.

You will need to access appropriate information to develop your ideas, source materials, negotiate use of any facilities required, request permissions for copyright material, and ensure that health and safety issues are not prohibitive. All this needs to be planned to include a time contingency in case of unforeseen problems.

Figure 7.1: The design cycle. You will find that you come across variations of this model from different sources but though terminology varies the structure remains similar.

The design cycle

Interpreting the brief – understanding the specifications within the intention and rationale of the project brief itself.

Research – historical and contextual background, background information, comparable work in the field.

Ideas development – generation of a range of ideas to contribute towards the solution of the brief/design problem.

Selection of ideas – choosing the ideas for further development.

Testing materials, techniques and processes – what are the best means through which to produce appropriate outcomes.

Production of visuals and maquettes – to effectively demonstrate ideas to client and test outcomes.

Presentation of ideas – to explain, describe, inform and persuade the client of the validity of your solutions.

Response to feedback – to refine and make appropriate adjustments in the light of client feedback.

Production of final outcomes

Evaluation – what have you learned to inform future practice?

Working with people

You need to establish a good working relationship with the client, and to gauge how much leeway there is in the interpretation of the brief. You may need to undertake market research, which could include talking to end-users, other parties interested in the design project, or team members if you are working collaboratively.

Contextualising the work

As part of your design development you need to have a comprehensive knowledge of:

* the historical context – how the design draws upon what has preceded it, and how it relates to contemporary work that is comparable

* similar work in the field

* methods, materials and techniques traditionally associated with designs of this kind, as well as new developments in the field.

PLTS

Independent enquirer

When working for a client, it is your responsibility to identify and research the information you need to fulfil the brief. This may involve consulting the client, industry experts, the public and end-users.

Producing a range of design solutions

The client will expect to see a range of ideas and experiments that have contributed towards your design. It is important to consider alternatives when presenting arguments to support your solution, which will provide you with additional options should your proposal be rejected. Initial ideas might include mind maps, mood boards, concept designs, working models or maquettes, visuals, proofs, mock-ups, and sample and test pieces. This will convince the client that you have been rigorous in your consideration of options, and have anticipated the possible impact of your design in the market place.

Modifying or developing your ideas in response to feedback

You may have a strong opinion about the suitability of your work for the brief, but be prepared for the client to disagree and request modifications, or even choose a different idea entirely. This is where documentation of your ideas and research can help support your preferred option. Alternatively, you may feel that the client is right and that you can develop a different idea you have already investigated. In a real working situation, your decision may be influenced by economic factors – an established artist or designer can afford to be less compromising. If you are less established it may be prudent to accept the client's wishes.

Functional skills

Mathematics

When undertaking a project, you need to provide an estimate of cost to the client, based on how long a job will take, including revisions, and hourly or daily rates of pay. For the latter, you need to take into account the fees of any other person contributing to the project, materials, wear and tear, travel and sundries. You should also be aware of the going rate for the job, and how this compares with your quotation, and make adjustments to ensure your figure is competitive.

Think of different ways to present initial ideas to your clients.

Make sure that your design meets the brief's specifications.

Producing the final outcome

Once you have established that your design has met the requirements of the brief, you need to produce a final outcome. If you are designing artwork for print, ask yourself whether your artwork conforms to the printer's specifications. If your product is a piece of public art, is it sufficiently durable for its projected lifespan? Is it likely to pose a hazard to the public, cause offence or contravene legal constraints?

Evaluating the process

Each time an artist or designer undertakes a professional commission, he/she should expect to learn something new that will contribute to personal development. It is worth reflecting on your project and assessing what has worked well and what needs further development.

Case study: How to find out what you need to know

Your course tutor has been approached by a business that wants its website redesigned. The client has arranged to come in and deliver a brief. You already know the name of the business and have a rough idea of what is required.

After the briefing, you realise you don't know as much as you thought and have missed a valuable opportunity to find out. You failed to take notes at the time and can't remember what was said.

1. **What actions can you take to retrieve the situation?**

2. **How are you going to find out what your client needs to communicate to his potential clients through the company website to enable you to do your job?**

Assessment activity 7.1: Planning your work schedule

In order to plan your work schedule, you need to establish each stage in the development process and allocate where this will fit in the production cycle.

- How much time are you going to allocate for each stage?
- Are you relying on responses from others?
- What can you do in the meantime?
- How will you ensure that you receive your responses soon enough to fit the schedule?
- Will you have access to the materials you need?
- Will you have access to the necessary facilities?
- What **contingencies** will you allow for unforeseen problems?
- Are there other team members to build into your schedule?

Create a working schedule for production, based on the design development cycle and incorporating immovable deadlines such as client meetings.

Grading tips

The production of a work schedule is one way you can evidence your understanding of the design cycle. Refer to the diagram on page 117 and use this to describe the stages **P1** and what you plan to do **P2**. Your schedule should be realistic, taking into consideration obstacles and time allowances **M1**. It should also respect the contributions of others and account for safety issues **D1**.

Proposed schedule for production
Circulation list for approval: Client, Design Group, Printer

Client briefing (all copy and pictures to Design Group)	**Monday 18 January**
Meeting to present initial ideas and concepts to Client	**Friday 5 February**
Revisions to design concepts and finished concepts/visual to Client for approval (via email)	**Friday 12 February**
Client to approve/make further amendments (via email). Further meeting necessary	**Tuesday 23 February**
Design concept confirmed to Design Group	**Friday 26 February**
First proofs to Client (via email)	**Friday 12 March**
Amendments to final artwork emailed to Design Group (via email)	**Wednesday 17 March**
Second proofs to Client via email for final amendments (via email)	**Monday 22 March**
Final amendments to Design Group (via email)	**Friday 26 March**
Finished artwork to Printer	**Wednesday 31 March**
Printer's digital proofs: meeting with Client, Design Group and Printer to check/approve/amend Printer's digital proofs for print	**Tuesday 6 April**
Delivery of Exhibition Guide to Client	**Tuesday 20 April**
Date of exhibition opening	**Friday 23 April**

Figure 7.2: Why is it important to create your own work schedule?

3. Be able to communicate ideas and intentions clearly

Collaboration with other artists gives you the opportunity to work outside your specialism, so you need knowledge of other creative industries and disciplines that have a potential link with your own, such as science, technology or business.

You will spend a lot of time talking about your work: discussions with peers, tutors and clients; studio critiques and presentations. The context and audience will determine the style and tone you adopt, as well as the appropriate level of formality.

Functional skills

English

Adapting your style of presentation to suit a particular audience is a fundamental communication skill. You cannot always anticipate your audience, so you will need to gauge their reaction to what you are saying at the time, and be prepared to adapt if you sense it is not being received well.

You will need negotiating and team-working skills when putting forward your ideas for creative solutions.

Functional skills

ICT

It is not always feasible to meet with your client to present ideas, and it is common nowadays to email proofs of design work for comments. It is your role to identify the most appropriate application in which to present your work. This may mean exporting files from InDesign or QuarkXPress to Acrobat Reader (pdf), PowerPoint or compressed file formats.

PLTS

Team worker

The ability to work productively with other people is a critical skill that will improve your employability. This includes maintaining clean and safe workspaces, being aware of others' needs and roles, and working with them to establish a common work schedule.

Assessment activity 7.2: Presenting your work

Presenting yourself as a credible professional can be intimidating and difficult. Tailor your delivery to match your skills and abilities, and focus on the following:

What is the purpose of your presentation?

- to present and explain the ideas behind your work and how they were developed.
- to convince your audience that you have produced a suitable solution to the brief.

In order to inform or explain, it helps to have a **logical order** and to **use examples**. To be persuasive you also need to **show enthusiasm**.

The audience should have a clear understanding of what has been said.

Rehearse your presentation

This will boost your confidence on the day. Rehearse it and **time yourself** in front of a friend or family member, and ask whether he/she understands what you are saying.

- Careful rehearsal helps you overcome nerves and clarifies what you want to say.
- 'Props' – you may want to use prompt cards or a computer slide show, to remind you of points to make.
- Think about your strengths and weaknesses and make sure you have everything you need – flipcharts and pens, data projector and laptop – and arrive sufficiently early to test out technology.

Grading tips

Although you may be assessed by a client or tutor, you need to produce evidence of your preparation for the presentation, which reinforces the points you are making P3 M1. Notes, computer slide shows and design sheets are good sources of evidence, and will help you to give your talk a coherent structure and deliver it with confidence M2. The design cycle should be evident in the presentation of your ideas D1

4. Be able to work safely with others

Remember

As an artist or designer, it is important to have a sound understanding of legal, health and safety, and **ethical issues**. Many artists practise freelance, which places the responsibility for these constraints on the practitioner.

Did you know?

When an artist, writer or composer produces a piece of original work, it is his/her 'intellectual property' and nobody has the right to use, publish or reproduce it without their permission for a specified period.

If you wanted to use another artist's work as part of your own, perhaps as an illustration of an idea, how would you ensure that you were acting within copyright law?

Recycling offers a number of opportunities to produce cutting-edge design at a low cost, in an environmentally responsible way.

Assessment activity 7.3: How safe your work space? BTEC

Think about the various environments in which you work: studio; workshop; computer bays; sewing room; darkroom; lecture theatre; on location.

Identify the potential hazards within each space and measures you could take to minimise risk.

- How can you ensure that your working practice does not impinge negatively on that of others?
- How can you ensure that your working environment maximises productivity and the smooth running of each area?

As a professional, you will have to make risk assessments. Try sourcing a sample risk assessment from your institution to see if there are any areas of risk you have overlooked.

Working environment

As well as health and safety considerations, you need to develop working practices that help you and your colleagues function responsibly and economically in the studio. This includes:

- taking care of equipment and making sure it is left clean, safe and ready for use
- ensuring that equipment does not endanger the personal safety of others, such as trailing flexes, close proximity of glue guns or wax pots, etc.
- avoiding wastage of materials
- taking advantage of opportunities for recycling.

Grading tips

You should always be aware of potential hazards for yourself and colleagues in your workspace **P4**, so should be constantly vigilant. You can make this evident by documenting issues arising in your work journal or sketchbook annotation, and develop the habit of producing a risk assessment **D1**.

Key terms

Contingencies – plans within a schedule that anticipate unforeseen events or problems.

Ethical issues – moral considerations, such as wasting resources, producing work in a way that is not environmentally responsible, risking harm or causing offence to individuals or groups.

Rob McDonald
Illustrator

Rob McDonald is an artist and illustrator who has designed book and magazine covers, and worked on projects for the BBC and Shell Oil.

'In all the work I produce, whether for a commission or exhibition, I use the same principles: undertaking in-depth research and analysing this information before carrying out an experimental programme of different processes and media. This helps me to generate more ideas and discover the best process for communicating my concepts.

This way of working is demonstrated in a book I created for an exhibition on how artists/designers are influenced by their children.

The project was a collaboration between myself and my three-year-old daughter, based on a day out to Margate. We took cameras and sketchbooks to gather research, and once we came home we explored our different ideas about what we had seen. We then analysed the information to create an outline of what we both wanted to say in the book.

This flat artwork represented some of the pages from the book Rob and his daughter created collaboratively. How many ways to construct an artists' book can you think of?

The next stage was how to unite all the different types of work we had produced – drawn and photographic. After playing with different processes, we came to the conclusion that printmaking and collage could be united to create a sequential story of our day, expressing both our individual ideas and the location. This was achieved mainly through colour, which reflected a typical British seaside town. The compositional structure was also important in indicating the passage of time within the book.'

Think about it!

- **What problems or issues do you think could arise from working collaboratively?**
- **What would you do with the ideas and experiments you reject for a specific piece of work?**
- **What might be the benefits of working in a creative team?**

Just checking

1. How would you define the design development process? Look back at this section and identify the various stages of the process.

2. How effective have you been in planning your project? Evaluate the strengths and weaknesses of your work schedule.

3. What are the most important skills for professional practice? Draw from your own and others' practice in this assignment to inform your evaluations.

4. How persuasive was the presentation of your ideas? What went well, and what was disastrous? How can you address any issues arising for future presentations?

5. Were there any legal issues that might affect your design?

6. How would you assess your studio practice in respect of working with others and health and safety issues?

edexcel

Assignment tips

Use your briefing session as an opportunity to gain good understanding of what is required – it may be your only chance of contact with the client.

- Come prepared – if you know who the client is, do some research on the business. Prepare questions about aspects of the business you don't understand, or about information such as target market, main competitors and how the company wants to be perceived in the marketplace.

- Make comprehensive and legible notes, and record any ideas you have at the briefing.

- Try to get a contact email or phone number, and check whether you can clarify points with the client later.

- Make a realistic production schedule at an early stage. There will be immovable deadlines such as client meetings, but you may need to build in contingencies and revisions.

- Make sure you document each stage, including justification of design decisions, so you can make a convincing case for the creative decisions you have made.

- Be professional and confident in your presentation style. Prepare well in advance and try to anticipate negative comments.

- Make sure that your final outcome conforms to the standards expected of the industry.

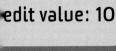

edit value: 10

12 Computers in art and design

The availability of digital technologies at affordable prices has revolutionised the way the creative industries produce work and increased the potential for creative innovation. Practitioners are now involved in a greater range of disciplines and in the various stages of production within those disciplines. This has allowed artists and designers to cross interdisciplinary boundaries, which is an increasing feature of contemporary practice.

In the past, for example, to set type you needed to have a highly sophisticated understanding of the properties of type and the aesthetics of letterforms and their relationship to each other. Today, everyone who has access to a computer can try their hand at being a film editor, photographic re-toucher or layout artist. The traditional skills that underpin art and design practice remain critical for the production of credible work and will set you apart as a professional rather than amateur user.

The computer in art and design is simply another medium used to produce creative outcomes. It enables artists to extend their range of techniques, develop their practice and expand their repertoire of skills.

Learning outcomes

After completing this unit you should:

1. understand the potential of digital media in contemporary art and design practice
2. be able to select materials for digital experimentation
3. be able to produce work using digital art and design techniques.

125

Assessment and grading criteria

This table shows you what you must do in order to achieve a **pass**, **merit** or **distinction** grade, and where you can find activities in this book to help you.

To achieve a **pass** grade the evidence must show that you are able to:	To achieve a **merit** grade the evidence must show that, in addition to the pass criteria, you are able to:	To achieve a **distinction** grade the evidence must show that, in addition to the pass and merit criteria, you are able to:
P1 review the potential for digital media in contemporary art and design practice **See Assessment activity 12.1, page 130**	**M1** explain the potential for digital media in contemporary art and design practice **See Assessment activity 12.1, page 130**	**D1** analyse digital media in contemporary art and design practice **See Assessment activity 12.1, page 130**
P2 select art and design materials for experimentation using digital techniques and processes **See Assessment activity 12.2, page 131**	**M2** carry out effective experimentation using multi-media techniques and processes purposefully **See Assessment activity 12.2, page 131**	**D2** carry out imaginative experimentation using multi-media techniques and processes independently **See Assessment activity 12.2, page 131**
P3 produce outcomes using digital art and design techniques **See Assessment activity 12.3, page 132**	**M3** present purposeful visual outcomes showing effective use of digital art and design techniques **See Assessment activity 12.3, page 132**	**D3** present sophisticated and imaginative visual outcomes showing sophisticated use of digital art and design techniques **See Assessment activity 12.3, page 132**

How you will be assessed

This unit will be assessed through internal assignments, designed to allow you to show your understanding of the unit outcomes. Any project work you undertake using computers can contribute to the assessment for this unit. This could be through:

- research into the uses of computers in art and design, identifying the methods, materials and techniques employed (with annotated evaluations of the effectiveness of the results)
- experiments from a range of primary sources underpinned by your research and relating to your chosen discipline and other disciplines
- imaginative digital outcomes demonstrating your acquisition of computer techniques, using these techniques to develop innovative work within a chosen discipline.

Mel

When we started our stop-motion animation film project, I had never used an Apple Mac before. Our group had decided to produce a film which combined sequences of drawn two-dimensional images with a three-dimensional set and figures made from Plasticine. This gave the whole team lots to do and we were able to play to our individual strengths. When we had produced the sets, characters and drawings, we began to shoot the stills working in pairs, each using different sections of the storyboards we'd produced. I was with Ricky working on the three-dimensional scenes; we had a camera hooked up to the i-mac and used a programme called Frame-thief to capture each still and then used it to make film clips which we imported into i-movie.

Once our clips were ready we all worked on editing the film and adding the soundtrack. We had to remember to document what we had done as individuals for the final assessment, as there had been so much to do. Although we had been using computers, we had actually produced lots of drawn and made work.

Over to you!

- What tends to be your 'role' in a team?
- In teamworking, can you identify each person's role within the team?
- If you were the team leader, how would you make sure your team worked together to meet their objectives?
- What action would you take if other team members did not fulfil their obligations to the team?

1. Understand the potential of digital media in contemporary art and design practice

Then and now

Think about all the various disciplines or combinations of disciplines in art and design. Look for examples in:
- fashion, photography and graphic design in magazines
- typography and the moving image in cinematography
- illustration, animation and three-dimensional modelling in children's films
- film and sound in fine-art installations.

Having chosen a few examples, try to find out how – or if – they would have been produced before the digital age. Compare pre-digital examples with contemporary work and think about the limitations of working in the pre-digital age compared to what is possible now: creatively, financially and practically.

Your exploration of the potential of **digital media** will concentrate on the impact of digital technologies on your own subject specialism. Artists and designers do not have to fully understand all aspects of computer programs used in art and design. Adobe Photoshop, for example, is multi-functional, and will be used in the context of a particular practice. A photographer will tend to use the tools that imitate traditional darkroom processes, such as the **dodge and burn** functions, the healing brush and redeye, and functions that enable control over colour balance, while an illustrator or designer might focus on layering and image manipulation. The more you understand, the more scope there is for innovation.

1.1 How is digital media used within current industry practice?

Film and video

There is a range of **hardware** to capture the moving image. Once you have your footage, this would be edited in a program such as Final Cut Pro, adding or editing a soundtrack, effects and credits.

A Photoshop designer working on an Apple Mac computer. Are you familiar with the different features of Photoshop, and the ways in which these may be used to manipulate photographs or scanned images?

Graphic design

Graphic designers producing artwork for print use three main programs:

- **Photoshop** is a **raster-based** program, which enables photographic and scanned drawn images or found items to be digitally manipulated.

- **Illustrator** is a **vector-based** program. It is ideal for producing logos or line-based images that need to be reproduced to different scales, from stationery to signage.

- **InDesign and QuarkXPress** are desktop publishing applications, into which images can be imported and combined with text elements in single or multiple page formats. Once a layout is complete it can be exported to a portable document format (pdf), compressing the file size and enabling it to be emailed to clients.

Key terms

Digital media – a blanket term for any data produced electronically.

Dodge and burn – used to lighten or darken areas of the image, based on the traditional technique for regulating exposure on particular areas of a print. Photographers hold back light to lighten an area on the print (dodging) or increase the exposure to darken areas on a print (burning).

Hardware – refers to the physical elements of the computer suite: processor, screen, keyboard, mouse, external hard drives, etc.

Raster-based or pixel-based graphics – represent images in the form of pixels: small coloured squares that make up the picture, typically photographic images. The quality of the image is dependent on the number of pixels in each square inch or square centimetre. The more pixels, the higher the quality of the image, and the larger the file size. This is referred to as the resolution. It is important to generate raster images at the right size for the end use and production method. For use on-screen, 72 dots per inch will be enough, but for a commercial printer, you would need to create images at 300 dots per inch at the size at which it will be reproduced.

Vector graphics – points, lines, curves and shapes to represent images using mathematical formulae. When the graphics are enlarged, the sharpness and quality of the image is retained, so they are excellent for signs and logos.

Animators and graphic designers working on film elements such as credits and concepts would use **software** packages associated with film, video and games design.

Key term

Software – refers to the varied range of programs that are used to generate data for specific purposes.

Separations – refer to the division of an image or design into single colours. This can be the four 'process' colours referred to as CMYK (cyan, magenta, yellow and black or 'key') or especially mixed spot colours. In lithographic printing, each colour would be represented on a plate, but in screen printing colours would be printed from separate screens.

Photography

Photographers still rely on their visual skill and ability to frame and capture suitable images. Digital photography has significantly reduced the cost by removing the need for film and processing. Photoshop provides the means to retouch photographic images digitally.

Fashion and textiles

Fashion promotion, branding and marketing tend to employ similar software packages to those used by graphic designers. They combine drawn, photographic or found images, scanned and imported into a file format such as Photoshop for manipulation, or InDesign or QuarkXPress for page layout. Nothing can replace the fluid, animated lines of fashion illustration, which still tend to be hand rendered before being incorporated into a design layout.

In textiles, Photoshop is increasingly used to reproduce created designs and **separations**, giving the designer a much more accurate visual projection of the finished piece.

Architecture

Adobe Creative Suite is a popular software package for general use in architecture. More specialised 2D drawing packages, such as AutoCAD, Microstation and ArchiCAD, enable you to create construction drawings and documentation using architectural design and drafting tools. 3D packages include Rhino, 3D Studio Max and Maya. Ability to use both a 2D and 3D package would be expected.

Web design

Web designers often use elements from the Adobe Creative Suite in the design of the site, and will use a programme such as Dreamweaver to build the site.

Games design

Approximately 30,000 people are employed in the games industry in the UK, which uses a vast range of hardware and software, whether for 3D modelling, animation or games programming.

The computer games industry is a fast-developing and exciting career option with an increasing range of job opportunities.

Fine art

Fine artists may use any of these software packages for their creative work, which might include video, film and digital images.

Gillian Wearing is an artist who makes extensive and highly creative use of video and digital work. Find out more about her and other prominent video artists such as John Baldessari, Willie Doherty and Sam Taylor-Wood.

Functional skills

ICT

Just as you need to know what media or material to use to achieve a particular effect, it is important to know which computer program to use for a specific purpose. Find out which programs are used in your industry, or linked industries such as the printing industry.

Assessment activity 12.1: Digital media impact

P1 M1 D1

Investigate how digital media has impacted on your subject specialism. Investigate:

- examples of professional work within your discipline produced before computer technology began to be widely used
- examples of exciting and innovative contemporary practice within your discipline.

Compare the work you have found within each category. Analyse and evaluate the aesthetic impact of digital technology on the work produced. You should aim to find out:

- what computer software industry professionals within your discipline use
- how digital methods of generating work have impacted on the nature of employment and working practices within the industry.

As part of your investigation, you could use books or the Internet, but you could also contact industry professionals or interview tutors on your course.

Grading tips

In order to achieve **M1**, your investigation should not only review the potential for digital media in contemporary art and design practice but should also include:

- comprehensive explanations of the processes used in artwork production, pre-digital and current to support your visual examples. Use diagrams and illustrations to support your findings
- comparisons between the visual examples, drawing on your research and understanding of processes.

At distinction level **D1**, your investigation should additionally include:

- in-depth visual analysis and evaluation of the wide range of work you have examined, demonstrating your understanding of processes and their application as well as an innovative approach as to how that could contribute towards the development of creative work.

2. Be able to select materials for digital experimentation

Work produced solely on the computer, without independent creative input, tends to be sterile, lacking in passion or innovation. When selecting elements for inclusion in your digital work, you need to apply the creative principles you have learned from core units. Read the mandatory units again and think about your practice with particular reference to:

• visual recording

• materials, techniques and processes

• ideas and concepts

• communication through art and design

• contextual influences in art and design.

Make notes from these units and see how they could be applied to your selection of materials for inclusion in your digital work.

Assessment activity 12.2: Extending your work BTEC

Re-visit some of your creative projects from mandatory and specialist units. Think about how you could extend and develop the work in the light of your research into the use of digital technologies.

Here are some examples from which you may want to draw:

• sketches or sections of drawings, prints or paintings

• hand-rendered text, calligraphy or formal typographic forms

• textiles, textured papers, found materials either natural or synthetic

• photographs, photocopies, newsprint or magazines

• footage from video cameras, mobile phones, digital cameras

• audio recordings, computer-generated music such as Garage Band, or live music, song and spoken word

• models, three-dimensional objects.

Think about how these could be combined. For example, three-dimensional work could be animated through stop motion or video, then edited with the inclusion of audio or lighting to achieve a specific atmosphere. Natural objects could be scanned and repeated to form patterns for fabric designs, which could then be wrapped around natural objects to create sculptural forms.

Grading tips

In order to achieve **M2**, your experimental work should include:

• visual analyses of how your experiments could be extended to contribute towards a larger body of work, by including a variety of outputs and software applications, such as discipline-specific applications as well as web-based outputs.

At distinction level **D2**, your investigation should include additionally:

• imaginative experimentation across a range of disciplines and software applications, fully exploring the potential to expand to generate innovate outcomes.

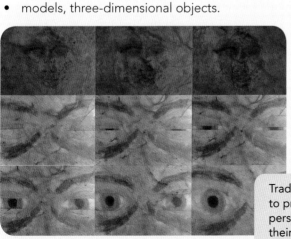

Traditional drawing and painting skills have been used to produce this sequence of illustrations representing a person underwater coming to the surface and opening their eyes. These have been scanned into the computer and used for an animated film. Try this for yourself.

3. Be able to produce work using digital art and design techniques

In order to make the leap to production of digital outcomes, you need to acquire as much technical knowledge as possible, and to combine this with key skills developed in the core units. To underpin digital work, you also need to reference the mandatory units, and utilise the design cycle – research, development, reflection and evaluation, and revision and extension of the work.

Remember

Develop the habit of analysing the images and objects you see in your everyday life. How have they been produced? What role has digital technology played in this? If you don't know the answer, use the Internet. Make sure you use creditable sources, such as reputable businesses, educational sites and galleries and museums.

Assessment activity 12.3: Documenting your design development process

P3 M3 D3   BTEC

The process of research, development, evaluation and revision may be repeated many times during the stages of production. How many times do you subconsciously go through this cycle when working on digital outcomes?

Refer back to Assessment activity 12.2. You have looked back at your previous work and considered your **research** and **development** processes. You have also made an assessment of images for development – **reflection and evaluation** – and are ready to revise and extend your work to produce a new piece – **revision and extension**.

Now you are ready to begin the design cycle again in the production of a final outcome using digital means, informed by the ideas you may already have.

Document this process visually and with annotation:

- **Research** – this time consider the capabilities of the software. Look at other digital work produced within your area and think about techniques you

may want to use – layering, repetition, turning or rotation, image manipulation, composition, use of narrative (you can refer to the unit specification for more ideas).
- **Development** – develop your work through experimentation using the software and techniques you have selected.
- **Evaluation** – are you managing to achieve your final outcome? If not, make some revisions, which may include more research and development.

The documentation of this process can be used as evidence of assessment and to feed future practice.

Grading tips

In order to achieve **M3**, your experimental work should include:

- demonstration of your ability to use software with a high degree of sensitivity and understanding of the medium and program, finesse in production and good reference to original visual intentions.

At distinction level **D3**, your investigation should additionally include:

- sophisticated development of ideas through to imaginative and effective final outcomes, underpinned by thorough and purposeful investigation and experimental work.

Neil Bottle
Textile designer

Neil Bottle is a printed textiles specialist with experience in design, product development and education. Since 1989, he has designed and manufactured fashion and interior accessories under his own label, Neil Bottle Designs.

Neil began to use digital techniques when working on a collection for the British Museum, which had decided to send the work to be printed abroad; it was thought that by producing the artwork digitally there would be more control over the colour and the work would be cheaper to produce. Neil had to acquire Photoshop skills to produce the work 'on the job', and was concerned that the hand-produced 'one-off' appeal of his previous work might discourage clients, but this fear was unfounded.

Section from 'Eclectic Script Rust', made for the Focus Exhibition at the Contemporary Applied Arts Gallery in London 2008. This wall hanging was created using a combination of hand generated and digital techniques. The design was then digitally printed on cotton sateen. The inspiration for the piece was drawn from a research trip to the Middle East, which focused on heritage crafts techniques and technical innovation in textiles. Size 60 x 220cm, printed with reactive dyes on cotton.

Neil comments:

'Digital techniques have advanced so quickly that the once-blurry images have rapidly developed a more refined quality. I have suffered from these improvements in mass-produced screen-printed textiles, which swept across fashion at the turn of the Millennium, prompting some stores to opt for cheaper products, capable of withstanding a higher mark-up, rather than hand-crafted prints made by UK-based designers.

Digital printing on textiles presents the opportunity to print only what is required, with no waste, and designs and patterns can be engineered to fit fabrics exactly. This precision is exciting and there is an element of improved sustainability of the process as there is less waste.'

Neil's current research focuses on the possibilities of combining traditional and digital design methods. His work has recently developed from typographical and architectural influences to more abstract designs.

Think about it!

- What are the benefits of using digital technology in this context?
- What do you think about the arguments for hand-crafted work versus digital technology in the context of the world today?
- What do you understand by a mark-up?

Just checking

1. What industry-standard software is used in your subject specialism?

2. How is it used within that discipline?

3. What is the difference between rastor and vector graphics?

4. What are separations? What is their significance in specific production processes?

5. What publications are available nationally to inform you about digital programs and techniques?

6. Where would you find out which courses might be suitable for you if you decide to progress to a degree course?

edexcel

Assignment tips

- Save your work regularly, not only on to the hard-drive of the computer – back up your files on a memory stick. If your computer 'freezes', or there is a problem with the power source and your work is not saved, you run the risk of losing hours of work and effort.

- It's important to be able to locate your work easily – get into the habit of naming your digital files and include your name or a word you will remember. By keeping a note of filenames you can utilise the 'find' function on your computer.

- It is wise to keep a copy of your work which can be transferred to other computers – invest in a key drive where you can store and keep your own work. Key drives are relatively cheap to purchase and store several gigabytes of information.

- Buy a small notebook and keep notes about how to achieve particular effects on the computer, which will save having to wait for a tutor or technician. When you discover something for yourself, share it with your friends and staff – it may be new for them too.

- Remember that many software packages have excellent 'help' facilities which allow you to find out or research the capabilities of the program.

Graphic design

Like many disciplines in art and design, graphic design has been revolutionised by the digital age. In the past, graphic designers would often have specialised in one particular area of design, but nowadays the speed and relative ease of production techniques allow designers to diversify.

Many graphic designers are self-employed and either work on their own or within a small design group, so it makes economic sense to undertake many different tasks within the field to avoid having to pay another designer. If a company employs you, it is likely that you will work within a small business. Many larger employers, such as Channel 4, tend to sub-contract work to smaller and/or regional businesses as required.

This section is designed to give you an overview of the range of creative activity that falls within the umbrella term of graphic design and includes:

* finding information about the sector
* information about job roles and careers and the necessary skills required
* case studies of students and young people who have just begun their creative careers
* case studies of experienced industry professionals.

Professional voices:
Tom, Toni and David

The advice below comes from young designers working in the graphic design industry, all of whom studied the BTEC Level 3 National course in Art and Design.

Tom:

Learn the basic things, such as printing techniques and setting up documents, or you will have to learn them on the job.

Toni:

Don't be afraid to say 'no' when you really disagree with something and have good reasons, and try always to work with a student mindset. The best designers I've met still think like students in that they want to be different and have fun with their work.

David:

* Scour the job listings to find out the software skills prospective employers are looking for. Do this early on, while you're still in a position to learn from your tutors.

* Be smart, and get good at what you love. There will be plenty of 'Jack-of-all-trades, master-of-none types', but there's nothing slicker than someone who really knows their coconuts!

* Get a website. A website cannot be destroyed, cannot get left on the bus and never looks like it was sabotaged. Even if you don't know exactly how, someone else will.

* When you finally land that golden goose of a job, always try to make some time for personal projects. Never lose sight of your goal, keep pushing, designing and creating! It's easy to get snowed under by work, so set aside time to blow off steam.

Over to you!

* **How will you find out about printing processes and document set-up?**

* **Have you produced your own website yet?**

* **How much time do you spend on personal creative projects?**

1. The graphic design industry

The UCAS website will give you some idea as to the breadth and number of degree courses relating to graphic design currently on offer in the UK, as well as helpful information about the key employability skills required. This offers some indication of the number of graduates hoping to join the workforce each year, but many arts practitioners work part-time in other jobs such as education, community arts work, museums and galleries, and across disciplines.

Skillset is the Sector Skills Council (SSC) for creative media, which comprises TV, film, radio, interactive media, animation, computer games, facilities, photo imaging and publishing. Visit their website at www.skillset.org

Creative and Cultural Skills is the SSC for advertising, crafts, music, performing, heritage, design and the arts and can be found at www. ccskills.org.uk. This site links to the Creative Choices website www.creative-choices.co.uk where you can access more job profiles and case histories, which may help to inform your choices for the future.

Example of magic marker visualisation.

Activity: Doing your homework

Go to the library and find a newspaper or magazine advertising employment opportunities for graphic designers, such as *Guardian Media* or *Creative Review*. Find a job that appeals to you. Try to find out as much as you can about:

- the company advertising the job
- the kind of work you would be doing
- the skills you would need
- other job roles within the company and how these relate to the job advertised.

When you apply for a job, the company might expect you to have found out something about them and what they do. This information will help you explain why you are ideal for the post.

1.1 What does a graphic designer do?

There is a huge range of creative activity falling under the umbrella term of graphic design. Many of the categories identified below are related to a graphic design pathway, but could also link to related disciplines, such as multi-media, photography or lens-based media.

Advertising

There are a number of job roles within the world of advertising, depending on the size of the organisation.

- **Visualiser** – traditionally, a visualiser would draw up rough images of advertisements, posters and other literature. Pre-digital, this would often be rendered in magic-marker pen to give the client an impression of how the piece would look. This might also include mock-ups and maquettes for packaging or point-of-sale concepts. The task of visualising has not changed, but now visual concepts can be produced on the computer and given a more finished look. Illustrations or concepts for photo-shoots may well be hand-drawn as they were in the past, and then scanned in and positioned digitally for the mock-up.

- **Artworker** – an artworker prepares the finished artwork for print, and may be working from a visualiser's concept. An artworker has to translate the concept into a format that will work on a practical and technical basis, and requires sophisticated creative skills. Prior to the computer age, this was a time-consuming job involving liaising with typesetters, pasting up type from proofs, and scaling and positioning images within the layout. It remains a highly skilled job, but is now cleaner, more flexible and less time-consuming. Items can be easily imported, positioned and scaled using industry-standard desktop publishing programs such as QuarkXPress and Adobe InDesign, and text can be altered and edited within the program.

- **Advertising campaigns** – an advertising campaign is a planned strategic set of actions intended to achieve a goal. It might include press and publishing, email, direct mail, television and public relations, in any combination within the budget. Graphic designers and art directors, either employed by the agency or freelancers, would work on the campaign.

- **Art director** – an art director will be an expert who organises and oversees the design concepts and sees them come to fruition. In the case of a music video, they might be responsible for: working to the designers' storyboards to ensure the set, location, costumes, make-up, lighting and other visual elements all gel together; directing the action; establishing continuity and being involved in the editing process. This model would also apply to the photographic shoot and presentation of printed material.

Activity: What's involved in a campaign?

Think about an advertising campaign that you consider has been particularly successful or a company whose advertising has caught your eye.

Find as many examples from the campaign or company as you can. You could do this by looking through magazines, taking photos of billboards or visiting the company website.

How many different specialist roles might have been involved in the conception, development and publication of the campaign?

- **Corporate design** – this might involve the design of a logo and the application of a design style to encompass websites, stationery, printed promotional material, television campaigns, vehicle livery and staff uniforms.

This billboard would be just one element of an advertising campaign which might include advertising and promotions in diverse locations. Can you think of an advertising campaign that has made an impression on you?

- **Photographer** – graphic designers are likely to have regular contact with photographers, or to be competent photographers themselves. Larger design companies will employ their own or freelance specialist photographers, but for a small company or sole trader it makes more economic sense to use your own skills, if possible.

  Whether or not you undertake photographic work yourself, it is essential to have a sound working knowledge of photography to know how to integrate it into your design work, and to understand its potential and limitations.

Activity: What it takes to be a graphic designer

The list below identifies the 'soft' skills (skills that are sometimes more difficult to define) needed to perform well as a graphic designer. From your knowledge of the sector so far, identify why these skills are important:

- creativity
- adaptability
- judgement
- influence
- attention to detail
- analysis
- personal development
- interpersonal sensitivity.

Signpost

Some of the content of the Graphic design pathway that is concerned with photography (Units 24, 29, 32, 48) is more fully covered in the Photography section.

Case study: Grant

Grant studied for a National Diploma in Art and Design, then undertook work experience which prepared him for full-time work in the industry.

'I am in sole charge of designing advertisements for prestigious clients at a medium-sized publishing company. We produce five monthly magazines, bi-monthly product card packs, wall-planners, calendars, graphics, vinyls and stationery, etc. As well as designing page layouts, I deal with printers and have to understand all the processes of my production team. I also help with web development and digital magazines. I am constantly learning new design techniques and am involved in business and negotiation. I still have much to learn, but have the perfect platform from which to develop.

'I would like to work next for a large publishing house in London, and maybe go abroad for a year.'

1. **How much do you know or can you find out about commercial printing processes?**
2. **What do you understand by 'vinyls'?**
3. **How many individual items of stationery might be produced for a large company?**

Case study: Gill, graphic designer

Gill produced these coloured pencil illustrations when Sealink British Ferries changed their name, and needed a set of leaflets for each vessel.

Following her degree, Gill worked on a local newspaper, creating advertisements and features, and reproducing line-drawings of customer products. The company typeset and printed the publications in-house, which enabled Gill to gain first-hand knowledge of print production. After two years, she started her own business. She compiled a professional portfolio and began cold-calling to build business contacts. As sole designer, she had to produce visualisation, finished artwork and illustration. Photographic elements were often supplied by the clients.

Her work also includes producing brochures, magazines, leaflets, posters and stationery for a range of clients, as well as book designs, layouts and jackets. When computer technology replaced traditional methods of artwork production, Gill bought a Mac and taught herself to generate artwork digitally.

'Having total control over typographic elements was amazing. Layout revisions can be done quickly and proofed on pdf files, saving time and money.'

1. **What do you understand by 'cold calling'?**

2. **How do changes in printing processes affect the work of graphic designers? Research some local printers and designers and find out how design and production staff work together.**

3. **Select three or four different typefaces. Can you find out who designed them? Where have you seen them used? What do you think makes them suitable in the context of the design?**

This kind of low-budget layout, with limited images available, would have been too expensive to produce before the digital age. Can you identify how this has been digitally produced, and work out what original material would have been supplied to the designer?

Animation

- **Artist** – an artist or team of artists could be responsible for **conceptualising** the scenes and deciding on colour and lighting, creating the characters and establishing their features or characteristics.

- **Storyboard artist** – would draw up the story or narrative in a series of frames, in a similar way to narrative in comic strips or graphic novels. As well as illustrating and testing out the story, this would give the team a framework for creating models and sets, or devising special effects.

- **Model makers** – these could be artists specialising in three-dimensional work, either producing physical models, or virtual characters through 3D modelling. Even contemporary animation films, which exploit the properties of computer-generated characters, use physical models to make characters look authentic.

- **Set designers** – create the concepts for stage and set designs and are often involved in the development of three-dimensional work.

Film and video

The roles of graphic designers in film and video could be very similar to those in animation. In addition they might include the creation of credits at the beginning and end of the film, as well as promotional work on posters, trailers, billboards, production and selection of stills and other promotional material for marketing the product.

Publishing and information design

- **Layout artist** – will take all the elements such as illustrations, diagrams, photographs and text and create a composition within a given format. Sometimes the layout artist will have also been responsible for creating the template for that format.

This poster advertising *The Matrix Reloaded* (2003), uses elements from other promotional literature, such as the typestyle and urban typographic decoration to retain a strong identity for the film.

Did you know?

Some contemporary animation films on DVD describe how the film was produced, providing a fascinating and entertaining insight into working practices in animation. Look out for these in the library or even among your own collection at home.

Activity: Deconstructing a layout

Find a magazine that you or friends enjoy reading. Have a look at the layout.

- Can you identify the grid format used in magazine work?

- Is it a standard two, three or four column format or a non-standard version?

- What are the 'common elements', such as page numbers, headers and footers?

- How has the designer used typefaces to establish a style for the publication?

- How has the designer made creative use of images or illustration?

- How do you think the magazine manages to appeal to its target audience?

Key term

Conceptualising – coming up with the defining idea, which establishes the mood or context and sets the scene.

- **Typographer** – a typographic designer will have a sophisticated understanding of the aesthetic properties of letterforms and their creative use, either independently or in combination with images. Typographers use scale, form, colour and texture to exploit the creative potential of letterforms, either to enhance the meaning of text or to create independent visual effects.

Functional skills

English

If you are working as a typographer, it is essential that you are able to spell. If you are not confident in your ability to spell and use grammar correctly, or appropriately for the context, make sure you ask a colleague to check your work before sending it to a client.

- **Photographer** – photographers create photographic or digitally manipulated images to illustrate the subject matter of publications. They may also source images, so need a working knowledge of what constitutes a good image. Harold Evans's book *Pictures on a Page* offers a helpful analysis of how the selection and cropping of an image contributes to the construction of meaning. See the signpost to Photography on page 139.

- **Illustrator** – an illustrator will produce artwork that supports and enhances messages in the text, or conveys a narrative independent of the text; he or she may also produce images illustrating 'how to' messages, such as instructive text.

- **Art director** – see Advertising.

Signpost

Many graphic designers specialise in New Media – interactive design, web design and games design.

More specific information about the job roles within these career pathways can be found in the Interactive media section. You can also access additional information about the sector on the Skillset website – www.skillset.org

New media

New media encompasses games design (concepts, sets, character development, narrative, etc.), interactive media and web design.

This is a comprehensive, but not definitive, overview of roles within the graphic design industry. You may find others from your own research, and inevitably there will be new roles as technology and working practices move on.

Case study: Dominique

Dominique studied for a National Diploma in Graphic Design and a Higher National Diploma in Graphic Design and Illustration.

'When I left college I worked temporarily for a small design team. I gained valuable experience of HTML and CSS and developed an interest in web design, so I applied for a junior design role at a web design company. As my skills have developed, I have become more involved and have ended up designing sites and following them through to web-build.

I also do web amends, manage new site-builds and design and build emails and storyboards for flash banners. The company I was working for aimed to make all their sites more accessible, which

has developed my knowledge of SEO. I currently work for a large communications company in London, where I produce MPU designs, newsletter advertisements, build emails – mostly monthly newsletters, competition headers and pop-unders for their site.'

1. **Where can you find technical information that would help support your web design work?**

2. **How might designing your own website or creating a blog help you to develop your own practice?**

3. **What do the acronyms HTML, CSS, SEO and MPU stand for? Find out what they mean.**

Brett Breckon
Illustrator

An example of Brett's early airbrush work, which was used as an Athena poster in the 1980s.

I have been self-employed as an illustrator for almost 30 years. My career followed no particular plan – I just wanted to illustrate.

Back then, I produced airbrushed images of Cadillacs and Wurlitzers, and looked up to a mixed bag of artistic heroes from airbrush legends to Pre-Raphaelite masters. Pop art and rock music were a big influence too, an odd aspirational mix that was incompatible with ad agencies and design companies. Instead, they paid me to do slick pictures of steel lintels, electric motors, computer components and other forgettable subjects.

The best things were the poorly paid jobs from publishers, which allowed me to read an unpublished novel and have greater control over a final cover image.

A computer-generated image in scraperboard style.

In design companies and ad agencies, art directors would produce ideas for their images, which a whizz-kid with Pantone markers drew up in rough, before I realised them with airbrush and inks. When the Mac first made its mark, dreadful 'airbrush' images appeared, which gave real airbrushing a bad name, and commissioned illustrations were replaced by computerised photo and type manipulation. Since then, I've moved on to using computers for image-making, usually in Photoshop. I prefer its parallels with airbrush illustration, not just because of the 'airbrush' tools, but the working in layers method is like masking off areas with frisk film in a real airbrush painting. The whole process is cleaner, quicker, healthier, more forgiving, and ultimately more versatile. However, I miss the satisfaction of holding a real painting in my hands at the end of the process.

Think about it!

- Brett produces a lot of work based on his own personal influences and interests. How do you bring these aspects of your life into your work?
- Brett implies that job satisfaction is more important to him than financial reward. What is your view on that?
- Working in layers is mentioned in this case study. What do you know about working with layers?

Just checking

1. How can you find out about the industry you want to join?

2. Do you fully understand the various job roles identified in the graphic design industry? How many can you list? Can you think of any more? How can you find out more?

3. Can you identify where there might be opportunities for cross-disciplinary work in graphic design?

edexcel

Assignment tips

Developing soft skills

You have looked at some of the 'softer' skills required and identified their place in the graphic design industry (see page 139). Can you think of occasions where you have demonstrated those skills or realised you needed to develop them further?

Below are the professional skills you can build upon to support your BTEC Level 3 National course and continue as part of your professional development:

- planning and organisation

- professional expertise

- commercial, financial and business awareness

- understanding of organisations

- technical understanding and application.

Analyse your skills against the headings above. What do they mean? How would you rate your current expertise? What would help you to develop those employability skills? How can you find out more?

Build your own library of examples of graphic design

We are bombarded everyday with examples of graphic design. As a designer, you should record examples which you find particularly effective or ineffective. This will help you to develop your practice and gain greater insight into what constitutes good – or bad – design.

Work experience

Try to get work experience with a design group. Look through the Yellow Pages, and write or email politely to ask for paid work. Get someone to check your spelling – first impressions are vital. Some larger companies, such as Channel 4, run work-experience schemes for students.

Fashion and clothing

Fashion is not only a search for something new, it is also a form of creative expression. The fashion and clothing industry is exciting, diverse, creative and inspirational, and is subject to constant change due to demands of the national and international market. Currently, there are an estimated 340,000 people employed within the UK industry, generating a total of £10 billion for the economy. Although forecasts indicate a further transfer of production activities overseas, it is projected that the sector will need to recruit an estimated 16,000 people before 2015 to replace those leaving through retirement.

The UK clothing industry is made up of a number of significant sub-sectors, which include knitwear and hosiery, corporate and work wear, outerwear, designer and branded fashion, and other clothing such as gloves, baby wear and headwear.

There are currently a wide range of roles and creative people within these fields, but for all thorough knowledge of the subject and mastery of the fundamental skills of the industry are essential. This section outlines the skills and knowledge required for a career in fashion, with reference to BTEC Level 3 National Fashion and Clothing specialised units, and provides some top tips for achieving high grades and success. Lastly, it provides examples of routes taken by students and professionals after completing the qualification.

This section is designed to give you an overview of the different activities within the fashion and clothing sector and includes:

- outlines of the skills and knowledge required for a career in fashion, with reference to BTEC Level 3 National Fashion and Clothing specialised units
- tips for achieving high grades and success
- examples of routes taken by students and professionals after completing the qualification.

Professional voice: Kirsty Doyle

Kirsty Doyle launched her career as a designer after winning the television programme *Project Catwalk* while completing a degree at Liverpool John Moores University. She started out selling designs at a craft market at 18 and launched her first label after her success on *Project Catwalk*. After six seasons making collections for retailers, she opened her flagship store in August 2009.

'Having my own business helped me decide which way I wanted my career to go. I make all of my pieces in 3D using card, paper or calico on the mannequin and concentrate on parts like the shoulder or the cuff. I then decide how the outfit would look with the details I have made. Discussing shapes with customers and clients helps develop collections to be commercial and sellable.'

Over to you!

- What qualifications might you need to become a fashion designer? Look at the courses on offer at universities.
- Audit your skills – have you got what it takes to work in this sector?

Kirsty Doyle's designs. Can you enter any competitions during your course to enhance your portfolio?

1. The fashion and clothing industry

Fashion-related businesses within the UK are dominated by small and medium-size employers, more than 80 per cent of which have ten or fewer employees. Although many of the larger companies operate internationally, there is still a demand for specialised technical skills and designers in the UK.

The industry is split between companies that supply 'private label' goods to retailers, and suppliers, such as Burberry and Henri Lloyd, who have developed their own brands. There are also businesses that produce collections with a 'signature' identity, such as Paul Smith and Vivienne Westwood.

With rapid changes in consumer tastes creating the need for flexibility, a growing global marketplace and the increasing importance of technology, fashion has become a globalised sector and demands a high level of craft, manufacturing and design skills.

1.1 What do fashion and clothing professionals do?

Fashion jobs have traditionally included designers, garment technologists, pattern cutters, pattern graders, sample machinists and production managers, but have now evolved to include wider roles, including marketing, buying, forecasting, styling, retail and promotion.

Fashion designer

Fashion designers need the technical skills to draw designs and produce samples. They can work for high-street stores or exclusive design houses, and may specialise in one or more areas, such as children's, women's or men's wear, outerwear, lingerie and so on. A fashion designer researches and collects ideas, follows trends and predictions, produces ideas and fashion designs either by hand or on a computer, develops ideas into patterns and often makes sample garments. Fashion design companies look for people who can demonstrate a strong portfolio of work, including practical drawing, computer-aided designs and technical (pattern cutting and sewing) skills.

Activity: Doing your homework

Find a newspaper or magazine that advertises employment opportunities for fashion and clothing professionals – *Guardian Media* or *Apparel* are two you could look at. Find a job that appeals to you, and try to find out as much as you can about:

- the company advertising the job
- the kind of work you would be doing
- the skills you would need
- what kind of other job roles exist within the company and the relationship they might have to the job advertised
- where in the UK you find concentrations of fashion and clothing activity.

Can you produce a technical drawing for this design?

It is essential that as a designer you have a creative eye for colour and shape, the ability to draw and show design ideas effectively, an interest in past and future trends, and skills in garment production and pattern-making.

Garment technologist

A garment technologist supports the design and buying team through all the stages of garment production and its development, from design to manufacture. Garment technologists can be involved with selecting the appropriate fabrics, trimmings and design within a budget. They also work with the pattern cutter and **pattern grader**

to oversee sizing, fitting and testing of the pre-sample garment and may be involved with product returns or faults.

It is essential for a garment technologist to understand the manufacturing or production process along with fabric properties and characteristics. They also need to be able to work both independently and as part of a team, often under pressure to meet deadlines. Graduates usually join a company in a junior role and progress to product development, quality control or buying, before becoming a garment technologist.

Pattern cutter

A pattern cutter is responsible for turning a design into a working pattern. The pattern can be produced by drafting as a flat pattern to given measurements, draped by using a dress stand or developed using a computer package. Most pattern cutters use a combination of two or more methods.

Pattern cutters need an understanding of current trends and the ability to interpret a designer's working drawing. In addition to good IT and numeracy skills, they therefore need a thorough knowledge of garment construction and pattern-cutting techniques, and the ability to work accurately and independently or as part of a team, often under pressure. Pattern cutters are often promoted to head pattern cutter or pattern grader and can also move into areas of garment technology.

Sample machinist

Sample machinists work closely with the designer, pattern cutter and garment technologist to create the first sample of a garment design and provide production details to the manufacturer. Some sample machinists may also be involved in making quality checks during the production process.

Sample machinists must have excellent sewing skills and a thorough understanding of design and pattern cutting, production processes and fabric types. Successful candidates are usually required to complete a BTEC with a strong technical base, usually followed by a higher degree.

Sample machinists can progress to a higher technical role such as garment technologist or quality controller.

Production manager

A production manager is responsible for ensuring that all products are produced to the required quality and meet both budget and deadlines. He/she will oversee the whole **production process**, planning and monitoring production schedules, overcoming faults and liaising with design, sales, buying and quality control teams and suppliers. As many companies now operate globally, the production manager may also be responsible for international supply chains. Employers would expect potential production managers to have a BTEC in fashion and clothing and a higher degree.

Have you investigated all the different roles in the fashion industry?

Fashion buyer

A buyer typically works for a large retail store or chain or a wholesale distributor, and needs a good understanding of the buying cycle and an awareness of current trends and forecasting. He/she will be required to work with both manufacturing companies and retail establishments and be able to analyse sales, markets and trends.

Good communication and IT skills are essential, as the buyer has to negotiate and liaise with numerous people on a national and possibly international basis. Buyers will normally have completed a BTEC in fashion and clothing or a business-related qualification followed by a degree in higher education.

To become a buyer, work experience within a retail environment is essential, and many buyers start out as sales associates. Within large organisations there may be teams of buyers with individual specialisms.

Fashion stylist

A fashion stylist creates images or settings for use in photographs for magazine articles or videos. They will work to a brief using accessories to complement garments, and may also be involved in public relations and networking. An awareness of current trends, design, photography, IT and good communication skills are all important.

Brand and fashion promotion

Promoters generally work for large or niche-market organisations or even for an independent designer wanting to promote a style, store or brand. Promoters need an understanding of promotional tactics and techniques, **target markets** and lifestyles. Good communication and IT skills are vital, along with an awareness of key trends and issues such as technology, sustainability and culture.

Key terms

Pattern grader – the person responsible for physical scaling of the pattern by either increasing or decreasing the size.

Production process – the process of manufacture which includes cutting, sewing, pressing and packaging of the finished garments.

Target market – the group of customers or clients that the retailer aims to sell to or the designer aims to market to.

Case study: James Nolan, fashion student, Central St Martin's London

In 2009, James won the Triumph Inspiration Award, an international competition based around the theme Icons. He was also accepted on placement to work with John Galliano in Paris in December 2009. James is inspired by unconventional sources and loves to discover new methods of pattern cutting. He is currently taking one year out in industry to qualify for a diploma in industrial studies.

James always approaches his work by looking outside the realms of conventional fashion. He enjoys having an initial conceptual idea and challenging himself to make it a part of the body: 'I think it is important to exploit all possibilities when designing clothes'. His processes involve extensive research of the initial idea. He loves taking photos of things that inspire him and works a lot with structures that usually derive from initial experiments that have been carried through from toiling, alongside his experiments in traditional pattern cutting. 'My fabric choices vary from project to project but I like an emphasis on texture and quality in my work'.

Tips from James:

'Work also in your free time as well as producing work for college, as this gives you the chance to gain more experience and discover new possibilities making you a better designer. Visit exhibitions to fuel your imagination and pay close attention to what is going on around you. Your environment can play a big part in creating your own signature designs.'

1. **Are you able to complete a work placement as part of your studies?**

2. **Have you visited any exhibitions or fashion shows recently?**

1.2 Research and recording

Many designers start their research by gathering information in a sketchbook or scrapbook. This will consist of primary and secondary source material, such as sketches, photographs, cuttings, photocopies and samples. Designers also research and record the history of fashion and watch trends and predictions for future seasons. Often a mood board or storyboard is used to support the research, which is then developed into a set of design ideas and illustrations accompanied by samples of fabrics and trimmings. This is known as the design development cycle.

How will a mood board support your research?

Signpost

See also Unit 127 Fashion visualisation and Unit 120 Fashion media, techniques and technology.

Activity: A winter season range

You have been asked to produce a range of designs for a US client for their new winter season clothing range. The client wants to echo extreme European fashion and flair. You need to present your design ideas in the form of a mood/concept board which includes a range of preliminary design ideas, fabric swatches and costings. Prepare a presentation that includes the following.

- research on European fashion
- evidence of trends and predictions for the following winter
- sources of inspiration
- information on the target market
- fashion illustrations and design ideas
- fabric sources and swatches
- technical specifications
- cost estimates.

1.3 Understanding fabrics

Designers have a wide range of fabrics and production processes at their disposal. The more you experience fabrics, the more you will understand the properties of different fabrics – weight, feel, performance, cost and suitability. You need to be able to identify woven and non-woven fabrics, and man-made and natural fabrics. Designers may select fabrics for their look, feel, colour, pattern or texture, but the choice may not necessarily be the most suitable for the design or manufacturing process. The fabric can be decorated with pattern, print and embroidery or even manipulated to create a three-dimensional effect such as by pleating or smocking. Each technique may or may not require specialist treatment during manufacture.

'I would not be able to create my designs without having an understanding of how fabrics work, their characteristics and how they work on the female figure.' – Paul Robinson, freelance designer and pattern cutting lecturer.

Start a fabrics sample collection and experiment to find the most suitable techniques for the manufacturing process.

- Keep a personal record of all fabric and yarns that you work with.
- Produce samples of a variety of decorative and surface techniques.
- Keep a directory of fabric and haberdashery suppliers and sources.

Signpost

See also Unit 128 Garment production, Unit 116 Embroidered textiles, Unit 117 Surface pattern, Unit 119 Printed textiles and Unit 111 Fabric manipulation.

Case study: Quality control managers

You may be surprised to find quality managers in the fashion and clothing sector, but quality control processes are an important and integral part of the industry. For example, quality control managers may work within the fabric production, checking materials for consistency, colour and strength. In garment production, processes can involve checking the quality and consistency of pattern cutting, stitching and finishing. Keeping detailed records, working with figures and identifying how processes can be improved are all part of the job.

1. **What do you think are the skills required to be a quality control manager?**

2. **Would this sort of work appeal to you? Why?**

1.4 Technical skills of pattern cutting and garment construction

Once designs or collections are finalised, the designer and technical staff interpret the design ideas into a series of working drawings to determine the exact details of the design. These drawings are then given to the pattern cutter and manufacturing team who will follow all the details, such as the exact position of pockets, stitch details, etc., during the manufacturing process. It will also be accompanied by fabric samples and technical information. A garment pattern is traditionally developed from a basic pattern block created for a range of garments. The block is then adapted for specific design features. In some circumstances, instead of a flat pattern, the pattern will be produced by draping fabric on a dress stand and pinning the design to it. This **toile** is then transferred on to a paper pattern. You may have access to computer packages such as Lectra, Ormus, or Gerber which generate patterns, but it is essential to understand flat methods in order to use these packages. Patterns can then

be graded to a variety of sizes. Again, this can be done manually or by computer. The patterns are then set out in a lay plan which is used to calculate the amount of fabric required for the garment. This accompanies the pattern, technical specification sheet and costing to the manufacturer.

1.5 Health and safety

There is a range of equipment used in the fashion industry, from industrial flatbed machines to specialist equipment such as overlockers, buttonholers and steam presses. Equipment ensures that garments are produced to a high standard and professional finish, and you should aim to acquire as many production skills as possible. However, when using industrial equipment, it is essential to adhere at all times to health and safety requirements, and carry out risk assessments on specialist machinery.

Signpost

See also Unit 121 Pattern construction for fashion and clothing, Unit 123 Pattern grading for fashion and clothing, Unit 120 Fashion media, techniques and technology, and Unit 128 Garment production.

Activity: Producing a sample

You have been asked to produce a sample garment for a fashion buyer so that they can consider the garment for part of their new seasonal range. The buyer wants to see the finished garment presented alongside the production documentation. Could you prepare a presentation which includes:

- the original design of the garment
- a working sketch or flat drawing of the garment
- a technical specification documentation
- a sequence of operation
- a full costing of the garment
- a pattern for the garment
- the finished garment.

1.6 CAD/CAM

To compete in the global fashion industry, the UK clothing industry uses the latest **CAD/CAM** computer technologies. These include visualising garments, accessories and fabrics, pattern drafting, pattern grading and cutting systems, garment and accessory sizing, 3D body scanners and product data management systems. It is essential to have an understanding of how this technology works, so if you have access to CAD/CAM packages while studying, learn to become competent in their use.

Signpost

See also Unit 120 Fashion media, techniques and technology, and Unit 125 Computer applications in fashion.

Activity: Computer applications in fashion

- Produce a working sketch/flat working drawing using a CAD package.
- Produce basic blocks using CAD pattern-cutting packages.
- Grade pattern blocks to a range of different sizes.
- Produce a range of pattern adaptations using CAD.
- Produce lay plans using a CAD package.

Key terms

Toile – a fabric sample used for fitting and checking a garment design.

CAD (Computer Aided Design) – computer software packages (such as Adobe Illustrator and Adobe Photoshop) that enable the designer to create fashion illustrations, flat working drawings, etc.

CAM (Computer Aided Manufacturing) – computer packages (such as Lectra and Gerber AccuMark) that aid the production or manufacturing process by producing patterns and lay plans, cutting fabric, etc.

1.7 Communication and presentation skills

From the process of research through to design, manufacture and sales, you will need to draw on people from other areas of the industry to achieve a successful outcome.

A key part of this is being able to present your work in a coherent manner, whether to a peer or client. Remember to:

- keep concise
- prepare
- make sure the presentation is relevant to your audience
- know your subject
- make a note of the time
- keep notes
- explore digital media as a resource.

Signpost

See also Unit 130 Fashion presentation techniques, Unit 131 Fashion presentation and Unit 133 Fashion styling.

Case study: Michelle, trainee product technologist

'A key part of my role is communication. I work in a team of thirteen technologists with responsibility for women's wear. I deal directly with our manufacturing base in Asia, which involves travel and communication via email and telephone. I also liaise regularly with the designer and give presentations. Most of our suppliers speak English, but knowledge of another language would be an asset, especially when on development visits.'

1. **Can you speak any other languages?**
2. **Are you confident in presenting your work to an audience?**

Activity: Developing your presentation skills

You have been asked to present a project within a specific time limit. The presentation must include an outline of the project from start to finish and an evaluation of the outcome.

- Research the work thoroughly.
- Plan the presentation to include all the relevant information.
- Prepare visual and written information as appropriate.

- Be creative in your approach.
- Practise the presentation beforehand.
- Speak confidently.
- Communicate clearly.
- Invite questions.
- Adhere to the time limitations of the presentation.

Case study: Jacob Donnelly, costume designer

Jacob is working at College Light Opera Company, in Falmouth, USA, as part of his summer vacation. He has completed a BTEC Level 3 National Diploma in fashion and clothing and a BTEC Level 4 Professional Diploma in costume management, and will return to continue his degree before pursuing work as a costume designer in the US. His work experience includes time at the Royal Exchange Theatre, Manchester and at a local Shakespearean festival.

'I have been working with the wardrobe team, which is made up from a number of university and college theatre departments. We have been designing and making costumes for ten musical theatre productions staged over ten weeks, and I have just completed 16 flapper dresses for *Lady Be Good*. I prefer to design my own costumes rather than work on other people's and like to use a wide range of materials, techniques and processes. In my last year at college I made a 17th-century man's costume in silk which I hand embroidered.'

1. **How can work experience help you to further your career? What plans have you got for work experience?**

2. **What are the pros and cons of working on your own designs? What about working on other people's designs?**

Millinery, beading and embroidery can enhance your skills in costume design and manufacture. Have you any knowledge of these skills and techniques?

Key term

Fashion forecasting – the process of predicting new and forthcoming trends.

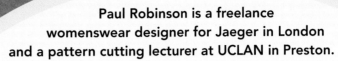

Paul Robinson
Womenswear fashion designer

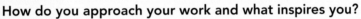

Paul Robinson is a freelance womenswear designer for Jaeger in London and a pattern cutting lecturer at UCLAN in Preston.

Some of my most recent work was for the Jaeger 2009 collection which is now available, and I also worked on Graduate Fashion Week 2009 with final year undergraduates.

Can you describe a memorable piece of work?

My MA collection – I pushed boundaries and it taught me to leave my comfort zone. Although it didn't feel natural at the time, it has given me far greater understanding and appreciation of design, pattern cutting and construction and has cemented all my work thus far.

It also gave me insight into fabrics, budgets, timescales, problem-solving and working as an independent designer.

How do you approach your work and what inspires you?

It's eclectic and diverse – architecture, atmosphere/moods and everyday things form primary research which then go on to form the basis of my designs.

Have there been any constraints in your work?

Good workspace and investment for your own work if you want to build your own business, which is something all new designers face. Private money or business support is crucial to starting up.

What materials, techniques and processes do you use?

Non-traditional fabrics like polypropylene in research, and chiffons and organzas for advanced use, employing classic tailoring where applicable.

What things have helped your career?

An appreciation of good, solid pattern cutting, construction, **fashion forecasting** and looking for shapes, silhouettes and ideas. Always stay ahead and read good magazines, understand how the industry ticks, network, network and network, know your market and stay focused and true to your goals and aspirations.

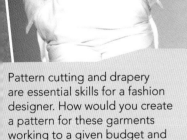

Pattern cutting and drapery are essential skills for a fashion designer. How would you create a pattern for these garments working to a given budget and deadline?

Think about it!

- **Can you find design inspiration from your surroundings?**
- **Which materials, techniques and processes can you source easily?**
- **Can you work to a given budget?**
- **Are you aware of current fashion trends?**
- **How can you register your designs for copyright?**

Just checking

1. What are the current trends and predictions for this year?

2. How can you be more experimental and innovative in your work?

3. How can you be more open and responsive to comments made by others?

4. What is the most effective way to refine your ideas to achieve the desired outcome?

5. Do you know the characteristics and properties of fabrics that you have used recently?

6. How can you develop your communication skills?

Assignment tips

- Read your assignment and ask for clarification if you have any queries.

- Produce a mind map based on your initial ideas.

- Record your starting points.

- Research your client.

- Be aware of current trends.

- Produce independently sourced research materials.

- Communicate your ideas clearly.

- Analyse and review your work.

- Present your work in a logical manner.

Photography

Since its invention, photography has undergone regular advances in technology. The introduction of the Leica in the 1920s allowed the camera to be carried rather than mounted on a tripod, which enabled photographers' work to become more candid.

The introduction of the Box Brownie made photography accessible to anybody who could afford it, and family snaps became commonplace. The digital age has brought fundamental changes to processes, and has made taking photographs a much more economical activity. Anyone who has a mobile phone can be a photographer, and the results are instantaneous and disposable. Pictures can be digitally enhanced and small errors easily rectified by re-touching.

This has placed greater pressure on professional photographers, many of whom are self-employed, but as you will see from the job roles highlighted in this section, photography is a highly skilled occupation requiring specialist knowledge and understanding – creative, technical and subject-specific.

This section is designed to give you an overview of the various categories of specialisms within photography and the type of work undertaken in each, and includes:

- finding information about the sector, job roles and careers, and the necessary skills required
- information about the specialist areas within photography, and what the work might entail
- case studies and observations from students and young people who have just begun their creative careers
- case studies of experienced industry professionals.

Professional voice: Lesley Davies-Evans

Lesley is a studio-based freelance photographer. She has worked in advertising, editorial and design photography and sold personal work to private collectors. Her job is to interpret briefs and visual layouts photographically, working closely with art directors to communicate their ideas.

The principal skills needed to work in the industry:

- motivation to develop a personal style that stands out
- being able to work as part of a team
- being able to present and adapt ideas, and make suggestions on how to achieve an outcome
- understanding the requirements of a brief or layout
- stamina to work unconventional hours and cope with the pressure of successful shooting in limited time
- being able to run a business, costing a job, organising the many aspects of a shoot and meeting deadlines, etc.

The impact of the digital age:

HUGE! Viewing your digital image instantly is fantastic but this has made clients more demanding. Photographers must understand technical information, which was once the responsibility of printers and re-touchers.

We are now used to viewing work live on monitors, which has changed the intimacy of the relationship between the camera and photographer. I find digital photography liberating and inspiring, although I feel lucky to have worked at a time when shooting on film was still standard.

Advice for students:

Nurturing your natural talent will ensure you bring something new and unique: pushing your ideas, re-shooting work when it is not up to scratch and using knowledge around you. Try to gain work experience; you need a lot of self-confidence AND good ideas.

Over to you!

- What do you consider to be the qualities needed to work effectively in a team?
- Which particular talents could you bring to the photographic industry?
- What do you think might be the best way to get a work experience placement?

1. Careers in photography

Public bodies and large organisations employ staff photographers, who serve the interests of the company or organisation and need to be versatile. Most photographers are self-employed or run their own studios, and need to have business as well as photographic skills. Like many creative sectors, photography is highly competitive, and fees are dependent on your client base, reputation and location.

When working in a studio, photographers must be able to communicate a **visual solution** based on the client's brief.

Specific and detailed information about the sector and related industries, including statistics, job roles and career pathways, can be found on the Skillset website www.skillset.org/photo/careers/photographers

Key term

Visual solution – creative interpretation that translates a concept into an image that conveys the meaning and intentions of the client.

Signpost

Contextual studies

If you are studying photography, a comprehensive knowledge of the history of photography (and its position within the visual arts) and developments in technology are essential to inform your practice. Creative practitioners draw extensively on what has happened in history to stimulate their ideas. Sometimes experimenting with a combination of processes such as pinhole photography and digital work can produce innovative results.

1.1 What does a photographer do?

Photographers normally specialise in specific areas, which can be broadly categorised as: advertising and editorial; general or high street; press or photojournalism; fashion; science; industrial and commercial; forensic; medical.

Some photographers will work across a number of categories but others have a higher degree of specialism – a photojournalist specialising in sports photography, for example, may only work across one or two sporting areas.

Photographic briefs may have very specific requirements or allow for creative interpretation in negotiation with the commissioning agent.

1.2 Specialist areas

Advertising and editorial

Advertising photography is used to illustrate and sell a product, location or concept, and will often be part of a wider advertising campaign.

Advertising photographers working on high-budget projects may find themselves in exotic locations, but much work is done in the studio utilising lighting effects, props and accessories, and involves skill, patience and attention to detail. Advertising photography can involve still-life, portraiture or landscape. Advertising campaigns that use television and video employ stills photographers to work on set and generate images for additional paper-based outputs such as magazines and newspapers.

Teamwork, whether through direct involvement or at a distance, is an important part of a photographer's practice and it is essential that a photographer is aware of all the stages between taking the picture and the end-user.

Editorial photographers generate images to illustrate or enhance stories in magazines, news publications, books or websites. Advertising and editorial photographers will often be commissioned by agencies and publishers, and may specialise in areas such as food, travel, interiors or transport.

Activity: Tempting your audience

Look for a range of advertising shots that you find particularly effective – Sunday supplements are always a good source. Record the following:

- Is the picture shot on location or in a studio?
- What do you imagine were the most difficult aspects of the photograph to achieve?
- What kind of problems or obstacles might the photographer have encountered? And what might have been the solution?
- What props were required?

Select some shots that could be replicated, such as food and drink, or smaller products such as toys, household items, etc.

Put together your own studio shoot thinking creatively about the best way to present the subject matter. How can you make it look tantalising?

Print and evaluate the results, recording them in a sketchbook or journal, or on design sheets, presentation boards or a website. Document the problems you encountered and possible solutions.

Functional skills

Mathematics

As a freelance, you will need to cost your work to include labour (your hourly rate and that of an assistant, if applicable), travel, wear and tear on equipment, and materials and props. Your quotations need to be accurate and comparisons drawn with the market price for the job. How would you cost the activity on the left?

Industrial and commercial

Also referred to as corporate photography, industrial and commercial work typically involves capturing images of company premises, industrial activities, company personnel and products, so the corporate photographer needs to be versatile. The work produced would be used for promotional and informational publications and public relations work. Some companies employ their own photographers, but use of freelance photographers is more commonplace.

Press and photojournalism

Newspaper and press photographers need to be able to work under pressure in order to capture images that will tell a story. Local press photographers would be required to cover a range of events, whereas national press photographers tend to specialise in areas such as conflict or war photography, politics or sport.

Some documentary photographers place themselves in the front line in world conflicts. Photographers such as Don McCullin have produced images which have moved the world and triggered campaigns against injustice.

Chris Lee
Advertising photographer

Chris has been running his business for over 25 years, and has seen the transition from traditional darkroom methods to digital work.

'Digitisation has doubled the amount of time I spend – one day in the studio has now turned into one day in the studio AND one day on the computer. Effectively, we are doing pre-press work. The bar has been raised and because the quality CAN be improved digitally, that is what is expected.

This photograph was taken using a long exposure, which has transformed the raging river into a soft, gentle flow; the camera was mounted on a tripod while the picture was taken, so the background has remained in sharp focus. The finished image has not been manipulated or cropped in any way.

You have to be extremely proficient in the use of Photoshop to be any good. Of course, photographers who have learnt through the medium of film and are trained to frame and compose their shots have the edge – you can't get everything back in Photoshop.

My business has changed – I have lost 40 per cent of my market through clients thinking they can do the more straightforward work – such as pack shots – themselves, so now I market myself in areas where I know original creative photography is needed.

There is no doubt that the quality is better and is constantly improving, and in some respects the medium has made the job easier. Low light-level shots, for example, used to be a nightmare, but work still needs to be done to solve problems with highlights and dirt on the sensor.'

Interestingly, Chris still finds the most effective way to get clients is through direct mail, using hard-copy brochures with images:

'Email is a waste of time – what do you do with your junk mail? I have a web presence, but that's not where the work comes from. A client would check out my website (www.chrisleephoto.com) after the initial contact has been made. And to keep a client, customer service is paramount.'

Think about it!

- **What does Chris mean by pre-press?**
- **What is direct mail?**
- **What do you understand by 'customer service'?**

161

Case study: Constructing a picture story

When a photographer covers a story or event, the editor will expect to see a range of pictures to tell the story. This should typically include:

- **Establishing shot** – this establishes the context of the picture and shows the viewer the location and situation of the event.
- **Portrait** – this would be a close-up featuring the main player or players in the story.
- **Relationship shots** – these would show the interaction of the main player in the story with other people. There might be a number of relationship shots to choose from.

The editor might choose from a range of shots to determine the 'slant' of the story and the way the main player is portrayed. You can see evidence of this every day in national newspapers, in the way that politicians and celebrities are presented.

Look carefully at a newspaper or magazine, and see if you can identify these photographic elements of a news story.

Example of an establishing shot, showing Archbishop of Canterbury Rowan Williams at a Christmas event in the cathedral. Can you identify the visual clues which set this scene?

A portrait of Archbishop Rowan Williams, the subject of the story. What impression do you have of the man from this picture?

A range of relationship shots – what do these pictures imply about the Archbishop's character and demeanour?

Sports photography

Sports photography is a highly specialised field of photojournalism, and sports photographers may specialise within just one sport. There is obviously a crossover with reportage in terms of reporting on sports activity in newspapers and sports supplements or magazines, as well as in advertising. Sport is heavily sponsored by business and high-quality images are required to publicise those partnerships.

Some press photographers are employed by publications, but many operate on a freelance basis. Many will supply words as well as photographs, seeking out stories for themselves and selling them to newspapers and magazine publications. Increasingly, images and text are sent via computer links and mobile phones.

Key term

Location photography – the photographer works at the site of the action, or in a REAL setting, rather than setting up shots in a studio.

What challenges are you likely to encounter when photographing sports? What else will you need to consider when working in this field?

Activity: Construct your own picture story

Now try this for yourself. You could choose to cover a local event, or even just document a day in your studio environment.

As you work, think about:

- Your establishing shot – how and from where can you shoot a picture that will tell the viewer what the story is about? What visual clues could you include?

- A portrait or portraits of the key people in your story – who are they? How do you want to portray them?

- Relationship shots – how are the people in the story interacting? How can you capture this visually? What do you want to say about the interactions? Is there going to be a focus for the story?

As the photographer, you can choose to give the editor a range of options that can be edited to present a particular slant on the story, or you could choose to present only the images which tell the story as you want it told.

Did you know?

If you are a photographer working for a client or a student photographer working on **location**, members of the public or the authorities may challenge you, particularly if you are taking photographs in a location where there might be children.

It is sensible to obtain an official letter from your client or the educational institution where you are studying which explains the nature of your work and confirms that you have obtained permission where necessary.

Photographers who are working at public events are often required – and would be strongly advised – to obtain public indemnity insurance which will provide cover should they inadvertently cause an accident during the course of their work.

Fashion

Fashion photographers are required to be innovative, creative, passionate and highly knowledgeable about the fashion industry, past and current. It is a very competitive area with few success stories at the top end of fashion photography, but the financial and material rewards are high for those individuals. Excellent interpersonal and networking skills are needed. Fashion photographers will often work within a team that includes art director, editors and other creative people, and need to communicate well with models, make-up artists and dressers.

Fashion photography also includes catalogue and mail-order work, where results need to be creative as well as efficient and highly competent.

Whether capturing images for haute couture or for a mail order catalogue, a fashion photographer must have a sophisticated understanding of the market and an ability to generate high-quality images to appeal to the target market.

General or high street

High-street photographers may be employed by the industrial, commercial and advertising sectors, but the majority of their work tends to be family portraiture and social occasions such as weddings and other family events. They may have their own studios or can sometimes set up temporary 'mobile' studios within shopping complexes

Medical

Medical photographers are usually employed and work in small medical illustration departments. The images they produce need to be accurate and objective recordings of injuries and diseases, and are used to inform treatment, and to educate and illustrate medical reports, articles or research papers. As well as having photographic skills, they need to have a sound understanding of the medical environment and understand how their images are used in order to fulfil the requirements of their brief.

Some medical photographers may also undertake medico-legal photographs or public relations or commercial shots for use by hospitals or institutions.

Forensic photographers work on assignments, which often relate to crime, accidents or injuries, and their work needs to be an accurate and detailed recording of data that can withstand rigorous investigation in law. They are employed by the police or other specialist services.

Science

Scientific photographers capture the world around us, documenting experiments and illustrating current practice in science and technology. This may involve the use of highly specialised techniques such as time lapse, thermal imaging, infrared and ultraviolet. The objective of the photographic image, as with medical or forensic work, is not necessarily aesthetic, but to provide specific visual information. Employment opportunities can come from research establishments or the government, and the photographer would work as part of a team. They would normally be required to have a degree in science as well as photographic qualifications.

Activity: Appealing to a particular market

Go to the library or Internet and research a selection of photographic fashion images from the following categories: haute couture, ready-to-wear and mass market.

How do the images differ? You can look for the obvious contrasts, such as the location, but look also for more subtle differences, such as props, situation, culture and location.

Create a visual record – design sheets or journal/sketchbook pages – and record your observations. Ask yourself the following questions.

- What is the purpose of the images?
- To whom do you think they are intended to appeal?
- How do they achieve this visually?

Remember

There are a huge range of magazines on the market for the keen photographer, whether amateur or professional, which feature useful tips on technique and equipment. Check out your library or associated websites.

Scientific photographers must be fully conversant with the aims and objectives of their work from a scientific perspective, as well as having all the relevant photographic skills to create their photographs.

Case study: Aaron

Aaron is currently in the final year of his degree course in photographic art after completing a BTEC Level 3 National course in Art and Design.

'The BTEC course helped me decide what I wanted to do. On my current course the practical work is mainly workshop based, learning different **photographic processes** and techniques and using different equipment – medium format, large format, digital backs and so on – to develop a wide range of skills.

I was lucky in being photographed by Rankin. I managed to get a two-week placement, which turned into four months working as a personal assistant to Henry Holland, after being recommended by someone leaving the same post. It mainly involved picking up garments from the PR company and delivering them to high-profile associates. I delivered one to Little Boots and got to stick some of the crystals on the garment she wore at Glastonbury Festival! I was also given the opportunity to go to London fashion week, where I met photographers from *Vogue* and *Attitude*. I already have a job offer for when I graduate.'

1. Do you know who Rankin is? Find out what kind of work Rankin produces.

2. Do you know who Henry Holland is? Find out about his company and look at some of the images produced to promote his work.

A photograph by Aaron of a garment designed by Ross Whittred (inspired by Balenciaga).

Key term

Photographic processes – the range of different formats and means through which images are produced, such as film, darkroom and digital work.

Photo agencies

Many photographers are members of agencies. Agencies have a bank of stock photographic shots and sell the rights to use their pictures to business or advertising clients. This is often much more economical for the client than commissioning a photographer. The photo agency would pay the photographer a percentage of the fee they collect.

Unit stills photographers

Unit stills photographers work on film sets to capture still images of the action for publicity material. Depending on the film's budget, they work a set number of days, and either capture the images while filming takes place or set up shots later that simulate scenes from the action.

The photo-imaging industry

In addition to taking pictures yourself, there is a whole industry of associated activities, such as photographic laboratories, picture libraries or photo agencies, retail, manufacture and equipment support services.

Signpost

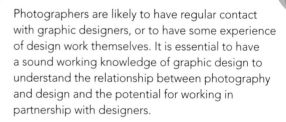

Photographers are likely to have regular contact with graphic designers, or to have some experience of design work themselves. It is essential to have a sound working knowledge of graphic design to understand the relationship between photography and design and the potential for working in partnership with designers.

Some of the units available through the Photography pathway (33, 38) can also be studied with Graphic design, are more fully explained in the Graphic design section.

George Wilson
Documentary photographer

A young girl at a community arts workshop event on Margate beach. Photographers have to work unobtrusively in order to capture candid pictures such as this.

George started taking photographs as a teenager, although he left school at 15 with no qualifications. After numerous jobs, he took an Open University foundation course in his thirties, followed by a degree in Drama at Middlesex Polytechnic. After a year, he decided to pursue his lifelong ambition to study photography and transferred to the Diploma in Documentary Photography in Newport South Wales, run by Magnum photographer David Hurn.

Asked what were the most important things he had learned at college, he replied: 'Wear shoes that don't make a noise – you can't be intrusive! I also learned how to work around a subject to get the right result – it's all about concentration. You don't take single photos, because the choice you make from your contact sheet determines your story and provides the information that you want to convey to your audience.'

When George first started work as a professional he processed all his black-and-white work and some of the colour using traditional darkroom processes. However, he totally embraced the digital age, although the act of taking a picture has not changed: 'The difference is that instead of spending hours in the darkroom, I spend hours on the computer.' He still uses film sometimes, which he feels gives a better tonal range to the image.

George commented on the difference between an amateur and a professional: 'It's not necessarily about ability, some amateurs are superb photographers. The difference is that a professional earns money and, when working to a deadline with only one chance at the shot, a professional has to produce the goods.'

Think about it!

- **What do you know about the Magnum Photo agency?**
- **What is a contact sheet? How would you make a contact sheet if you were shooting on film?**
- **How do you make a contact sheet in Photoshop?**

Just checking

1. What does a photographer do? In the light of this section, what have you learned about being a photographer?

2. How would you go about submitting your work to a photo agency or library?

3. What kind of shots would you need to put together a picture story for a newspaper or magazine?

4. What are the three broad areas of the fashion market?

5. Think of an image used for advertising. What would you have to include in the costing for a similar shot?

edexcel

Assignment tips

*   Know your subject, past and present. Photography draws on knowledge of the past – knowing its history, and photographers who have made an impact, will help you understand what constitutes a good picture.

*   Keep yourself well-informed on current affairs. If you are interested in editorial work and you have no idea what is going on in the world, you stand little chance of gaining employment with agencies whose job it is to inform.

*   If you are interested in a particular area of photography, find out who the top photographers are, what makes their work respected and how they progressed their career.

*   Develop the ability to network with people. Aaron (featured) offers the following top tip: 'Networking will get you job opportunities. Offer your services to people to get experience. I offered to do photographic work for fashion students when they graduated – I got the experience of working a fashion catwalk, they got the images. If they do well, you could do well too…'

*   Learn about the industries related to photography, such as journalism, graphic design or film. You will frequently find yourself working as part of a team. You need to understand the potential and limitations of other disciplines to fulfil your role. Develop skills in other areas and you will increase your versatility.

*   Take opportunities to gain experience as a photographer, or photographer's assistant, even if unpaid. You can add this experience to your CV. If your shots are good, they will contribute towards your portfolio.

*   Be sensitive to issues around child protection and health and safety. If you are undertaking work as a student, make sure you have identification such as a student card or letter of authorisation. If you are working in the public domain, make sure your activities are not posing any danger to the public.

Fine art

Fine art is perhaps the broadest of all the art and design disciplines. It can embrace an enormous range of skills and media, from the more traditional disciplines of painting, sculpture and printmaking, to more contemporary forms such as installation, film, sound and performance.

The major difference between fine art and other areas is context: fine artists make work primarily for galleries and other site-specific locations, as well as commissions for private or public clients via advertsing and websites, rather than for industry. They also have to define their own briefs, evolve an individual style and develop an experimental approach to media and techniques.

This section is designed to give you an overview of the various categories of specialisms within fine art and the type of work undertaken in each, and includes:

* finding information about the specific areas within fine art, what the work might entail and the necessary skills required
* case studies of experienced professional fine artists.

Professional voices:
Chris Rutter and Evelyn Bennett

The sculptor Chris Rutter, and Evelyn Bennett, who has a background in textiles and illustration, have worked together since 1996, as Rutter and Bennett, making large-scale three-dimensional work. Most of their work is commissioned, with some of the most exciting pieces produced for Goodwood Sculpture Park, where they have been given a large budget and a brief to create what they want. Goodwood pays the production costs of the sculptures, which, when sold, generate the artists' fees. Chris and Evelyn work mostly with steel and fibreglass, with the help of fabricators for large-scale work, but produce the models and smaller-scale steel sculptures themselves. Other recent commissions include a piece for a Bow housing development and a project in Gosport. Their practice encompasses other media including two-dimensional work and sound. They also have an agent who finds them commissions and gallery exhibitions, while other work has come from the Axis website, an artist database supported by the Arts Council. They avoid being tied to only one gallery so as not to restrict the development of their practice.

A Rutter and Bennett sculptural installation in the landscape.

Over to you!

- Can you think of some of the practicalities and disadvantages of working collaboratively? Try researching other fine-art partnerships, such as Gilbert and George, Jane and Louise Wilson, Jake and Dinos Chapman, the Boyle family, and Jeanne-Claude and Christo.

- How would you find a market for your work if you wanted to make large-scale sculptures?

- How would you cost a piece of public art? Think about all the production stages you would need to factor into your fee.

1. What does a fine artist do?

Fine art covers an enormous range of possibilities, many of which are listed below. Some of these are specialist and have specific demands and outcomes, but whichever category you pursue you will need to make research and critical analysis of your own and others' work a key component of your practice.

As a fine artist you will normally be devising your own project within the boundaries of a unit assignment, gallery criteria or site-specific limitations.

Signpost

Refer back to Unit 5 to help you investigate some key art works that have been sited in a variety of locations. Try to find out whether or not these pieces were commissioned, and if so by whom, and consider the impact they have today. You will also find it useful to review ideas around visual recording and ideas and concepts in Units 1 and 3 to support your work for this pathway.

If you are working in **two dimensions** you could be working in any of the following:

- For many artists, drawing from observation is paramount, and for some it remains the sole focus of their practice. As a student, many of your assignments will begin with drawing. Research some observational drawings by leading contemporary artists and compare these to more historical images.

- You could be a painter making work in a variety of media and scales and using a traditional figurative format – look at the landscape-based, densely painted imagery of Peter Doig. Or you could make abstract or gestural work in the spirit of Catalan artist Antoni Tapies, referred to in Unit 3. Both artists have successfully translated their work into printmaking. Printmaking could also be the sole focus of your practice and could take the form of etching, lithography, screen-printing or wood- or lino-cuts.

- You could use an array of media to create graphic or narrative images. If you work within one of these pathways you might also produce storyboards for developing your work into film, animation or book formats.

- As a fine artist you could also be working with photographic processes. You might specialise in experimental imagery photography, using a variety of scales and forms and different lens-based processes. You could also explore image manipulation using computer techniques – this could involve a range of starting points, from painting to print to photography, which are then digitally reconfigured.

Observational drawing is a useful starting point for any fine art outcome.

Printmaking could also be the sole focus of your practice and could take the form of etching, lithography, screen-printing or wood- or lino-cuts.

- You could also explore lens-based processes through film, video and interactive media: look at the work of the American performance and video artist Bruce Nauman, who explores language and communication. You could also use video and sound installation – try researching the American artist Bill Viola, who uses video as an art form but is also concerned with music and sound.

If you are working in **three dimensions** you could explore some of the following methods.

- We have already referred to three sculptors in Unit 2 who work in very different ways, but you could also look at the casting techniques of Eva Hesse and Henry Moore, or the archiving of found material by Mark Dion. You could research artists who use constructed forms, such as the large-scale welded works of Anthony Caro, or the fragile impermanent sculptures composed of natural materials by the land artist Andy Goldsworthy.

- Many fine artists use ceramics in their practice – try investigating the sculptures of Turner prize nominee Rebecca Warren, whose work includes finely crafted forms emerging out of roughly modelled blocks of clay. You could research the vessels of Grayson Perry, whose vase forms appear traditional, but are covered in anarchic decorations.

- Grayson Perry has also made designs for tapestries and textiles. Many artists use three-dimensional textiles, exploring processes such as embroidery and felting to develop sculptural outcomes – look at the architectural constructions of Annie Sherbourne to give you a sense of other possibilities.

- Public artists develop work primarily for public spaces and corporate environments. The professional voice at the beginning of this unit looked at the publicly sited work of Rutter and Bennett. In a similar vein are the large-scale projects of Jeanne-Claude and Christo, who have wrapped major buildings such as the German Reichstag.

- You may be making multi-disciplinary work, which means working in different media. Think of the French artist Louise Bourgeois, whose work includes large-scale installations, sculpture, painting, printmaking and tapestry, although her themes of childhood and the role of the mother in society remain consistent.

An example of work by the multi-disciplinary artist Louise Bourgeois. What do you think this sculpture is constructed from? Can you find examples of her work in other media?

1.1 Fine art principles

While your specialism will determine the form of your final outcome, there are elements within fine art practice common to all disciplines. Key to all work is a coherent composition, which means ensuring that the overall look of your piece is satisfying. Consider your final outcome: how is your composition working? Is your eye led around it satisfactorily, or does your eye wander off the edge of the work? Is there coherence to the shapes and forms that you have used? Are there good contrasts, such as light and dark, or areas of intricate mark-making juxtaposed with more simplified sections? If you have used colour, is this working, or has it got muddy or discordant?

Functional skills

ICT

Several of the fine art units have an emphasis on computers (32 and 34) and will help develop your ICT skills. However, even in other fine art areas you can document your work, or manipulate outcomes, to build on your technological skills.

Activity: Making a composition

This is a paper-based activity, but you can decide whether to use pencil/charcoal/graphite/ink/paint/collage, and/or a combination of these.

Take a sheet of A1 paper and make a quick drawing of your studio. Now turn the paper 90 degrees and draw something completely different on top of the first drawing: for example, plot everything that you can see in the studio red. You could use a different media for this, such as paint, if your first drawing is in charcoal.

Now turn the paper another 90 degrees (so your original drawing is upside down) and draw something completely different on top of the first two layers, such as a portrait. Again, you could choose a different medium for this. Turn your paper another 90 degrees for one last drawing: you might think about adding collaged materials this time to show up over the existing layers.

You now have a densely built-up picture surface. Analyse this and decide what to do to make it more coherent. You could try the following.

1. Paint out sections that seem too 'busy'.

2. Cut into the surface of the paper; remove areas and/or push new textures or surfaces from behind.

3. Add new sections, either by collaging these on top or recycling discarded sections of drawings.

A medium such as compressed charcoal is excellent for developing mark-making and reworking drawings.

Kevin Jones
Painter/designer

A detail from one of Kevin's paintings of wind turbines, which gives a contemporary take on a traditional landscape format.

Kevin Jones studied Fine art at Kent Institute of Art and Design in Canterbury, where his work centred on wall-based, site-specific drawing and installation. After graduation, he was invited to do some teaching on his former degree course, which gave him the impetus to do a PGCE (Postgraduate Certificate of Education). Teaching is now his main source of income.

Kevin's work has changed significantly since college. While making site-specific work was possible in a college environment and allowed him to be ambitious, he couldn't transfer this process easily to his studio.

He tried to think of ways of changing his working methods to allow more autonomy, and consequently moved towards painting.

Owing to his experience of Photoshop and multi-media, Kevin has become interested in using photography to record part of the painting process. As his work contains a lot of landscape imagery, the photography component enables him to process the subject matter. He has now started exploring pinhole and cyanotype photography, and aims to investigate film and sound.

Kevin has exhibited widely in London and the South East, but has also begun organising exhibitions in order to access more unorthodox spaces. He has curated several shows in empty shops and houses, which he sees as a means of presenting innovative work.

Think about it!

- Can you think of any unconventional spaces where you could exhibit your work?
- What would you need to do to organise such an exhibition?
- How could you ensure that the work exhibited was safe from theft and that its installation posed no risk to the audience?

1.2 Generating fine art ideas

Sometimes the hardest aspect of being an artist is generating an initial idea exciting enough to trigger a whole body of work. Artists develop different strategies for producing ideas – some have routine systems in place while others exploit the random and/or spontaneous response. The next activity gives you a framework to work with while allowing for the unexpected.

Activity: Deconstruction

Pick two inanimate objects which have no value and can be taken apart easily and safely, such as an electronic keyboard, an old telephone, a section of rope, etc. See what happens if you start to deconstruct the objects – what kind of shapes and forms are revealed? Are there unexpected elements, and, if so, do they give you ideas for future use? While taking these objects apart, document your progress through drawing, photography, film or a combination of these.

1. Now try to find ways of bringing these two objects together. Think about the following:

- What are the connections between the two objects? Do they share any of the same media/ forms/construction methods?

- What are the contrasts between the two? Think about the materials they are constructed from – are they fragile/solid, man-made/natural, soft/ hard, smooth/sharp?

- Do they share a particular aesthetic? If so, how could you use this?

2. Once you have combined your objects in a reconstructed form, make drawings/paintings/ photos/film of your outcome. Try doing this on a variety of scales and formats to give your work ambiguity; and try to be as innovative as possible in your making. For example, you could make something sculptural, then project light on to it and use the photographic documentation as your outcome.

Key term

Cyanotype – a photographic printing process resulting in a cyan-blue print. Photosensitive chemicals are applied to a receptive surface and allowed to dry in a dark room. On exposure to sunlight or ultraviolet light everyday objects placed on this surface create photograms – stencil-type images, which are revealed when the photosensitive chemicals are rinsed off.

1.3 Developing and realising fine art ideas

An important part of any artist or designer's practice is to generate information about the subject matter of their work. The next activity is designed to help you make preparatory work leading to a more considered outcome.

Activity: Location work leading to a triptych

Make a triptych about a particular location – that is a sequence of three linked sections. You will need to gather lots of information to determine what to place in each.

Carry out a series of studies about your chosen location, after first creating a series of grounds to work on. Take a range of different kinds of papers, or pieces of canvas and card (you might need to prime these first), or found matter, such as newsprint and packaging, and use ink/charcoal/collage, etc. to change the surfaces.

On location, make drawings about your environment in different media on the various grounds. Your outcomes could be fast paced or more intensive. To trigger imagery, think about the shape and size of the surface you are working on, look at small details as well as large architectural features.

When you have a range of preparatory work, start planning your triptych by sketching ideas in your sketchbook. You might think about blowing up one drawing for each section, in which case you will need to consider how to link these together into three panels. Or you could integrate several studies together within one panel, in which case you'll need to consider the picture space carefully – think back to the first composition activity. You will also need to think about:

- the size and shape of your triptych panels
- media
- the feeling or information you want to convey about the location, and how your imagery and use of media reinforce your emotional responses.

What materials and equipment would you take with you on location work?

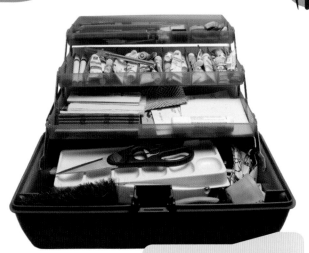

Sketchbook experimentation exploring ink on collaged paper pieces.

1.4 Presenting fine art

One of the characteristics of fine art is the range of possibilities for presentation. We have seen that artists are not confined to presenting work within galleries, but can also install work within landscapes or public spaces, in 'found' buildings, and can sell work via fairs, websites and agents.

- Try to organise a show at college. Consider how to present work innovatively in even the most banal space.

- Document the outcome and use it as the basis for a presentation.

Signpost

Fine artists are increasingly using computer technology. Some of the units available through the Fine art pathway (Units 32 and 34 in particular) are more fully explained in the section on Computers in art and design.

Activity: Transformation - making art outdoors

This activity involves making work in an outdoor location. It may be something in your college grounds, or in a specific location. In either case you will need to seek permission first and to make a rigorous risk assessment before starting. It will also be useful to research artists' responses to the landscape, and to visit places such as Grizedale Sculpture Park or Kings Wood in Kent, where you can see site-specific work. This is a very open brief – your task is to respond to the outdoors in a way of your choosing. You will need a range of materials to work, but might want to limit yourself to materials sympathetic to the environment, such as chalk, charcoal, twine and paper. You might need to take water with you, as well as cameras to document your processes and outcome.

Once in your outdoor environment, find an area that intrigues you, such as a gnarled tree or an area of undulating ground. Consider how to make an innovative response to this, whether through conventional representation or more unusual means. See if the area around your chosen spot gives you any ideas – there may be leaves growing in a particularly vivid colour which suggest a land art outcome, or the shape of a tree may suggest making paper constructions to place on it. Whatever you do, you should be sensitive to the environment and avoid damaging existing plant forms.

1. Could you make a piece of work using materials from the location? For example, could you mono-print with mud, or use leaves to make colour to stain a drawing?

2. Can you suspend work within this environment? What would you use? How does this transform the location?

3. Try investigating the land art movement and use this research to develop ideas for work in other outdoor locations.

Installing work outside can create a totally different dynamic compared to exhibiting it indoors.

WorkSpace

Andy Malone

Book artist

Making a living solely from fine art can be challenging, and although some fine artists undoubtedly achieve this, many more find different ways of supplementing their income.

Andy studied Fine art/Sculpture at Canterbury College of Art (now UCA) before following a postgraduate course at Central St Martins in London. While at college he made large constructed wooden sculptures, often using a chainsaw. He took on a large studio in Canterbury where space is more affordable than in the capital.

To support himself when he left college, Andy registered on a government scheme to encourage new businesses and worked as an assistant to established sculptors. He also applied for funding to develop his work, taught at Wimbledon School of Art and undertook Arts Council-supported residencies in schools. He now teaches full-time at Canterbury UCA and exhibits his work widely, both in this country and abroad. His work has developed in dramatically different ways, and is now formed by cutting shapes, usually figurative, from maps and books and juxtaposing these within book formations. He regularly presents his work at artists' book fairs and specialist art bookshops/galleries; his books have been purchased by the Tate Gallery and other organisations with artists' book collections.

A detail of one of Andy's books, incorporating cut-outs of found bird egg imagery.

Think about it!

- How could you find out about grants or bursaries to apply for?
- Are there any skills that you have learned at college that would help you secure paid work?
- Can you think of formats for your own work that you could develop alongside a job schedule?

WorkSpace Ian Bottle

Fine artist

Ian Bottle works in a range of media and formats. Before taking a degree in Fine art at Newcastle Polytechnic his work revolved around ideas for environments for which he made maquettes, but at college his focus shifted to painting.

While still a student, he took part in the Northern Open and was subsequently awarded a student bursary and a solo exhibition at the Northern Centre for Contemporary Art in Sunderland. He was also selected for 'One Year On', a feature section at the International Contemporary Art Fair at Olympia in London.

One of Ian's paintings, which combines shapes and forms referred to in his sculptural pieces.

The experience of having a solo show and stand at a prestigious event led to other exhibitions and gallery contacts. Ian's work consisted of large-scale figurative imagery that served as allegories for wider personal and political concerns. Ian went on to do an MA at Chelsea School of Art where he was awarded a Boise travel scholarship to study Italian painting.

Since then, Ian has established his own studio in Kent and works fulltime as a lecturer. Although he still paints, digital media, particularly digital photography, is now an important component of his work, which he manipulates in Photoshop to create grounds for his paintings. He also projects photographs of fragmented shapes and forms in his studio, which become the basis for paintings as well as sculpture. Computer programs such as InDesign allow him to translate paintings into layouts for artist's books, which he sells as an affordable alternative to paintings and drawings.

Think about it!

- Can you think of any other formats for Ian's work that could combine his interest in sculpture, painting and digital media?
- How would you exhibit a diverse body of work like this in an empty gallery space?
- How would you price the different types of work that Ian makes?

Just checking

1. Make sure that you are keeping a sketchbook full of your ideas, drawings and reference points. This is essential for you as an artist, whatever medium you use, and provides a useful insight into your thought processes for tutors and/or galleries who want to review your work.

2. Try to keep abreast of current exhibitions and shows. Even if you can't get to see them in person, most galleries have comprehensive websites providing information about artists showing with them: this is a really useful means for you to keep abreast of contemporary practice.

edexcel

Assignment tips

- Throughout your career as an artist you will be required to provide statements about your work and to submit information about your practice for interviews, exhibition proposals and grant applications. To do this, you will need to confront what your work is about, what has inspired it and how you make and present it. Keep your statements clear and concise, and make sure you stick to any word limit.

- You will also need to produce a CV (curriculum vitae). This should list your date of birth, education, qualifications, exhibitions you have participated in and any awards or prizes you have won, as well as any exchange schemes or overseas projects you have undertaken.

- Make sure that you keep good documentation of all your work.

- Keep this in a range of formats: download images on to a CD-ROM, keep updated email images and print out good-quality A4 photos.

Interactive media

Interactive media is where science meets art. Interactive objects existed long before the advent of digital technology – a football is an interactive object: kick the ball and you can observe cause and effect – but objects such as this were more the product of craft than technology. Interactive digital media goes much further than craft in the degree to which it allows us to manipulate our world. By using interactive media, artists and designers can also reach a much wider audience and use existing skills to develop new forms of creativity. For example, designers can use interactive media to make work that moves or uses sound, or that addresses social issues. You could be designing a website for a local dentist or a lighting scheme for the Moscow State Circus; you could be a tester for the latest holographic world-dominance immersive game, or help your education authority produce strategies to support vulnerable members of the community. Moreover, recent developments in computers mean that it is possible to make work in this medium with relatively little technical expertise.

Interactive media and its applications are still developing. However, changes in individual needs coupled with technological discoveries mean that whatever interactive media is today it will be different tomorrow.

This section looks at those areas where a designer with interactive skills might find employment, and includes:

- information about the sector
- information about job roles and the skills that may be required
- case studies of students and young people who have just begun their creative careers
- case studies of experienced industry professionals.

Professional voice: Antony Bliss

Growing up with computers from an early age, and leaning more towards the technical side of life, I was constantly pulling things apart, then rebuilding them. Having a keen interest in art and design, I also specialised my skills in the creative world.

After gaining a BTEC National Diploma in Multimedia Design, which gave me multimedia skills such as digital and model animation, video editing and use of Adobe's Creative Suite, three years ago I began to specialise in photography. Since then I have begun to explore the world of photography and the digital manipulation of images in greater detail. I enjoy learning new things, exploring different styles of marketing and advertising, online and off, and what can be achieved with different techniques and processes.

I am currently employed by G-Forces Web Management in Bearsted, Kent, initially as a CSS Designer then progressing to the role of Online Marketing Executive, developing the online marketing strategies for numerous top automotive dealerships in the UK. The work includes search engine optimisation, link building, email campaigns and creative social media advertising. Previously, I was employed as a designer at the award-winning website design company SiteWizard, based in Kent. This role involved building, designing and maintaining websites for their in-house content management system at a very fast turnaround, allowing me to refine my skills in logo design, interactive Flash, stationery design and e-commerce website design.

Over to you!

- When you look at a website are you most interested in what it does or what it looks like?
- How many things do you do every day that do not involve computers?
- Try to plan your future without 'new technology' – what sort of business would you be in?
- As far as computer technology goes, any guess about the future is likely to be correct. Take a guess about some future development and then hide it away to dig up later – see if you were right or if it happened a lot sooner than you predicted. What will the next computer operating system look like?

Future operating systems will look more like the imagined ones we see in films like *Minority Report* (2002) with Tom Cruise or *Déjà Vu* (2006; pictured above) directed by Tony Scott.

1. The interactive media sector

Interactive media can certainly be understood as part of the skill set of an artist or designer. But the sector can also include people who do not belong to this field. They may be linguists, scientists, archaeologists, publishers, medics or explorers – the list is endless. Interactive media is transformative – just as it has changed the nature of modern art and design, it can also change the practice of many other specialisms.

Signpost

Links to the Graphic design discipline are very strong and many of the skills and activities common to the graphic design industry are shared with interactive media. See also the Graphic design unit.

Activity: Educational institutions

Find out how interactive media is being applied by visiting the websites of some of the great educational institutions in the world.

- In the UK, the Royal College of Art, London College of Communication and the Lansdown Centre for Electronic Art at Middlesex University are important centres for education and research in this area.
- MIT (Massachusetts Institute of Technology) in the US is also a key place to look.
- In Italy, IVREA (Interactive Design Institute Ivrea) near Turin runs projects that investigate what interactive media could be in the future.
- FutureLab based in Bristol is a government-funded research centre that looks at how interactive media can help primary and secondary schools and learning in general. Artists and technicians work together to see how their combined knowledge and skills can transform our world.
- Arts Catalyst is a group that looks at the environment, travel, physics and biology. They commission ambitious projects that combine art and science using interactive media.

Case study: Richard Smith, Jannuzzi Smith Design

Michele Jannuzzi and I started the business (a cross-media design company) in 1993, after graduating from the Royal College of Art. Communication is more difficult today than it has ever been – technology challenges what it means to communicate. Never before have we been able to cross-reference such a wealth and diversity of information, or faced such difficult questions about how information is delivered and accessed. We try to focus on the fundamental requirement of our discipline – helping people to communicate more effectively. We also try to define how a medium can be used for a specific end, and how media can be managed collectively. If we can enrich the process of communicating and convey the message clearly and interestingly, we have done our job.

1. In Richard and Michele's book they have spelt out the word 'supercali fragelisticexpialidocious' using a font that has nothing to do with traditional type design. See if you can make a series of letterforms out of abstract patterns that you can use to make something readable.

Type can be liberated from the great print tradition now that the look of words on the screen has become so important.

1.1 The skill set

General art and design skills are important for anyone aspiring to work in a creative environment.

You will need:

- confidence with imagery
- ability to draw and understand composition
- a good eye and willingness to experiment and resolve problems
- a sense of order and structure
- a love and feel for good typography.

High-level computer skills are not generally necessary, but familiarity with basic computer functions is essential. The latest software may be appealing, but most digital tasks can be done with older, cheaper versions – some applications are so ambitious that few designers use all the tools available. Applications are usually temporary and employers will be more interested in your ideas and thought processes.

Computers can store and test ideas but they do not have a vision. The logic gates in a computer are either on or off. Human emotional responses draw us to explore the areas of life that are just possibilities – not on or off. Leonardo's helicopter idea did not fly in his own time – but it does now.

1.2 Getting started

Interactive media practitioners rarely set out to specialise in this area. Most have other skills, such as typography, illustration or animation, which also enable them to make a living. Interactive media is likely to be just part of the products and services that a design group provides.

- Small Design is an international US company that makes interactive displays for museums. Their work involves 3D design, graphics, animation and video.
- Studio Tonne in the UK makes print graphics but also designs and makes interactive sound toys for the websites of pop groups.
- Babel Media, based in Brighton, outsources technology for the games industry.

Companies working with interactive media are very interested in today's school leavers and graduates, because computers have been part of their lives from birth. But these companies want more than mere users or technicians – they are looking for original ideas and design skills, and the ability to conceptualise.

Many companies advertise for start-up positions as a web designer or **Flash** programmer. You may already have these skills, but if your passion is for performance art you should look for companies making work for film, theatre or music, and develop appropriate software skills. However, software skills are not crucial to finding employment – many interactive products run with quite basic technology, and design companies often have their own software; if they are interested in you they will give you training.

Key term

Flash – a simple animation application that can be scripted to provide interactivity and is popular for making websites and games, but is incompatible with new web standards as demanded by the World Wide Web Consortium (www.w3.org).

Case study: Andy Edwards

I studied BTEC HND in Multimedia before taking a BA in Video Art. Though I never felt good at making narratives, the ideas behind moving imagery intrigued me – I had always loved film and spent my student years working in video stores. I also found it easy to work on computers and was constantly downloading free applications. I am hoping to build up contacts in the TV and video industry using my digital skills.

From September until December 2009, I was a trainee through Screen South (funded by Skillset) at Filmscape Media, a company that hires cameras, lighting and other equipment to film and television productions. This work has developed my understanding of the media industry immensely and given me the hands-on skills to pursue further work in this sector.

1. **Do you have a family story you would like to make an animation or video for?**

2. **Can you prepare a plan for a famous story with a running time of 30 seconds?**

3. **What do you think is the most important skill today for a film director?**

Saul Bass (1920–96) brought graphic ideas to the screen and transformed the film title sequence into an art form of its own. The effects that he invented were technically very difficult to achieve and also highly expensive. These effects can now be made on many home computers with video software.

Programmer

Programming is, of course, an important part of interactive media. However, many professionals are not programmers and buy in software skills when required. The tasks of web designer and web builder are now considered separate.

Software applications and what constitutes essential software are constantly changing. However, many high level programming languages, such as HTML and its subsets, XML and Javascript, are worth learning. C++ is a language commonly used by artists for installations, and Lingo and ActionScript – both derivatives of Javascript – are robust and easy to learn for anyone wanting to work in the computer games industry. You can see the coding for web pages by looking at 'Source' in the 'View' menu of any browser.

Specialist programmers are often employed on a freelance basis, but they also work alongside visualisers as a two-person creative team, and may have an art and design training or a purely technical background. Programming can be a way to work in exciting and challenging creative areas without having to be creative yourself. Easy-to-use programming software available for free trial includes Max5 from cycling74: www.cycling74.com

PLTS

Team worker

You will need to develop strong team-working skills to succeed in this field. Work on understanding the different roles and responsibilities during your group assignments. What are the characteristics of a successful team?

Did you know?

Web standards and usablity issues are well covered by the Worldwide Web Consortium (www.w3.org). Here you can also find descriptions of programming languages, and access the blog of the person who invented the web as we know it – Sir Tim Berners-Lee. You can also copy and paste codes from this and other sites to use for your own projects.

Visualiser

Visualisers are 'ideas people', and often are either artists or come from a theoretical academic background. The visualiser creates the concept for the project and sees it through from start to finish, and will also sometimes combine the roles of artworker, writer and project manager. As well as having a lot of craft skills, they will liaise with other makers such as architects and fabricators to achieve the required result. Visualisers may have some programming ability but are can also commission the technical aspects from others. The **CSS** (styling sheet) file for a website may also be the responsibility of the visualiser.

Visualisers are often the people who find work for the studio. They tend to have a wide knowledge of interactive media and want to push the medium in new directions.

Artworker

Interactive media projects require highly finished graphics. Where the budget allows for more than a programmer and visualiser, an artworker would be hired to produce the graphics. These may involve not just images but moving graphics, videos and animations. An artworker would have competence with Adobe applications including Web, and in stop-motion 2D and 3D animation. They may also have to be familiar with new 'codecs' (**compressions/decompressions**) and other file formats for moving material, and will be highly organised and able to produce large quantities of material to budget and on time. An artworker may also produce graphics for other purposes, such as packaging and advertising for the project, and will therefore require experience in print as well as screen.

Activity: Strange, expensive and amazing?

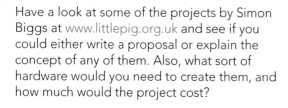

Have a look at some of the projects by Simon Biggs at www.littlepig.org.uk and see if you could either write a proposal or explain the concept of any of them. Also, what sort of hardware would you need to create them, and how much would the project cost?

Activity: Content is king

Look at any piece of interactive media and count the number of still and/or moving images. Work out how long each piece would take to produce and then calculate how many hours has been spent making the graphics alone. Remember it is almost impossible to make interactive media without content.

Key terms

CSS (Cascading Style Script) – CSS in websites allows the content to be separate from the style of the pages. This makes the data more accessible and reduces the amount of coding for each page. CSS is the way forward for better web standards and it allows the same content to be viewed on different hardware devices.

Compression/decompression – hardware and software 'codecs' that enable large files to run on computers or TVs. The ideal codec is slow to compress and quick to decompress, and is usually the smallest file you can have for video. Some codecs produce files that can be edited, like DV PAL, but others are so compressed that you can only distribute and watch them – like MPG4.

Project manager

Some interactive media projects can be very large – managing a website such as those for the BBC or *Guardian* involve organising and controlling hundreds of people. The project manager needs to be familiar with all aspects of the job and take responsibility for any problems. Even when only a small team is involved someone needs to allocate the work and manage the budget and client. Sometimes the subject matter of the project also requires the skills of a project manager. In the case of the *Guardian* website the manager is likely to have a background in journalism, whereas project managers for education sites will probably have started their careers in teaching. Project managers may also work with other managers if, for instance, the product is part of a large advertising campaign.

Activity: Ever tried herding cats?

Organise a team in your class studio to work on a project together. It can be a simple task and does not have to be done on computer. Allocate the work so that each member has sole responsibility for a set of tasks for the finished product. Find out how difficult it is to keep the team together and focused.

Case study: Ben Price

I studied for a BTEC National Diploma in Multimedia and then took an HND in Youth Culture at Chichester University. I now work as a Substance Misuse Youth Worker on a project with young people looking at issues of drugs and alcohol on the streets and in the classroom. My official role is DISP worker for West Kent.

A DISP is a one-day programme for young people under 18 who have issues with Class B drugs and below, and have been referred to me by teachers, police and parents, or as self-referrals. It is a multi-agency project also involving the youth service, police and ex-offenders. The programme is a last chance for some young people, who can go on a DISP instead of getting a criminal record.

I host the programme and deal with assessments. This might seem far from interactive media but it makes sense when you consider my other interests. I have skills as a street performer and entertainer, and realised that, while not the best way to make a living, these were very useful in engaging disaffected young people. Computer and presentation skills are also important in helping youngsters form social bonds and get into work. I regard myself as an informal educator rather than a social worker, and hope that my confidence with interactive practices will help to influence educational policy for young people.

1. **Do you think computers are socially enabling?**
2. **Do you put things on Facebook that you would not want your mother to see?**
3. **Have you ever solved a personal difficulty with a computer search?**

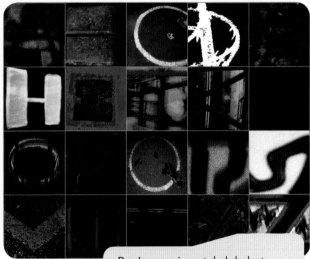

Ben's experimental alphabet – you can find thousands of alphabets like this on the web. Why not create one and post it up there?

User tester

User testing is a specialist area of interactive media. Testing interactive media has become essential as products have become ever more complex and detailed. The user tester may work as part of a team looking at all the aspects of the product, even testing the concept, but will not have been involved in the production – the more they know about the project beforehand, the more likely it is that problems will be missed. User testers not usually expected to fix things, just to point out where something doesn't work or is wrong. They can come from an art and design background, particularly product design, but may just have skills and experience linked to the subject of the product. Many games designers find that a lot of their work is testing other games products. Others are experts in understanding how we think and what motivates us, and have helped improve what is called the **human–computer interface**. The user tester may have to write clear and lengthy reports on projects, so writing skills are a huge advantage.

Key term

Human–computer interface – buttons, switches and levers have long been part of the way we control machines. Computers have emulated them on screen because they are useful visual metaphors, but this style of interface may soon disappear. We are understanding more and more about the human interface – expression, gesture, ideas linked through meaning, etc. – and the computer interface will start to be influenced by these more human ways of communicating.

Did you know?

Useful texts include *Paper Prototyping,* Carolyn Snyder (Morgan Kaufmann, 2003) and *The Essential Guide to Computing,* E. Garrison Walters (Prentice Hall, 2000).

Paper prototyping

Paper-prototyping is an important skill for interactive media. Many of the most complex projects will have started out and even been tested on paper before any artwork or programming has taken place. If you have a great idea but don't have the technical skills to carry it out, make it on paper. Paper-prototyping is cheap and effective, and interactive media companies can put a lot of resources into this area. A well-produced paper prototype shows you can think flexibly and focus on the problem at hand. Examples of interactive media on paper can include favourite websites or games, and are very useful in your portfolio.

Did you know?

Games like Zoombinis are fun and hide the real, serious purpose, which is to learn maths. Games are also great to sell advertising on the web – look at Games for Girls (www.girlgames1.com).

Activity: When will your mobile take you to Mars?

You will all have mobile phones or MP3 players. Do a comparison test on two different brands and see what makes one better than the other. Do a web search on the items and find out whether anyone else has noticed the differences. Or do a visit to a local place of interest and compare the real place with its website. Does it seem the same? Is it more or less interesting? Did the website tell you about what you found intriguing when you made a visit?

Paul Farrington
Interactive designer

I did a BTEC before taking a BA and MA at the Royal College of Art.

I love print and typography and still do traditional design commissions, but have always loved music as well. On my BA I started working with computers to develop a form of typography based on sound. I didn't know if it was a new form of cyber-art or if it had commercial possibilities, but a visiting professor – Brian Eno – encouraged me to believe that my experiments had worth.

If you had found this image on your screen, what would you think it was? Is it a logo? Is it a game? Are you meant to explore it? Are these buttons? Which would you click first – the black shape or one of the green ones?

Now working as Studio Tonne, I am also known for music festival posters and CDs, and belong to the generation that bridges old and new media. I love printing and paper, ink and varnish, as well as accidents and things that age. Although complex, the digital world risks becoming complacent and sterile – my current projects are moving into areas of theatre and dance.

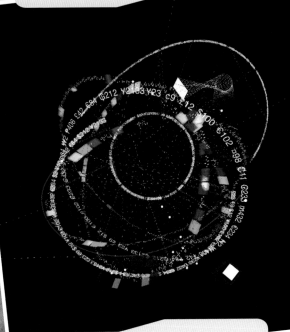

Paul's website (www.studiotonne.com) is full of ideas that use colour, text and sound. He has divided the site into an area for work and an area for play. It is interesting to see how many of the work ideas have come out of play.

Think about it!

- **Find a piece of well-known art and make it interactive. Mona Lisa's eyes follow visitors around the room – but could you tell her a joke? Tickle her? Make her laugh? What would she sound like?**

- **What digital toy would you like to see on the website of your favourite band? What would it look like? How would you persuade the band that they should have it on the site?**

Just checking

1. What are the main job roles in the interactive media sector? Can you identify the key skills and aptitudes needed for each of them?

2. How will you develop your skills to keep up with changes in technology that affect interactive media?

3. Have digital developments really made the world a 'global village' and is this a good thing?

4. What digital device has most profoundly affected your life and has it been good for you?

5. Can you think of ten areas of life that will never be influenced by digital processes? What should you never do with a computer?

6. Now that you can write your own biography and publish it on Wikipedia, what are you going to tell the world about yourself – and will anyone be interested? Can you find ways to make this personal data help you advance your real life?

7. In a digital world your 'domain name' will probably be more important to you than your own name – it will represent your personal profile and your brand. Your domain could be worth millions at the end of your life. What name are you going to choose and when are you going to create it and grow it?

8. If you could make a digital Avatar of yourself to release into the digital world, what would you have it do? Would you make it a force for Good or for Evil and how would you arrange this?

9. Modern computers work using billions of electronic logic gates. Human beings work using similar but biological or chemical systems. When we make computers work like we do, will they look like us?

edexcel

Assignment tips

- Get familiar with as many applications as you can – concentrate on what you need to know in order to create your ideas. Never learn a whole application for its own sake – if you see someone use a technique that you think may lead to an idea, then learn it. It may be useful, or it may be just an impressive trick. Either result is good for experience.

- Always use your own imagery, and make sure it looks good for the purpose you intend – screen or print. Take your digital camera with you all the time as well as your camera phone.

- Experiment constantly and save your experiments! You never know when they may be useful.

- Make files and folders on your web browser to build a database of sites you have found inspiring or useful. Make notes elsewhere about what you think about these sites.

- Try to remember that interactive media is the creative part of information technology, but is not synonymous with it. If IT is not your thing then IM may be.

3D design

3D design covers a multitude of disciplines and areas of art and design activity. Those working in industries such as architecture, product design, interior design, sculpture and installation art all call on the core skills and understanding that lie at the heart of 3D design practice. The practices and processes that 3D design practitioners use have changed due to technological advances, but at the heart of their work remains an appreciation of the nature of working in three dimensions to create artefacts, buildings and experiences that can be practical or beautiful – or both.

Whilst there has always been a strong emphasis on the initial expression of ideas in two dimensions, technological developments have altered the way 3D designers carry out many of their design processes. Computers have introduced computer-aided design software, such as ArchiCAD, which allows a designer to create 'virtual' versions of their design on screen before moving on to creating a maquette or prototype. By being able to view objects in three dimensions on a computer screen, designers can gain a more realistic preview of how their ideas will look when finished and alter or adjust their plans. Designers can also demonstrate their prospective work to clients or commissioning bodies and obtain feedback before translating designs into three dimensions.

This section is designed to give you an overview of the range of creative activity that falls within 3D design and includes:

- information about the sector
- information about job roles and careers
- case studies of students and young people who have just begun their creative careers
- case studies of experienced industry professionals.

Professional voice: Ellie Foster

Ellie Foster completed a BTEC Level 3 National course and BA (Hons) in 3D Design, specialising in furniture design. She now works for a company creating staging and props for the theatre and television industry. She offers the following advice.

1. Document all your ideas and the development of your designs, making sure that you keep detailed sketchbooks and annotated mood boards. This is essential to ensuring success, and will make changing ideas or working on future briefs easier by allowing you to refer back to development work; you can also often find inspiration in things you initially discarded.

2. Don't focus too much on one idea or solution to a problem – you will often need to adapt and change designs according to a client's needs. Developing and exploring a range of solutions to a problem will give you plenty of options.

3. Be professional. Make sure you have prepared thoroughly for meeting clients and conduct yourself professionally in all your dealings with people in the industry. Even little things, like spell-checking emails and annotations on design boards, will help to present you as a reliable professional.

Do you think you would enjoy working as a 3D designer for the theatre and television industry? Where else could you work as a 3D designer?

'I have found working in this sector rewarding and exciting, but it is a competitive field. Being professional and organised as well as creative will give you an advantage over other people competing for the same roles.'

Over to you!

- Ellie points out that conducting yourself professionally is important. Can you think of three reasons why it might be a bad idea not to spell-check your writing?
- As Ellie states, this is a competitive field. How will you ensure that you have an advantage over others competing for work in this area?

1. The 3D design sector

The 3D design sector is made up of a network of companies that produce products, furniture or artefacts on a large scale for mass markets, and smaller businesses that provide specialised services to specific audiences. There are also a small number of freelance individuals who provide services to clients.

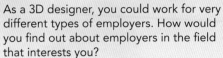

As a 3D designer, you could work for very different types of employers. How would you find out about employers in the field that interests you?

If you are interested in the design process behind large, expensive products such as, say, cars or motorbikes, you would need to look at employment in a company that produces on a mass scale. If you are more interested in architecture or interior design, there may be opportunities in smaller firms, or you could look into working as a freelancer.

1.1 Career pathways

Career pathways in this sector often mean moving on from Level 3 courses, such as BTECs, to higher education – usually in the form of a degree. The UCAS website will provide you with detailed lists of courses available in the areas that interest you. Sandwich courses offer opportunities to work in the industry for a year, enabling you to gain experience and build up contacts that can help you find employment when you graduate.

Skills councils are also useful places to gain information, such as Creative and Cultural Skills (www.ccskills.org.uk), which supports the cultural and creative sectors, including 3D design. CCS has also set up Creative Choices (www.creative-choices.co.uk) to give guidance and support on working in the industry, and enables you to see videos of designers offering advice on how to build a career in the design industry.

1.2 Areas within the 3D design industries

The 3D design sector covers a wide range of disciplines and areas of practice. The following is a guide to those that feature most prominently.

Architecture

Architects follow a highly specialised training in higher education, which usually focuses on the aesthetic dimension of structural design, either in pure architecture or subjects such as spatial or interior design. Architects need to have excellent organisational skills and an ability to communicate well with clients and team members. The field is also heavily reliant on understanding the technical aspects of design, so architecture-related degrees often ask for good grades in mathematics and possibly engineering skills. Maths Functional Skills studies could therefore be very useful if you didn't gain good Maths grades at GCSE.

Places on architecture courses are in high demand and universities usually ask that students provide a high grade in Level 3 studies and a good portfolio of work.

Signpost

In any form of design, a thorough understanding of historical design movements and schools is essential. In the Contextual influences in art and design unit you will learn how the work produced by established designers was influenced by the circumstances that surrounded them. Understanding the effect of context on the work of a designer will help develop an awareness of your own design practice. The analytical vocabulary and reference terms provided by this unit will be essential to communicating with other designers and clients.

Key terms

Prototype – a working example of a particular product or artefact that is used to demonstrate how a design might function or operate.

Ergonomics – the science of understanding how objects or space relate to the human body.

You will need more than strong design skills to succeed in the design industry. Do you have the necessary communication skills to interpret clients' ideas requirements and convey your ideas?

Case study: Charlotte

Charlotte completed a BTEC Level 3 National course in 3D design followed by an HND at university. Charlotte says she never realised how important her BTEC contextual studies would be: 'I didn't appreciate at the time that I would refer to the design movements and practitioners we looked at constantly once at Uni and working in the industry. A lot of what I learned has become shorthand when communicating ideas. For example, I can describe a feature as having an "Art Deco sunburst" look to it, and my colleagues know immediately what I mean. I wouldn't be able to do this without my contextual studies folder, which I still use today, six years after finishing my BTEC course!'

In the Contextual influences in art and design unit, you will look at a wide range of movements and practitioners. By doing some brief Internet research, can you discover how looking at the design movements suggested might be useful to a designer working on the following briefs?

Design brief	Movement
Designing functional office furniture	The Bauhaus School
Designing the interior of a luxury cabin on a cruise liner	Art Deco
Designing a range of jewellery based on natural forms such as flowers and insects	Art Nouveau

Table 1: Investigating design movements.

Product design

Product design is a wide and varied field. The scale and nature of products demanded by the industry will dictate the role of the designer. Usually driven by a client brief or market need, product design can supply the end user with a service, assist with a task or provide an entertainment or activity.

An example of a designer responding to human need can be seen in the Anglepoise Lamp, designed by George Carwardine in 1932. This style of lighting, designed to direct light towards a specific area, has become a design classic and is still the **prototype** for much lighting in offices and homes today. Other carefully designed everyday objects include the Evian 'Active' water bottle, redesigned in 2001 by the PA Consulting Group to answer the needs of people using the product 'on the move', whether working or exercising. The designers added a leak-proof drinking spout and an **ergonomically** designed shape, which provided indentations and a textured surface for gripping the bottle at the centre, a style that has since been adopted by many different drinks manufacturers.

Innovations in product design may be practical, beautiful or both.

Those working in product design will usually rise through the ranks of a design organisation, beginning as a junior designer, assisting with project work and providing design support for others' ideas. They may then progress to a design team, creating their own ideas and solutions, and carrying these designs forward for consideration by a client or senior design team. Eventually, some product designers move into a senior design position, focusing mainly on selecting and guiding the work of others.

Functional skills

Mathematics

In all forms of design, precision can be essential in ensuring that your designs are produced effectively and the finished item is fit for purpose. When designing items such as exhibition stands or stage sets, measuring and calculating space, size and volume accurately is crucial to working professionally and effectively. Miscalculating the size of an object for use on stage could result in an item that is useless and wasting money and time. When working in such areas, the skills of accurate measurement and calculating scale, which you will gain from Functional Skills Maths, will be essential for functioning professionally.

Activity: Role play

Design is about fulfilling the need of a client or market. Imagine you are employed by a company specialising in disability needs similar to the one that Jane works for (see WorkSpace, p. 199). You have been approached by an organisation that works with the visually impaired. They have highlighted some day-to-day tasks that are difficult for those with limited vision and asked you to generate ideas for design solutions.

Task 1

To gain an insight into the challenges faced by those with visual impairment, working with a partner select a safe environment indoors and blindfold one of you with a cloth; the one wearing the blindfold should then attempt to perform a series of simple tasks, such as using a mobile phone or opening a bag and removing a given item. A blindfolded person will discover how difficult this is without the sense of sight, and an observer will see how other senses are used to compensate for the missing visual information.

Task 2

You will now use this experience for the next stage of the activity. For each of the challenging situations highlighted below, work in pairs to find out why these activities may be difficult for a partially sighted person and what dangers or risks they may present. Then consider how you could overcome these challenges through clever design and by making use of other senses. How could touch or sound by used to replace visual information?

Challenging situation	Associated dangers and risks	Potential design solutions
Selecting the correct control switches on a cooker hob		
Operating the locks on standard double-glazed window fittings		
Checking the level of water inside a kettle		
Using a wristwatch		

Table 2: Solutions to challenges for people with a visual impairment.

Signpost

Product designers often need to work closely with those using 2D techniques, such as graphic designers, to develop a product's aesthetic quality. For example, a product designer creating a range of food containers may need to collaborate with a designer developing the logo and labels for the containers. Because both graphic and product designers will have different ideas about how the item should look, careful teamwork is needed to ensure that their respective ideas are considered and that they produce a product they can both feel proud of and is fit for purpose. Although you may not have skills in graphic design, you need to be aware of what the field involves to work effectively with graphic designers when developing 3D products. See also the Graphic design unit.

Interior design

Interior designers usually work as freelancers, either operating as small businesses taking commissions from clients or providing services to larger companies on a contract basis.

The work of a freelance interior designer usually involves identifying how a space is to be used and its aesthetic requirements. In most cases a budget will be discussed early on to ensure that the client has a clear idea of project costs, and the designer is aware of the financial parameters.

There will usually be a stage when the designer formulates some initial ideas and plans, such as mood boards, to reflect the overall tone of the work. They will also map out some sketches and have regular meetings with the client to ensure that the designs meet requirements. The designer may then transfer some of their designs to a software package in order to create a virtual version of the finished 3D design. The designer then moves on to implementing the plans, selecting furniture, wall coverings, soft furnishings, decorative features, lighting, and accessories and fixtures such as windows and doors to complement the completed space. At this stage they may also commission bespoke pieces from furniture, glassware, ceramic or textile designers, to create a specific aesthetic or tone.

Some interior designers obtain contracts with companies that undertake regular interior alterations. Many hotel and restaurant chains, shop franchises, department stores and supermarkets will have in-house interior design teams, whose designs are replicated identically in different locations. Such designers will usually have the ability to create a strong corporate identity and visual style and use this to give an organisation an individual look.

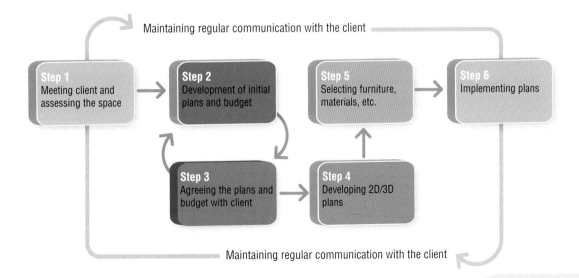

Figure 1: Stages of working on a brief as an interior designer.

Activity: Investigating corporate identity

Corporate identity is a feature of many design briefs, and large organisations will often have strict guidelines over how their business should look. Make a list of some major organisations or multinational companies, and of visual items related to them, e.g., McDonalds: the 'golden arches' M logo, the Ronald McDonald mascot, the colours red and yellow, and so on.

Using the Internet, try to locate images of head offices or administrative buildings for these companies. Can you see elements of their corporate identities within the images?

Print out your images and annotate any examples of corporate identity you can identify.

What challenges could you face as a 3D designer working in the film industry?

Theatre, television and film design

Some 3D designers work within the media industry, building props, sets and staging for theatre, television or film productions. In the theatre, most designers will work under a director, who will have a view of how the play is to look. He/she will communicate what is required of the designers, who may work as part of a larger team with a costume designer and hair and make-up artists.

In the television and film industries, an art director will usually decide what is to be produced visually and what is to be expected of the designs. He/she will communicate with the director and producer to ensure that all designs are appropriate. Many roles, from prop maker to art director and beyond will be contracted on an ad hoc basis to different companies. Though there may also be permanent design positions in theatre companies or media organisations, most companies will employ freelancers according to their previous work and experience.

Success in this area depends on the ability to work professionally and to very tight deadlines. The live nature of theatre and the expense involved in television and film production demands that designers work fast and efficiently to prescriptive briefs.

Activity: Professional behaviour

Several design professionals discussed in this section mention the importance of maintaining a professional attitude. In the table below, see if you can explain how you would demonstrate professionalism in the area given. There is an example to help you.

Challenge	Action
Maintaining time effectively	Always arrive for meetings five minutes early
Effective communication	
Appropriate personal presentation	
Courtesy	
Ability to adapt	

Table 3: Solutions to professional behaviour challenges.

Jane Singleton
Product designer

Jane Singleton is a product designer, working for a company that makes items that support people with limited mobility within their home.

She first came across the concept of ergonomics and the importance of creating designs that work with the human body while studying for a BTEC National course in 3D design. Jane continued her studies at degree level, where she specialised in looking at how designers comply with accessibility and disability discrimination laws and guidelines.

'I love my job as it really pushes me to be creative. Often clients working with those with limited mobility give us guidance on the tasks and activities that people find difficult, and I then have to generate workable solutions to these issues.

The greatest reward is knowing that something I have designed might be used by someone every day, and could in a small way help make their life better.'

Jane finds she uses what she learned on her BTEC course on a daily basis in her work.

'Before my BTEC I really didn't appreciate the importance of considering the human form in design. Now, with every design, I use what I learned about ergonomics as well as the practical skills the course gave me in using ArchiCAD and Photoshop.'

Products such as this can make a huge difference to the everyday lives of people with limited mobility. How would you develop and refine your ideas for a product like this?

Think about it!

- Have you completed any briefs that considered how an item/room/product will be used by people?
- How did this influence the decisions you made?
- Can you think of any designs that would involve considering ergonomics and human interaction?

Just checking

1. Where would you go to find more information about how to get into the area of 3D design that interests you most?

2. Why is behaving in a professional manner so important for a successful 3D designer?

3. Why might it be useful to gain an understanding of other design fields, such as graphic design, when preparing to work in the industry?

4. Which areas of the industry are you most likely to be working in on a freelance basis?

edexcel :::

Assignment tips

- Always maintain up-to-date information about the sector and developments in the design industry. Libraries often stock industry journals and publications, and there is a vast amount of information available on the Internet. By its nature, design is something that moves with the times. You need to maintain a current understanding of design trends and fashions.

- Keep a visual diary of things that inspire, intrigue, interest or please you visually. Collect them together and create a source book of items, including postcards, leaflets, product labels, photographs or any other visual references you find. This can be very inspirational as you develop new designs.

- Stay observant. If you ever find yourself frustrated by something that doesn't work as it should, is difficult to operate or you find particularly aesthetically offensive – make a note of it. See if you can come up with solutions for how these things could be improved. Developing ideas is a skill that improves with practice, so get thinking, and when the time comes to answer a brief you will be ready!

Textiles

From the production of raw fibres to the making and trading of fabrics and clothes, textiles are a major global industry, employing designers, scientists, technologists, engineers, manufacturers, and marketing and sales specialists. The textile industry also includes the manufacture of accessories such as shoes and bags, and the textile service industry which includes laundry, dry cleaning and repair services.

The work of textile designers can be applied commercially to fashion, clothing, accessories, interiors and stage and screen costumes, and can be sold in shops and galleries or made to commission for individual clients.

As part of your Textiles pathway, you may find yourself exploring the following activities:

- fibre spinning and weaving
- making knitted and crochet fabrics
- making non-woven fabrics by bonding fibres
- making felted fabrics from fibres or knitted cloths
- producing designs for fashion, interiors and other surfaces such as paper and ceramics
- manufacturing articles including household textiles, clothes, knitwear and accessories such as bags and footwear.

This unit is designed to give you an overview of the various specialisms within textiles and the type of work undertaken in each, and includes:

- information about the sector, job roles and careers and the necessary skills required
- information about specialist areas within textiles and what the work might entail
- case studies and observations by students and young people who have begun their creative careers
- case studies of experienced industry professionals.

Professional voice: Marnie Miles

Marnie Miles studied for a BTEC in Art and Design specialising in textile design, followed by a degree course at university in constructed textiles; she now produces woven fabric which she sells to commercial and private clients. Her inspiration comes from colours found along the coasts of Britain and Jamaica.

Marnie's woven cloth is used for fashion accessories such as silk scarves and clutch bags and for exclusive curtain and upholstery fabric. Twice a year, she also designs a collection of weaves which she makes up as sample cloths. These samples are exhibited at trade fairs throughout the world, either through an agent or by Marnie herself working with a group of other weavers. If a sample is sold to a commercial weaver, she may be asked to develop the idea further, or her work will be commercially produced for curtains or upholstery or adapted using different colourways and yarns. Marnie works freelance and has to follow contemporary trends and ideas in order to create fabrics that are different and exclusive.

'As a weave designer I have to know about the ideas that fabric makers are producing and be aware of trend forecasting.'

Over to you!

- Examine some woven textiles that are used for upholstery fabrics. Then compare and contrast these with different textiles used for curtains. Why are these fabrics often very different?
- How do weavers reflect their inspiration in their work?

What seasons do these colours make you think about?

What might have inspired this fabric?

1. The textile industry

The UK textile industry is thriving and generates almost £6 billion per year for the national economy, yet most British textile businesses employ fewer than ten people.

Textile services sector

- Money this sector contributes to the UK economy each year: £1.1 billion

- Businesses in sector: 13,000 enterprises of which 11,000 are sole traders with no employees. 50,000 employed in the industry. 55% female

Figure 1: Pie chart showing the relative sizes of the sectors based on the total number of businesses in each sector. 75 per cent of textile companies employ fewer than ten people. Only 7 per cent employ more than 50 people. How might this affect your choice of textile career?

Textiles sector

- Money this sector contributes to the UK economy each year: £4.1 billion

- Exports: £3 billion

- Businesses in sector: 26,000 enterprises of which around 20,000 are sole traders with no employees. 105,000 employed in the industry. 64% male

Footwear and leather sector

- Money this sector contributes to the UK economy each year: £700 million

- Exports: £1 billion

- Businesses in sector: 4,600 enterprises of which 3,000 are sole traders with no employees. 27,000 employed in the industry. 61% male

Key terms

Textiles sector – this sector includes spinning, weaving, knitting, dyeing and finishing, carpets, narrow fabrics, ribbons, technical textiles, man-made fibres and wholesale textiles.

Footwear and leather sector – this sector includes fellmongery, which is cleaning and preparing hide for leather, leather processing, manufacture of leather goods, footwear, shoe repair and wholesale leather.

Textile services sector – this sector includes commercial and in-house laundries, dry-cleaning services, work wear and linen rental for the hospitality industry.

Historically, the greatest concentration of industrial activity was in West Yorkshire and Lancashire, and was linked to the cotton mills of the industrial revolution. Other parts of the UK also have a long tradition of weaving, knitting and textile production.

Over the last 25 years much textile production has moved overseas, which has meant fewer jobs in

the UK. Skillfast, the textile sector skills council, says that 25,000 skilled professionals will be needed over the next few years to replace older workers retiring. As 73 per cent of the workforce is aged 35 or over, there is therefore a need to attract new, young talent into the industry, and skilled personnel are also in demand in technical development, management, administration, sales/marketing and research.

Figure 2: Map showing the location of historical/traditional centres of textile production in the UK.

Most textile companies specialise in producing a specific type of product:

- Flexitec Structures in Fareham, Hampshire, produce engineered flexible textile structures for transporting liquids such as wine.
www.flexitec.com

- Axminster carpets, based in Devon, have been producing high-quality goods for over 250 years.
www.axminster-carpets.co.uk

- Heathcoat Fabrics, also in Devon, make bridal nets and tulles, as well as fabrics for healthcare, sail cloth, and flame retardant and camouflage fabrics for the military.
www.heathcoat.co.uk

- Offray specialise in high-tech fabrics for things like parachutes, and fabrics integrated with electronics. Their advanced engineering work has also led to the development of smart textiles, which could make wearable computers a reality.
www.osnf.com/p_smart.html

- Mulberry in Somerset makes handbags, luggage and accessories.
www.mulberry.com

Did you know?

Designers may take the credit, but their work wouldn't be the same without the finishing touches of the embroiderers and other handworkers who transform an outfit into a work of art. The House of Lesage is the oldest embroidery atelier in Paris and here you will find seamstresses and embroiderers stitching hundreds of tiny pearl, crystal and glass beads onto fabrics for catwalk shows.

Activity: Starting points for textiles

Visit your local department store, where you can see fashion clothes produced by a variety of companies. Department stores are useful for this activity because they host a variety of fashion houses under one roof. Choose fashion houses that offer different specialisms – Phase Eight, Kaliko, East and Wallis all offer day and evening wear. For each fashion label you have chosen:

1. Look at and note down the fabrics used for different garments. You will have to look carefully at the label or price ticket for this information.

2. Record how the fabrics are made. Are they woven, knitted or felted?

3. Record how the garments are decorated. For example, if a garment is knitted, see if it includes a pattern, such as Fair Isle, cable or other fancy knit stitch, or has a design been printed on the fabric?

4. Record the colours, patterns, embellishments, the feel of the fabrics, their name and the scale of patterns.

5. How suitable is the fabric and decoration in relation to the purpose of the garment? Has the designer made a good choice?

You might choose to narrow your research to one type of garment such as women's outer wear, leisure wear or children's wear.

Present your findings to your group. You will need to make sure your notes are clear and that you concentrate on the fabrics and their decorations.

Did you know?

Painters and sculptors have designed textiles for many years. Henry Moore was a sculptor but he collaborated with textile manufacturer Zika Ascher during the Second World War to produce coloured silk scarves that helped to brighten up outfits in the post-war era.

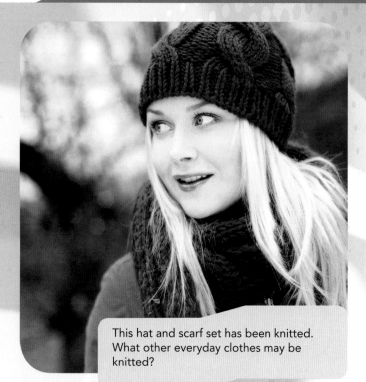

This hat and scarf set has been knitted. What other everyday clothes may be knitted?

Case study: Textiles and the economy

Dr Paul Holdstock of Holdstock Technical Services says: 'Technical textiles are an integral part of our everyday lives and form a vital part of the UK and world economy. The high-performance textile sector alone generates over £1 billion for the UK economy every year. We use and interact with technical textiles from the moment we are born, and rely on their performance and protection throughout our working lives and during our leisure time. The development and production of technical textiles requires dedicated scientists, engineers, technologists and designers. The traditional textile technologies of spinning, weaving, knitting and surface decoration are just the start. Physics, chemistry, materials science, human physiology and many other disciplines are all essential elements.'

1. **Name some examples of high-performance clothing that require higher-level design and technical roles to produce.**

2. **Why are technical roles important?**

3. **What are the technical skills valued by the industry?**

1.1 What does a career in textiles mean?

Working in the textile industry can mean a role in any of the following areas:

- **Design** – textile designers who specialise in fashion might be producing ideas for commercial mass production, exclusive fashion houses or one-off ideas for private clients, boutiques and galleries. Designers who specialise in interiors could be producing ideas for curtains, carpets, upholstery fabrics, accessories or decoration.

- **Manufacture** – specialist roles include spinners, dye house operatives, weavers, fabric bonders, knitters, printers and leather producers. Operatives are skilled and need specialist process knowledge. Footwear manufacturers supply different market levels from high-street brands to Jimmy Choo, as well as sports and orthopaedic wear. Leather goods and accessories include the manufacture

Leather goods production includes shoes, belts, handbags and luggage.

of luggage and handbags. The bulk of UK leather production is found in South Wales and Scotland. Technical roles include textile technicians who are responsible for the upkeep and maintenance of equipment and machinery. There is already concern over technical skills shortage, particularly in the footwear and leather industries.

- **Research and development** – textile technologists develop and test fibres, fabrics, colourants and machinery. Much of their work will cross other industries. For example, smart fabrics are of interest to a wide range of scientists, designers and engineers, such as those involved in electronics, medicine, sport, communication and fashion. There are opportunities for degree and postgraduate study in textile technology and for those with qualifications in textile and fabric technology and in fabric development and design.

- **Service industry** – this includes laundry and dry-cleaning operatives, clothing alteration workers, shoe repairers and pressers. All these jobs are supported by technical staff and engineers who maintain and keep the industry operating. Customer service is important in the textile service industry and there are also management positions available. As with other sectors, the service industry also has a skills shortage.

- **Sales, retail and marketing** – wholesalers supply yarns and fabrics to manufacturers of the clothing trade, while retailers sell finished products. There are careers available in management administration, sales, warehousing and distribution. The largest concentration of textile wholesalers in the UK is in north-west England.

Remember

Textile artists, designers and craft workers need to understand and have experience of a wide range of materials and technical skills to help them create original work.

Case study: Nina Fraser, textile artist

Textiles art often combines fabrics with mixed media.

After doing a BTEC course, Nina Fraser took a degree course at Winchester School of Art which allowed her to experiment with techniques ranging from animation and screen-printing to model making and computer-aided design. Nina often creates individual pieces that become part of a larger picture when combined in an installation, an approach that is integral to all her current projects. Global and social issues and concerns are a major influence in her ideas, which she often combines with nostalgic childhood references to create an attractive yet uneasy juxtaposition of imagery. Her awareness of the textile industry and, in particular, the sweatshops in developing countries, drives her to create work to inspire social change, in collaboration with the UK-based anti-sweatshop campaign, No Sweat. Nina has also created a series of pieces for a show at a non-profit arts café she helped to set up. This project was supported by other skills learnt during her degree course, such as time management, criticism and self-promotion.

1. **What skills have you learnt throughout your textile course?**

2. **What does ethical trading entail?**

3. **Research the ethical policies of leading textile firms. What can you find out?**

Activity: Skills audit for the textile industry

There are significant skills shortages in the textile industry which will increase over the next few years as people retire. Currently, about 50 per cent of employers report skills shortages.

1. List your transferable skills. Think about how well you work in a team, and if you enjoy research.

2. What sort of role would suit you? Are you interested in science or technology? Do you enjoy designing or making?

3. What additional skills will help you in a textile career? How can you improve the skills you have?

Find out more about textile careers by looking on the Skillfast website:

www.skillfast-uk.org/justthejob

Many people in the textiles sector are self-employed. They might be designers, makers or craft specialists, such as those who make hand-stitched decorations, quilts, hats, pictures and toys. Self-employed people are multi-skilled because they have to handle all the different areas of their business, from making to sales.

Handstitching is used to produce unique pieces of work.

Job	Description
Weaver	Produces collections of sample woven fabrics to sell to commercial buyers at trade fairs. Buyers either use the ideas as they are or pass them to production designers to adapt.
Quilt maker	Makes one-off quilts to sell to commission or through exhibition.
Textile artist	Makes and sells one-off pieces to commission or through art galleries.
Museum curator and researcher	A specialist textile curator understands how textiles were made in the past and how to preserve printed fabric and paper designs for future generations.
Technical textile designer	Specialises in research and development of performance textiles, which involves testing fibres and fabrics and recording results.
Textile production engineer	Responsible for making sure textile manufacturing equipment and production processes run safely and cost-effectively, and for troubleshooting problems.
Textile scientist	Devises new products to meet certain specifications. May work in a range of industry sectors including dyeing, the medical industry or laboratories developing synthetic fibres, all of which require knowledge of chemistry. Scientists may also be active in developing flame- and heat-retardant clothing for industry, the military and fire services. Also investigates customer problems and faults and keeps up to date with new technologies.
Laundry manager	Services large hotels and hospitals as well as dry-cleaning fine items such as evening dresses. Responsibilities include customer service as well as technical knowledge of processes.
Quality control inspector	Oversees, for example, fabric printing in a small factory that designs and prints fabrics for independent textile designers. Checks that colours are correct, print is accurate and fabric is finished to a high standard.
Forecaster	Highlights style trends in fabrics, textures and patterns, and helps businesses to analyse trend forecasts and use them to maximise product sales.

Table 1: Job roles in the textile industry.

Activity: Colourways

Colourways tend be seasonal to reflect collections at different times of the year. If you were asked to design two collections based on treacle and candy colours:

- what time of the year would each collection be staged?
- what colours would you use for each collection?

Predict colours for next summer and link them with patterns and designs from other cultures.

Did you know?

Textile conservators are essential to establishing the history of textiles. We know from conservators about ancient fabric styles and designs, and about dyestuffs used on textiles made in biblical times. Some of the oldest fabrics have been found in Egypt and China. Even 20th-century fabrics need conserving from daylight and wear and tear.

See www.vam.ac.uk/collections/textiles/caring_textiles for more information.

Activity: Fibre technology

Fibre technologists study the properties of fibres. These include the strengths and flexibilities as well as the chemicals and colours used to make permanent colours or patterns.

In a simple table like the one below, write a list of the fibres, fabrics and yarns you use in your textile work.

Name of fibre/fabric	Dyes/paints used	Type, e.g. woven, knitted, bonded	Fixing methods	Washing qualities	Finish

- Analyse each fabric/fibre/yarn and fill in the chart. Keep the table going as a technical reference and note which dyes work well, gradually building up this information in a small technical file. Look at websites to understand more about fibres and fabrics, such as www.fabrics.net/cotton.asp or http://en.wikipedia.org/wiki/Fabrics.

Now look at performance fabrics. You have been asked to recommend a fabric to a fashion designer to produce **one** of the following:

- an outdoor one-piece waterproof suit for a toddler for winter and spring. The fabric needs to be tough but light.
- a fabric to make a warm but lightweight hip-length jacket for a teenager, to be worn from autumn through to spring.

Do this by researching performance fabrics. You will find these in sport shops and outdoor activity shops. Look at **six** different garments and take notes under the following headings:

- name of garment and manufacturer (e.g. ski jacket)
- fibre/fabric, especially noting how fabric construction and properties contribute to end use – is it stretchy/firm/warm/light/heavy?
- finish – such as waterproof, showerproof, waxed
- cleaning instructions.

All this information should be found on the label. Make a simple table with these headings and record your results.

Produce a statement that explains your choices.

1.2 Textile design techniques

Fashion textile designers work either as **freelancers** or for a fashion house, and will specialise in specific areas of making and decoration.

Printed decoration is where a design is applied to the surface of a plain cloth, and includes digital printing, screen printing, dyeing, painting, block printing and resist methods such as batik. These can be used in a range of applications, including home fabrics (curtains, bed linen, upholstery) and fashion and paper (gift-wrap and wallpaper).

Woven, knitted, felt, hooked and knotted textiles are examples of constructed fabrics that integrate pattern into the material itself. Felt, which is one of the oldest forms of fabric, is composed of wool, but may also be combined with silk and other materials.

Embroidery is the art of embellishing fabrics using hand and machine stitches, and is produced for fashion, accessories and interiors. The Embroiderers' Guild UK provides embroiderers with a member's network and exhibition opportunities, and has a collection of over 11,000 embroidered objects housed at Hampton Court Palace in London (www.embroiderersguild.com).

Key term

Freelancer – someone who works for themselves and is not commited to one employer.

Compare and contrast the work of Zandra Rhodes (right) and Cressida Bell (left). What types of repeat patterns do they use?

Caroline McNamara
Textile designer

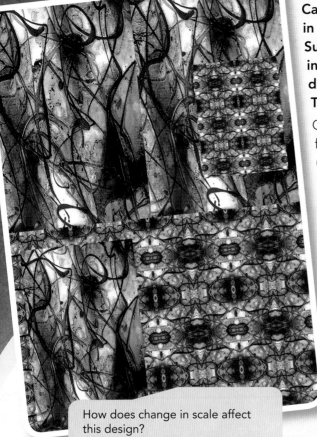

Caroline McNamara took an HNC in Textiles, followed by a BA (Hons) in Surface design and a postgraduate Diploma in Digital surface design. She now specialises in digital surface design and is studying for an MA in Textile culture.

Caroline draws inspiration from many different sources for her textile work, such as the Warner Textile Archives (Braintree, Essex), the Victoria and Albert Museum Print Archives (London) and local textiles in Carrow House, Norwich.

Caroline produces a huge amount of photography to support her designs, which include wallpaper patterns, ceramics, purses and bags; she also creates digitally produced designs for goods such as china tableware, wallpaper, gift-wrap, cushions and clothes.

How does change in scale affect this design?

She sells her work through exhibitions and museum shops, and works freelance in a variety of textile/surface design disciplines including teaching embroidery. By being an active member of the Wallpaper History Society, the Textile Society and the Eastern Region Textile Forum, Caroline regularly updates her skills and ideas to make sure her work looks different and keeps current.

What type of repeat pattern is this? What forms of repeat pattern can you identify in other designs?

Think about it!

- **When producing paper textile designs, can you visualise them on a variety of items?**
- **How might a change of scale affect your work?**
- **Explore repeat patterns. Can you repeat a design using a CAD package?**
- **What are your sources of inspiration?**
- **How can you make use of your photographs?**

Did you know?

Hand knitters are an important part of the knitwear industry, where designers work for yarn houses such as Rowan, Sirdar or Patons. See the UK handknitting website for more information, www.bhkc.co.uk or www.ukhandknitting.com

Hand & Lock (London) have been making hand-embroidered **embellishments** for fashion and ecclesiastical garments and military insignia since 1767. See their website at www.handembroidery.com

Functional skills

ICT, Mathematics and English

Researching seasonal collections will help develop your ICT skills. Scaling patterns up and down, and working out dye, yarn and fabric quantities will all evidence your Mathematics skills.

Writing reports on textiles and textile designers, or completing applications for higher education, apprenticeships or employment opportunities will demonstrate your English and ICT skills.

Key terms

Embellishment – something that adds interest to a design piece such as shiny threads, beads or sequins.

Did you know?

Orla Kiely is a UK textile designer who produces work across a range of applications. Her visual language has been developed through graphic patterns that have become a signature style. Designs can be found on womenswear, household textiles, travel and homeware, as well as on bags and accessories (see www.orlakiely.com).

Constructed and stitched textiles have a long history that cuts across cultures and continents.

Sara Impey
Quilt designer and textile magazine editor

Sara Impey trained as a journalist, before exploring textiles and starting to make and exhibit quilts and patchwork. She is interested in repeat patterns and oppositions of positive and negative, and prefers to work with simple geometric designs inside a grid system.

Sara says she is led by technique – taking a particular method and exploring it over a number of quilts. In the past, inspiration has come from patterns in landscape or the weather, but in the last five years her quilts have incorporated stitched text in a simple format of one letter per square. She also derives ideas from social commentary and Internet blogs. A current piece of work contrasts dance performance with digital imagery and quilting.

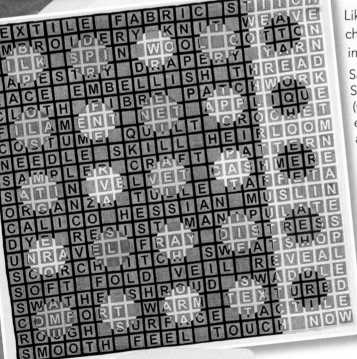

Like dance rehearsal for a choreographer, the process is as important to her as the finished object.

Sara sells her work through exhibitions. She belongs to European Group Quilt Art (www.quiltart.org.uk), which has regular touring exhibitions in Europe and the UK. Her work is also represented in the American Museum of Arts and Design in New York and she has been commissioned to make a quilt for the Victoria and Albert Museum in London. Sara co-edits *Textiles Perspectives*, which covers textile subjects past and present, especially the sociological context of their making and how they affect women's lives.

This quilt is called *Context* and it is extremely detailed. Go to www.quiltart.org.uk/saraimpey.html and run your cursor over the quilt to see an enlarged view.

Think about it!

- How important is the process of thinking through an idea and understanding a technique to your textile work?
- Can you name some painters and textile designers who have been inspired by geometric shapes?

Just checking

1. What are the properties of the threads and fabrics you use in your work?

2. Do you know which textile dyes and paints are permanent? How are they fixed to the fabric? Can they be washed?

3. How many ways can you make a repeat pattern?

4. Are the materials you use affected by sunlight? What difference would this make to your outcomes?

5. Which textile markets do you sell samples to and why?

6. Which textile markets do you sell paper designs to and why?

7. What is a colourway and why are colourways important?

Assignment tips

- Understanding techniques enables textile designers and makers to ensure the quality of their work. Perfect your techniques – keep a special notebook for recording the dyes you use on fabric, note down recipes, fixing methods and times, and attach samples against your notes. Dyes are variable and many textile pieces can be ruined by unstable dyes – test yours by leaving a small piece on a window ledge for at least two weeks with one half covered up. Then compare the two sides.

- Keep cards and coloured papers with interesting colours and patterns to use as collage materials; be aware of current trends; find designers that re-use imagery in their work.

- Designers often study the past to get ideas. Look at the textile work of these designers to see if your work can be inspired by theirs. Many of the designers listed below use strong repeat patterns.

  - Baron and Larcher

  - Enid Marx

  - Lucienne Day

  - Vanessa Bell and Duncan Grant

  - Marianne Straub

  - Kaffe Fassett

  - Sasha Kagan

  - Candace Bahouth.

Design crafts

Design crafts is a vast creative sector covering many disciplines and involving numerous creative businesses. A large number of people set up as sole traders and work for themselves as designer-makers of jewellery, ceramics and woodwork. The sector also includes artists and designers specialising in, for example, glass-making, graphic crafts, textiles, toys and automata. According to Creative and Cultural Skills, the craft sector employs over 88,000 people in the UK and contributes approximately £3 billion to the economy each year.

The Crafts Council is the national development agency representing crafts; this agency commissions economic studies to assess the employment and financial output of the sector. Creative and Cultural Skills is the sector skills council for craft, which has developed the Craft Blueprint, how craft will be taught, and the National Occupational Standards for Crafts (in association with the Crafts Council).

A design crafts background can also take you into a wide range of industries such as architecture, textiles, fine art, sculpture, surface pattern design, product design, packaging design, automotive design and interior design. Among design crafts students there is often a synergy between their use of design skills and material and technical knowledge to create products.

This section is designed to give you an overview of the different activities, crafts and designers that make up the design crafts sector. It includes:

- opportunities for developing your career
- skills you might need within your specialism
- activities to try out
- case studies of designer-makers.

Professional voice:
Tanvi Kant

The award winning jewellery maker Tanvi Kant, who has a BA in crafts from Derby University, makes jewellery from reclaimed fabrics and hand-formed ceramics, using both design and craft skills. Tanvi exhibits her work at selected craft fairs and international exhibitions.

'Old saris, which are bound and lined with hand-formed ceramic discs, are among my favourite fabrics to use. My work has a sustainable and ecological ethos, and shows that re-purposed materials can be made into subtle contemporary pieces.'

Drawing is also a strong theme in Tanvi's work; she has just completed an international residency using visual studies based on drawing and photography to gather information, and developing these through drawing and illustration. These designs were then translated into three-dimensional pieces using textiles and other materials.

Studying design crafts gave Tanvi a multi-disciplined background and helped her develop both making and transferable design skills. Tanvi is a good example of how an artist's career develops and changes over time depending on the types of opportunity available. She also demonstrates how the skills needed to design and make work can be applied to different materials and techniques.

Over to you!

- **What skills do you think Tanvi needs to work in the materials she uses?**
- **Have a look at some of Tanvi's work at www.tanvikant.co.uk. Who do you think the audience for her work is?**

Necklace made from recycled, bound materials. What materials could you use to make jewellery?

1. The design crafts sector

About 80 per cent of craft businesses employ fewer than five people. Traditional ways of earning a living are through making and selling work at markets, craft fairs and exhibitions, as well as through the Internet, either via your own website or through online galleries and marketing sites such as Etsy and Bigcartel. Another way to make money is through licensing and selling design ideas and rights, so your products can be made into large-volume productions. Teaching can also supplement your income and is a useful way to keep your skills up to date and make contact with people – it can be very lonely working on your own in the studio every day.

Websites – the Crafts Council is the national development agency for promoting the crafts in the UK, which publishes the magazine *Crafts* and has a very useful website (www.craftscouncil.org. uk).

Other sources of support and information include the British Council, which can help promote your work overseas, the Design Council and the Arts Council. There are also regional development agencies, and some local councils provide funding and support for small businesses. Visit www.britishcouncil.org, www.artscouncil.org.uk and www.designcouncil.org.uk

1.1 Careers

There are many specialist design crafts which have close links with each other. Popular areas are jewellery, metalwork, forged metal, glass (fused/ stained/ blown), ceramics (functional/sculptural), toy making (puppets/wooden/ fabric), automata, furniture, woodwork, mixed media and musical instruments. Related areas can include fine art, animation, set design, prop-making, animatronics, architecture, packaging design, product design, surface pattern and carpentry. All include making as well as design skills. Some artists will work in more than one material, but many will specialise in one technique and material to make their work unique.

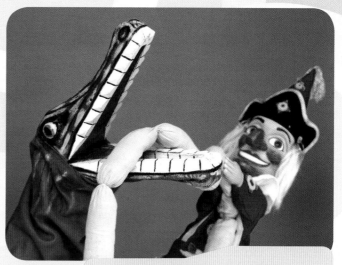

Have you investigated all the areas relating to design crafts?

Designer-makers

Jeweller – many jewellers work alone, sometimes from home or in shared studios, producing work to their own designs and selling them through retail outlets. They may also work to commission for customers, making objects such as wedding rings. The case study on Rachel Galley shows how she developed her business after working for other people and is now a limited company selling through luxury shops and a television shopping channel. Tanvi Kant is also a jeweller but has a different approach and each product is unique.

How did Rachel Galley develop her business? Read the Case study on page 219 for more ideas.

Ceramicist – pottery and ceramics are made by ceramicists. The work produced can be either functional, like tableware, or sculptural and decorative. Designer-makers use a range of techniques, including slip-casting (using liquid clay and moulds), hand-building (using slabs or coils of clay) and throwing (using a potter's wheel). Work is then glazed and fired in a kiln and sold through shops, galleries and craft fairs. Larger companies employ designers who use CAD computer programs to design a prototype which can be a design, an image of what the final product might be or a 3D model. This can then be used to make moulds and slip-cast pots for mass production. Surface-pattern designers create designs for transfers and decals which are printed in sheets before being applied to work which is then fired again in the kiln to make the pattern permanent.

What specific conditions are necessary when working with wood?

How many different types of places can you think of where you could sell design crafts products? Read the case studies in this chapter to give you some clues.

Did you know?

CAD computer programs: Companies may use a program such as Rhino/3D Studio Max to design the form, which is then made in resin and called rapid prototyping. The model is then reviewed or a mould is taken in order to make the final articles.

Woodworker – wood can be turned on a lathe to make bowls and containers, or can be used to make furniture. This is a popular sustainable material and woodworkers have a very environmentally friendly image. Handmade furniture is usually bespoke – made to order to meet a customer's needs. Wood is highly versatile but requires a lot of skill and equipment, and woodworkers often need a lot of space to store and work the wood. They also need workshops with extractors and ventilation for a safe working environment. Customers can be found at trade fairs and exhibitions, and through advertising and word-of-mouth.

Activity: Skills audit

What kind of skills do you think you will need to study design crafts? Would you be best suited to working as a sole trader or as a designer for a company?

- Read through the case studies and list all the skills described, such as drawing, making, etc.

- Skills audit – make a list of your skills, including personal skills like 'organisation' and any work experience skills you may have, such as customer service, cash handling, etc.

- Look at your skills and identify areas that are strengths and those you need to develop to work towards your career goals.

www.prospects.ac.uk lists job descriptions along with the relevant skills needed, which may be useful for completing your skills audit.

Case study: Rachel Galley, jeweller

Rachel Galley (www.rachelgalley.com) studied jewellery at Central St Martins School of Art in London, and then worked in industry designing and making jewellery for large companies. After three years, she decided to set up her own business and become a limited company, which helped to give her work a professional profile in a competitive marketplace. While working in industry, Rachel learned techniques for creating sophisticated and unique designs that could be made in large quantities. These also allow her time to produce bespoke commissions and develop new designs.

Rachel shows her jewellery at trade fairs and high-profile jewellery shows, and has a network of shops in the UK and abroad that sell her work. She has also launched a collection on a jewellery shopping channel and uses social media such as Twitter to market her work. She has a studio in London at Cockpit Arts – a charity that helps set up creative businesses.

Movement and tactility inspire Rachel and within her designs there is often an ability to interact with the pieces by changing the stone, length or the look of the piece to personalise and make each piece individual to the wearer.

1. **How would you get started if you were going to design a piece of jewellery?**
2. **What materials could you use?**
3. **How could you use social and interactive media to promote your work?**

Rachel Galley, jewellery maker and designer.

Activity: Glossary building

There will be new technical terms that you encounter on a specialist pathway. Here are ten common terms – list them in the back of your sketchbook and find out what they mean. Add to this glossary each time you encounter a new word or phrase:

- anneal
- solder
- weld
- flux
- bisc
- glaze
- slip
- laminate
- pierce
- vacuum.

1.2 Research and development

The processes that underpin all the units in the design crafts pathway are similar, even though the techniques and media vary. These include research, development, experimentation, completion and review. Most successful designers and companies spend time on research and development before starting to work with expensive materials.

Research

Research is key to getting your work off to a good start. Gather information by drawing, taking photographs, collecting data on artists that work in a similar way and on the materials and techniques you will be using.

By drawing with lots of different materials, you can collect visual information such as colour, texture, scale, weight, application and cost. Good research can also show where your ideas come from and how they can be used and applied.

Research can be presented in sketchbooks, note books, technical folders, visual diaries, presentation sheets, or even in a computer slide show. Keep returning to your research as your ideas develop.

Key term

Development – ideas can be developed through experimenting and exploring. Use design skills to problem solve, and play with and explore materials and techniques to build confidence.

It is important to test your ideas to make sure they work and are not harmful, and to record any findings and solutions. If you are making a ring, for example, is it too sharp or heavy to wear? How can you make it more comfortable?

You may be able to form a time plan for the development process, which will also help you forecast costs and resources.

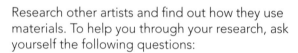

Activity: Research

Research other artists and find out how they use materials. To help you through your research, ask yourself the following questions:

• Who is their audience?

• Where do they show their work?

Why is it important to test your ideas before starting your project?

Develop

As your work evolves, it is important to list any constraints relating to your project:

• Are there any health and safety or legal considerations?

• Are you working to a budget or for a particular place?

• Who are you designing/making for?

• What are the best materials to use?

• What skills will you need?

• What are the manufacturing issues and will you need professional help?

Functional skills

Mathematics

Use spreadsheets to keep track of your budgets. Create a spreadsheet that shows your budget for research, materials, time, experimentation, manufacturing for example. Then make sure you itemise what you actually spent.

Activity: Joining without glue

This activity will help you develop your problem-solving skills and introduce you to a range of materials and techniques. You will need small sections of different materials, ideally cut to the same size, such as card, copper, glass, MDF, Perspex, fabric, hessian, plastic, wood, aluminium and recycled materials.

Make sure you are aware of safe working practices and any health and safety issues.

Key words for this task are stitching, slotting, cutting, carving, bending.

Now create a container that uses three materials in an interesting way but does not use glue to join them. Here are some suggestions depending on what is available:

Metal work

- annealing – use a blowtorch to soften the copper
- centre punching and drilling – use a pillar drill and hand drill
- piercing, fitting a saw blade.

Wood, metal or plastics

- sanding and polishing.

Plastics

- use the heat gun to bend Perspex
- cutting and filing.

Fabric and mixed media

- join by making links, stitching, bonding, weaving, wrapping and wiring.

In your sketchbook you should show initial ideas, artists you researched and characteristics you noticed about the materials. Use technical terms to describe the techniques used.

Bisc fired ceramics cooling down inside the kiln.

Using photographs and drawings to create a moodboard for your research is a great way to communicate your ideas.

Explore/extend

Many specialist units have a section 'Explore' and another to 'Extend'. You may decide to try lots of materials and techniques, or to spend time developing one or two over several projects. Testing, analysing, recording and trying new combinations will all help extend your understanding of materials.

As you learn about materials, record your findings and techniques. This could be in the form of charts, tables, photographs or drawings, but they don't all have to be written down – images and samples can also be a valuable resource. Keeping a sample board of materials and techniques is a good way to try out and remind you of techniques and help finalise decisions.

How could you use drawings and models to develop ideas and solve problems before you begin work on your final designs?

Activity: Exploring and extending

This activity will help you develop transferable skills and solve problems using different materials and techniques.

Task 1

Produce an A2 sheet of line drawings from observation of an organic structure, such as leaves, rocks or plants. Make sure you fill the sheet.

Task 2

Make a viewfinder, select an A5 area of your drawing and photocopy this section four times. Now recreate three 3D versions of your selected section using the following techniques and materials:

- copper wire and lead solder
- string, thread and sticks
- stitching, gluing, soldering found objects and mixed materials.

Task 3

Set up a plaster frame the same size as your photocopied section, mix some plaster and fill the frame to make a plaster slab. When this has set, carve the motif from your photocopy into the plaster and leave to dry.

Task 4

Roll pieces of soft clay over your plaster slab and manipulate them to make soft cylinders and forms. They will have a raised area to match the carving on your plaster slab, which can then be decorated with slips and scratched on to develop designs.

To make constructed clay pieces, roll slabs over your plaster work and leave them to dry until they are leather-hard. They can then be cut to size and joined with clay slip to form boxes and frames.

Task 5

In your sketchbook, take photocopies of your drawing and develop your ideas in two dimensions. Enlarge, reduce and repeat sections; add colour and mark-making; rip edges; add found materials; weave paper sections; and stitch, glue and fold, to make 20 alternative samples from the same starting-point.

Task 6

Identify which outcomes were the most successful and why. What health and safety issues did you encounter during this activity?

1.3 Finish

In addition to the research, planning, developing and making, you will need to finish your work. It is important to leave yourself enough time to **complete** your outcomes. Sometimes the first few pieces can have a poor finish which can be disappointing and affect your overall grade.

Time planning and good preparation can help overcome these common errors.

- Make sure you know health and safety guidelines before you start so that you don't lose time.

- Ensure that joins to be soldered are cleaned with wire wool or 'Pickle' to get a good join.

- Smooth edges that will be visible or come into contact with the user.

- Plan how your item will be stored and transported between workshops, to avoid damage before assessment.

- Allow time for clay work to be fired before assessment.

- Photograph ceramics at each stage in case they get damaged in the kiln!

1.4 Evaluate

Evaluation is a skill and needs to be learned. Simple evaluations at a pass level may be step-by-step accounts of what you did during the project. These are often factual, backed up with photographs and illustrations, but often don't use evaluative language or include thought processes and decisions.

Evaluation and **reviewing** can start early in a project. You could include a weekly summary or notes at the end of each session, which might include the following:

- examples of problems you faced and how you overcame them

- how you checked and tested your work against goals

- materials and techniques you used and why you chose them

- practitioners or stimuli that influenced you.

You could number your sketchbook pages and refer to them in your evaluation to illustrate points. Explain why you made decisions and how you developed your ideas. Include drawings, photos, illustrations, examples, recordings, models and samples.

Functional skills

Mathematics

In all forms of design, precision can be essential in ensuring that your designs are produced effectively and the finished item is fit for purpose. When designing items such as exhibition stands or stage sets, measuring and calculating space, size and volume accurately is crucial to working professionally and effectively. Miscalculating the size of an object for use on stage could result in an item that is useless and wasting money and time. When working in such areas, the skills of accurate measurement and calculating scale will be essential for functioning professionally.

Key terms

Completing – to complete your work, you should use finishing skills to make and finish well-presented pieces of work, designs and design sheets.

Reviewing – at the review stage, you should ensure that you check your work, test your ideas, problem solve, look at how you can improve or develop work throughout the design process so that the finished piece is well designed and considered.

Rachel Dormor

Ceramicist

Rachel Dormor studied a BTEC National Diploma in Art and Design before completing an HND in Design Crafts which enabled her to develop her passion for making things by studying ceramics, jewellery, woodwork and sculpture.

Rachel carried on learning after studying by working as a potter's assistant for several years until she set up her company, Rachel Dormor Ceramics (www.racheldormorceramics.com), with the help of the Prince's Trust. Rachel's tableware company, based in Stoke-on-Trent, produces handmade porcelain tableware which is sold throughout the UK and abroad.

Functional ceramics – cups, plates and bowls all made on a potter's wheel.

Rachel makes beautiful, functional everyday items such as bowls, cups and milk jugs which are all simple shapes and glazed in soft contemporary colours. After several years of selling through craft fairs and galleries, Rachel took time out to go back to university and study an MA in industrial ceramic design. Learning about industrial design and how products can be manufactured on a large scale as well as producing design work for ceramic companies helped Rachel to develop new ranges and start exporting her tableware abroad.

What would you say the biggest challenges are to craft-makers?

'Being able to make the time to research, develop and test your ideas is very difficult when you work for yourself. It's important to keep ahead of changing trends and to keep developing fresh ideas.'

How should designers/craft-makers promote their work?

'Customers are interested in the story behind the product, who made it, what inspires them and what they are like. I use a website, a blog, a photosharing account and social media to tell people about the story behind my work and help them feel connected with the business.'

Think about it!

- How could you use social media to keep in contact with your customers?
- How do you think designers and craft-makers can work with manufacturers and industry?
- How could you find out about new trends to help you develop new ideas?

Hannah Lobley
Environmental artist

Hannah Lobley completed a BA in Decorative Arts and an MA in Applied Art and Visual Culture before launching as a sole trader.

Hannah uses layers of wastepaper and recycles the laminate pages to form blocks which can then be carved and manipulated. When finished, the colour and textures of the recycled papers form a unique and distinctive surface. Products range from small, turned bowls and decorative pieces, sold through galleries and exhibitions, to public art and large-scale commissions.

Hannah's unique work and innovative use of materials have won her international acclaim.

What is your unique selling point?

'Being sensitive to environmental issues and creating stunning sculptural commissions that are ecologically sound.'

Hannah Lobley uses a lathe to carve her work. What health and safety equipment would you use in your school or college workshop?

Think about it!

- Scale up your ideas on your design sheets to see if they would work as large-scale public artworks – use Photoshop to mock up backgrounds.
- What techniques and materials could you use that are safe and environmentally friendly?
- What could you recycle to make a new material?

Just checking

1. Make a list of resistant and non-resistant materials.

2. Describe health and safety factors to consider in design crafts.

3. List five ways of developing your work.

4. What similarities and differences did you notice in the case studies?

edexcel :::

Assignment tips

- Plan your project before you start by listing any resources you may need, such as equipment, storage space, transport, and any safety and installation issues.

- Keep technical notes in a folder or sketchbook.

- Take photos of your samples and work as it develops – annotate these with captions.

- Present your developmental work, using presentation sheets, slide-shows, etc.

- Test your ideas – try things out to see if they work and are fit for purpose; include this in your evaluation.

- When things change, discuss why or how you overcame the problem.

- Merit and distinction grades in this pathway are awarded when research and development work are thorough and well documented, and samples and/or finished work are well made and designed, with end use in mind.

Endorsed routes – optional units

The tables on the following pages list the optional units that are available for each of the endorsed routes. Your centre may offer a selection of these units for you to choose from. Remember – you **must** do the mandatory units specified for your Level 3 qualification (Certificate, Subsidiary Diploma, Diploma or Extended Diploma).

Table 1: These are the optional (professional specialist) units. You will do a selection of these with any of the endorsed routes (or the general Art and Design route).

Unit	Optional units (Professional specialist)	Credit value	Level
6	Application, exploration and realisation	20	3
7	Design methods in art and design	10	3
8	Design principles in art and design	10	3
9	Professional practice in art and design	10	3
10	Personal and professional development in art and design	10	3
11	Freelance work in art and design	10	3
12	Computers in art and design	10	3
13	Art and design specialist contextual investigation	10	3
14	Community art	10	3
15	Fundraising for art and design	5	3
16	Promoting art and design work	10	3
17	Management of art and design projects	10	3
18	Collaborative working in art and design	10	3
19	Educating through art and design	10	3
20	Developing business models for the art and design sector	10	3
21	Starting a small business	10	3
22	Setting up an art and design studio	10	3

Art and Design (Graphic design)
Table 2: These are the optional units for the endorsed Graphic design route.

Unit	Optional units (Graphic design specialist)	Credit value	Level
24	Photographic studio techniques	10	3
27	Digital image capture and editing	10	3
29	Photography location techniques	10	3
32	Experimental imagery in photography	10	3
33	Lens-based image making	10	3
34	Image manipulation using computer applications	10	3
37	Graphics media, techniques and technology	10	3
38	Mixed media image making	10	3
39	Typefaces and letter forms	10	3
40	Typographic and layout design	10	3
41	Words and images in graphic design	10	3
42	Design for advertising	10	3
43	Graphics for 3D application	10	3
44	Website design	10	3
45	Graphic image making	10	3
47	Factual writing in art and design	10	3
48	Narrative image making	10	3
49	Specialist illustration using computer applications	10	3
50	Information graphics	10	3
51	3D computer modelling	10	3
53	2D animation production	10	3
57	Human-computer interfaces for computer games	10	3
58	Sound in interactive media	10	3
97	Product design	10	3

Art and Design (Fashion and clothing)
Table 3: These are the optional units for the endorsed Fashion and clothing route.

Unit	Optional units (Fashion and clothing specialist)	Credit value	Level
49	Specialist illustration using computer applications	10	3
75	Drawing from observation	10	3
93	Small-scale working	10	3
94	Small-scale design	10	3
95	Human-scale working	10	3
96	Human-scale design	10	3
117	Surface pattern	10	3
118	Repeat pattern	10	3
119	Printed textiles	10	3
120	Fashion media, techniques and technology	10	3
121	Pattern construction for fashion and clothing	10	3
122	Pattern development for fashion and clothing	10	3
123	Pattern grading for fashion and clothing	10	3
124	Production techniques for fashion and clothing	10	3
125	Computer applications in fashion	10	3
126	Fashion marketing	10	3
127	Fashion visualisation	10	3
128	Garment production	10	3
129	Accessory production	10	3
130	Fashion presentation techniques	10	3
131	Fashion promotion	10	3
132	Fashion in retail	10	3
133	Fashion styling	10	3
134	Fashion buying	10	3
135	Developing costume design skills	10	3
136	Make-up application skills and creative uses in performance	10	3
137	Hair styling and dressing for performers	10	3

Art and Design (Photography)

Table 4: These are the optional units for the endorsed Photography route.

Unit	Optional units (Photography specialist)	Credit value	Level
23	Photographic media, techniques and technology	10	3
24	Photographic studio techniques	10	3
25	Studio photography	10	3
26	Specialist studio photography	10	3
27	Digital image capture and editing	10	3
28	Commercial photographic laboratory operations	10	3
29	Photography location techniques	10	3
30	Location photography	10	3
31	Specialist location photography	10	3
32	Experimental imagery in photography	10	3
33	Lens-based image making	10	3
34	Image manipulation using computer applications	10	3
35	Darkroom practice	10	3
36	Darkroom applications	10	3
38	Mixed media image making	10	3
48	Narrative image making	10	3
54	Film and video editing techniques	10	3
59	Stop motion animation production	10	3
60	Single camera techniques	10	3
79	Multi-disciplinary work in fine art	10	3
135	Developing costume design skills	10	3
136	Make-up application skills and creative uses in performance	10	3
137	Hair styling and dressing for performers	10	3

Art and Design (Fine art)
Table 5: These are the optional units for the endorsed Fine art route.

Unit	Optional units (Fine art specialist)	Credit value	Level
32	Experimental imagery in photography	10	3
34	Image manipulation using computer applications	10	3
45	Graphic image making	10	3
48	Narrative image making	10	3
49	Specialist illustration using computer applications	10	3
54	Film and video editing techniques	10	3
56	Producing video installation work	10	3
58	Sound in interactive media	10	3
59	Stop motion animation production	10	3
60	Single camera techniques	10	3
75	Drawing from observation	10	3
76	Generating fine art ideas	10	3
77	Fine art principles	10	3
78	Developing and realising fine art ideas	10	3
79	Multi-disciplinary work in fine art	10	3
80	Painting in fine art	10	3
81	Printmaking	10	3
82	Sculpture	10	3
83	Public art	10	3
84	Presenting fine art work	10	3
88	Extending specialist ceramic techniques	10	3
91	Large-scale working	10	3
92	Large-scale design	10	3
109	3D sculptural textiles	10	3

Art and Design (Interactive media)
Table 6: These are the optional units for the endorsed Interactive media route.

Unit	Optional units (Interactive media specialist)	Credit value	Level
34	Image manipulation using computer applications	10	3
44	Website design	10	3
45	Graphic image making	10	3
46	Digital storytelling	10	3
52	3D animation	10	3
53	2D animation production	10	3
54	Film and video editing techniques	10	3
55	Understanding video technology	10	3
56	Producing video installation work	10	3
57	Human-computer interfaces for computer games	10	3
58	Sound in interactive media	10	3
59	Stop motion animation production	10	3
60	Single camera techniques	10	3
61	Pre-production techniques for the creative media industries	5	3
62	Interactive media authoring	10	3
63	Interactive media design	10	3
64	Introduction to music technology	10	3
65	Audio production processes and techniques	10	3
66	Digital video production for interactive media	10	3
67	Computer game engines	10	3
68	Computer game design	10	3
69	Sound for computer games	10	3
70	Computer game story development	10	3
71	Soundtrack production for the moving image	10	3
72	Drawing concept art for computer games	10	3
73	Web animation for interactive media	10	3
74	Principles of software design and development	10	3

Art and Design (3D design)
Table 7: These are the optional units for the endorsed 3D design route.

Unit	Optional units (3D design specialist)	Credit value	Level
43	Graphics for 3D application	10	3
49	Specialist illustration using computer applications	10	3
51	3D computer modelling	10	3
83	Public art	10	3
85	Exploring specialist techniques	10	3
86	Extending specialist techniques	10	3
90	3D design media, techniques and technology	10	3
91	Large-scale working	10	3
92	Large-scale design	10	3
93	Small-scale working	10	3
94	Small-scale design	10	3
95	Human-scale working	10	3
96	Human-scale design	10	3
97	Product design	10	3
98	Design for moving parts	10	3
109	3D sculptural textiles	10	3

Art and Design (Textiles)

Table 8: These are the optional units for the endorsed Textiles route.

Unit	Optional units (Textiles specialist)	Credit value	Level
34	Image manipulation using computer applications	10	3
75	Drawing from observation	10	3
79	Multi-disciplinary work in fine art	10	3
84	Presenting fine art work	10	3
107	Exploring specialist textile techniques	10	3
108	Extending specialist textile techniques	10	3
109	3D sculptural textiles	10	3
110	Papermaking and printmaking	10	3
111	Fabric manipulation	10	3
112	Feltmaking and felting	10	3
113	Textile installation	10	3
114	Woven textiles	10	3
115	Knitted textiles	10	3
116	Embroidered textiles	10	3
117	Surface pattern	10	3
118	Repeat pattern	10	3
119	Printed textiles	10	3
121	Pattern construction for fashion and clothing	10	3
122	Pattern development for fashion and clothing	10	3

Art and Design (Design crafts)
Table 9: These are the optional units for the endorsed Design crafts route.

Unit	Optional units (Design crafts specialist)	Credit value	Level
75	Drawing from observation	10	3
79	Multi-disciplinary work in fine art	10	3
85	Exploring specialist techniques	10	3
86	Extending specialist techniques	10	3
87	Exploring specialist ceramic techniques	10	3
88	Extending specialist ceramic techniques	10	3
89	Developing and realising design craft ideas	10	3
90	3D design media, techniques and technology	10	3
93	Small-scale working	10	3
94	Small-scale design	10	3
98	Design for moving parts	10	3
99	Exploring resistant materials	10	3
100	Extending resistant materials	10	3
101	Exploring non-resistant materials	10	3
102	Extending non-resistant materials	10	3
103	Exploring specialist glass techniques	10	3
104	Extending specialist glass techniques	10	3
105	Exploring specialist metal and jewellery techniques	10	3
106	Extending specialist metal and jewellery techniques	10	3
107	Exploring specialist textile techniques	10	3
108	Extending specialist textile techniques	10	3

Glossary

Action Painting – a radical demonstration of the concept that painting was a series of highly physical actions and was no longer dependent on the easel.

Aesthetics – when we talk about how aesthetically pleasing an artwork is, we mean that we find an enjoyment or appreciation in its formation.

Analysis – detailed and careful consideration of something in order to understand it better. This may be through examination of its individual parts, or study of the structure as a whole.

Armature – a metal framework on to which a material such as clay or plaster is moulded to form a sculpture.

Art – works produced through creative human endeavour rather than nature, and which reflect the skill or ability to do something well.

Bibliography – a bibliography used to refer to the list of written sources used by an author but can now also include other sources such as the Internet and television broadcasts. Your bibliography will demonstrate the breadth of your research and also point the reader towards sources for future study. It is important to try to identify the key works in any subject you are studying, including primary sources.

CAD (Computer Aided Design) – computer software packages (such as Adobe Illustrator and Adobe Photoshop) that enable the designer to create fashion illustrations, flat working drawings, etc.

CAM (Computer Aided Manufacturing) – computer packages (such as Lectra and Gerber AccuMark) that aid the production or manufacturing process by producing patterns and lay plans, cutting fabric, etc.

Cogent – forceful and convincing to the intellect and reason.

Collage – the process of using fragments of sometimes unrelated printed matter and photographs to make compositions.

Completing – to complete your work, you should use finishing skills to make and finish well-presented pieces of work, designs and design sheets.

Compression/decompression – hardware and software 'codecs' that enable large files to run on computers or TVs. The ideal codec is slow to compress and quick to decompress and is usually the smallest file you can have for video. Some codecs produce files that can be edited, like DV PAL, but others are so compressed that you can only distribute and watch them – like MPG4.

Concept – the notion or idea that underpins and is communicated by an artwork.

Conceptualising – coming up with the defining idea which establishes the mood or context and sets the scene.

Contingencies – plans within a schedule that anticipate unforeseen events or problems.

Creativity – the ability to use the imagination, or to draw on your knowledge of a subject, to develop new and original ideas or outcomes.

Critique – a considered judgement of or discussion about the qualities of a creative work.

CSS (Cascading Style Script) – CSS in websites allows the content to be separate from the style of the pages. This makes the data more accessible and reduces the amount of coding for each page. CSS is the way forward for better web standards and it allows the same content to be viewed on different hardware devices.

Cyanotype – a photographic printing process resulting in a cyan-blue print. Photosensitive chemicals are applied to a receptive surface and allowed to dry in a dark room. On exposure to sunlight or ultraviolet light, everyday objects placed on this surface create photograms – stencil-type images, which are revealed when the photosensitive chemicals are rinsed off.

Demographics – refers to a study of life in communities through looking at births/deaths/diseases/average income/average age, etc.

Design – to create or plan a form or structure in a skilful or artistic way, usually for a particular purpose.

Development – ideas can be developed through experimenting and exploring. Use design skills to problem solve, and play with and explore materials and techniques to build confidence.

Digital media – any data produced electronically.

Dodge and burn – used to lighten or darken areas of the image, based on the traditional technique for regulating exposure on particular areas of a print. Photographers hold back light to lighten an area on the print (dodging) or increase the exposure to darken areas on a print (burning).

Embellishment – something that adds interest to a design piece such as shiny threads, beads or sequins.

Ergonomics – the science of understanding how objects or space relate to the human body.

Ethical issues – moral considerations, such as wasting resources, producing work in a way that is not environmentally responsible, risking harm or causing offence to individuals or groups.

Explicit – clearly expressed, leaving no doubt as to the intended meaning.

Fashion forecasting – the process of predicting new and forthcoming trends.

Flash – a simple animation application that can be scripted to provide interactivity and is popular for making websites and games, but is incompatible with new web standards as demanded by the World Wide Web Consortium (www.w3.org).

Footwear and leather sector – this sector includes fellmongery, which is cleaning and preparing hide for leather, leather processing, manufacture of leather goods, footwear, shoe repair and wholesale leather.

Freelancer – someone who works for themselves and is not committed to one employer.

Ground – the surface artists work on, usually applied to painting and thus referring to paper, canvas, wood or walls. Preparing ground means making the surface suitable for painting on, such as by priming canvas for oil/acrylics, or applying gesso for tempera painting.

Hardware – refers to the physical elements of the computer suite: processor, screen, keyboard, mouse, external hard drives, etc.

Human–computer interface – buttons, switches and levers have long been part of the way we control machines. Computers have emulated them on screen because they are useful visual metaphors, but this style of interface may soon disappear. We are understanding more about the human interface – expression, gesture, ideas linked through meaning, etc. – and the computer interface will start to be influenced by these more human ways of communicating.

Icons – traditionally images of religious figures, but can mean anyone who is widely admired and looked up to. The term is also used to describe symbols or graphic representations, such as icons on a computer screen.

Imaginative – new and original, or not likely to have been easily thought up by somebody else.

Implicit or implied – not obvious, but open to interpretation. (Meaning may be confined to a privileged or elite group of people with prior knowledge or experience, which gives them an advantage.)

Innovation – the act or process of inventing or introducing something new, or a new way of doing something.

Installation – an artwork which is installed within a gallery or found space and as such relates to the entire specified exhibition area, as opposed to a single wall space or floor space.

Isolate – by picking out a detail, and enlarging it, you can enhance and clarify its features, and create a composition within a space.

Language – a system of communication with its own set of conventions, encompassing spoken or written words, signs, gestures or sounds.

Lowlights and highlights – the darkest and lightest areas, respectively. By identifying the lowlights on a subject in your mark-making, you can help to recreate a three-dimensional structure on a two-dimensional surface.

Maquette – a smaller, preliminary model made by an artist, before embarking on a full-scale, final piece of work.

Metaphor – describing something in a way that does not have literal meaning, for example, 'raining cats and dogs'.

Monoprint – a straightforward means of making a simple print by rollering printing ink on to a flat, wipeable surface, such as glass or Perspex, and laying a piece of paper on top. By drawing on the back of the paper, a mirror image of the original drawing is achieved on the reverse side. Although the name suggests that only one print can be achieved, it's usually possible to get a least one additional print – the 'ghost' print – from the residual ink remaining on the wipeable surface.

Myth – a traditional narrative involving supernatural or imaginary characters. It can also mean a widely held but false idea.

Negative space – the shape around an object. The object can sometimes be distracting, and analysing negative space can help you identify the shape or structure.

Pattern grader – the person responsible for physical scaling of the pattern by either increasing or decreasing the size.

Personal research – this is independent research supported by organised trips and visits to museums, galleries, etc.

Photographic processes – the range of different formats and means through which images are produced, such as film, darkroom and digital work.

Production process – the process of manufacture which includes cutting, sewing, pressing and packaging of the finished garments.

Prototype – a working example of a particular product or artefact that is used to demonstrate how a design might function or operate.

Raster-based or pixel-based graphics – represent images in the form of pixels: small coloured squares that make up the picture, typically photographic images. The quality of the image is dependent on the number of pixels in each square inch or square centimetre. The more pixels, the higher the quality of the image, and this makes the file size larger. This is referred to as the resolution. It is important to generate raster images at the right size for the end use and production method. For use on-screen, 72 dots per inch will be enough, but for a commercial printer, you would need to create images at 300 dots per inch which is the size at which it will be reproduced.

Reflection – careful thought, especially the process of reconsidering previous actions, events or decisions.

Repeat – a way to explore the additional properties of an object.

Research – a methodical investigation into a subject to discover facts, establish or revise a theory and develop a plan of action based on what is discovered.

Reviewing – at the review stage, you should ensure that you check your work, test your ideas, problem solve, look at how you can improve or develop work throughout the design process so that the finished piece is well designed and considered.

Rotating – enables the artist to examine multiple viewpoints simultaneously to create a feeling of movement.

Semantics – relating to meaning.

Separations – refer to the division of an image or design into single colours. This can be the four 'process' colours referred to as CMYK or especially mixed spot colours. In lithographic printing, each colour would be represented on a plate, but in screen printing, colours would be printed from separate screens.

Simulate – to reproduce a physical experience.

Software – refers to the varied range of programs that are used to generate data for specific processes.

Sustainable – the word sustainable is applied to materials and manufacturing processes that can be easily obtained and replaced, and therefore have a less harmful effect on the environment. If you are using timber, for example, look for wood that comes from a sustainable source.

Tacit – understood on an intuitive or subconscious level without being verbalised or consciously defined.

Target market – the group of customers or clients that the retailer aims to sell to or the designer aims to market to.

Textile services sector – this sector includes commercial and in-house laundries, dry-cleaning services, work wear and linen rental for the hospitality industry.

Textiles sector – this sector includes spinning, weaving, knitting, dyeing and finishing, carpets, narrow fabrics, ribbons, technical textiles, man-made fibres and wholesale textiles.

Toile – a fabric sample used for fitting and checking a garment design.

Toiles – the different cloth surfaces, such as canvas and linen, used to paint on.

Typography – letterforms and their use within a graphic design and layout were an important aspect of the Bauhaus School, with influential work designed by László Moholy-Nagy, Herbert Bayer and Joost Schmidt.

Vector graphics – points, lines, curves and shapes to represent images using mathematical formulae. When the graphics are enlarged, the sharpness and quality of the image is retained, so they are excellent for signs and logos.

Visual communication – how you communicate your ideas without words, such as by drawings, thumbnail sketches, working drawings, photos, photos of design development, design sheets and annotation.

Visual language – how you communicate meaning in your work through mark-making and using the formal elements – line, tone, form and colour.

Visual solution – create interpretation that translates a concept into an image that conveys the meaning and intentions of the client.

Index

WITHDRA

WITHDRAWN